*f*P

SMALL WONDERS

HEALING CHILDHOOD TRAUMA WITH EMDR

Joan Lovett, M.D.

THE FREE PRESS

THE FREE PRESS
A Division of Simon & Schuster Inc.
1230 Avenue of the Americas
New York, NY 10020

THE FREE PRESS and colophon are
trademarks of Simon & Schuster Inc.

Designed by MM Design 2000 Inc.

Manufactured in the United States of America

10 9 8 7 6 5 4 3 2 1

Library of Congress Cataloging-in-Publication Data

Lovett, Joan.
    Small wonders : healing childhood trauma with EMDR / Joan Lovett.
        p.   cm.
    Includes bibliographical references and index.
    1. Eye movement desensitization and reprocessing for children.
    I. Title.
    RJ505.E9L68   1999   98-30742
    618.92′8914—dc21   CIP

ISBN 0-684-84446-X

To John, Evan, and Sasha,
with love

CONTENTS

ACKNOWLEDGMENTS

I want to express my thanks to those who have inspired and helped me. John, Sasha, and Evan have sustained me with love, encouragement, patience, entertainment, editorial comments, and help with the computer.

I want to express my gratitude to Landry Wildwind for generously sharing her wisdom, expertise, and care. Her help made this book possible.

I appreciate Francine Shapiro for her vision, courage, and perseverance in developing EMDR. Her comments on this manuscript contributed to its accuracy.

Other colleagues whose ideas have contributed to mine and enriched my work include Adrianne Casadaban, Sandy Dibbel-Hope, Robbie Dunton, Bob Gilden, Karen Harber, Phyllis Klaus, Phil Manfield, Vivian Mazur, Zoe Newman, Thelma Peck, Peggy Thompson, Bob Tinker, and the staff at the West Coast Children's Center.

I would like to acknowledge Gabby Weiss and Hal Holman, both of whom influenced my medical career. Their passion for practicing medicine with creativity, compassion, and objectivity inspired me.

Thanks to Thomas Sampson for urging me to tell my story; to Laurel Parnell for encouraging me to write this book; and to Debbie Carton, Ann Moritz Chesnut, Harriet Sage, and Molly Selvin for reading parts of the manuscript and offering comments and encouragement.

I am grateful to Sheryl Fullerton, my literary agent, for her guidance in developing my proposal and shepherding me through this process with good humor; to Naomi Lucks, for expert editorial assistance and for being touched by the children's stories; and to Philip Rappaport and Caryn-Amy King of The Free Press for believing in this project and promoting *Small Wonders*.

I owe special thanks to the children whose courage and creativity inspire me and to the families who shared their stories so that others will benefit from their experiences.

FOREWORD

Some children eat too much and are overweight. Some get so anxious that they can't do their best in school. Some worry every time they try to fall asleep and as a result are chronically sleep deprived. These dysfunctional behaviors are common. They become part of the daily concerns of good parents, who try everything they know to help their child. Parents may be told, "It's just a stage; the child will grow out of it," but professional help may be needed to guide children along their normal developmental path.

Small Wonders is a book of short stories about children who have not outgrown their abnormal behaviors despite their parents' best efforts. Trauma precipitated these children's ongoing troubles. To the general public, the word "trauma" is associated with war, violent crime, earthquakes, hurricanes, fire, rape, and AIDS. However, more commonplace experiences, such as a grandparent dying, head lice, or being publicly criticized by a teacher, may cause persistent and profound symptomatology in a young child. If left untreated, these problems often get worse over time. The children do not grow out of them. But the children in Dr. Lovett's stories do get better when they are treated with EMDR.

What is EMDR? It is a comprehensive method of psychotherapy addressing problems that are based on earlier life experiences. There are more controlled studies supporting the use of EMDR with psychological trauma than for any other treatment method. The abbreviation stands for Eye Movement Desensitization and Reprocessing, which turned out to be a poor choice of name given the complexity and comprehensiveness of the method. The treatment approach emerged from my chance discovery in 1987 that eye movements had a distinct and beneficial effect on my thoughts and emotions. As I began working with this phenomenon, I discovered that in order for it to consistently reduce psychological disturbance and increase positive emotions, I had to develop a series of procedures around the eye movement. Eventually these procedures included aspects of all the major psychological orientations. Furthermore, experiences with blind patients and children who wouldn't or couldn't make eye contact taught us that the effects of the eye movements could be achieved as well with other types of repetitive stimulation, including tapping and auditory tones.

If I had to do it over again, I would probably name the method simply Reprocessing Therapy; however, the therapy now has such worldwide recognition that we keep using the letters EMDR for the same reason that AT&T retains its initials. Telegraphs aren't used anymore, but the name remains. It might be more useful, however, to think of the letters as standing for Emotional and Mental Development and Reorganization. That is, what is useful in an experience is learned, stored with appropriate emotions, and capable of guiding the person in the future, while that which is useless is discarded. Basically the client's psychological health can emerge on all levels—emotional, cognitive, and physiological. In other words, although some experiences may be retained in the brain in a way that causes dysfunction, the primary message of EMDR is that the client is intrinsically healthy: once experiences are processed with EMDR, the client can quickly return to a state of equilibrium. Learning occurs as the client's negative memories become less salient and less valid, while positive experiences become more vivid and empowering.

As of 1990, when the first EMDR training was given to mental health professionals in the United States, the method began to evolve with input from a wide range of experienced clinicians. One of the most exciting areas of development and ongoing research over the years has been the use of EMDR with children. As this book so clearly and eloquently demonstrates, children are wonderfully resilient. Although symptoms may initially baffle both child and parent, a sensitive clinician trained in EMDR can generally unravel and clarify these mysteries of mind and body. Most importantly, children can often be returned to a state of psychological health that otherwise might have been persistently derailed or, if appropriate, they can frequently be carefully raised to a new plateau of wholeness and well-being that far surpasses their earlier status.

Dr. Lovett has written an extremely important book for both parents and therapists. Her considerable clinical expertise has led her to develop a new strategy for the use of EMDR, one that incorporates storytelling, along with play therapy and the more familiar EMDR protocols. Through careful explanations and detailed case histories, she illustrates how EMDR may be used for problems as wide-ranging as nightmares, trichotillomania (hair pulling), phobias, depression, sibling rivalry, grief, and a variety of complaints that can be traced to a child's lack of self-esteem and trust in the world. If left untreated, these problems can stunt the child's development regardless of how loving, nurturing, and concerned the parent may be. Just as it is clearly the parents' responsibility to provide their child with appropriate medical care, there is equally a necessity to find appropriate psychological care when symptoms do not remit despite loving parental attention. As Dr. Lovett so amply illustrates, co-participation among parent, child, and therapist is often vital to allow a return to health—and potentially to peak achievement.

The comparison between medical and psychological care is particularly important for the developing child because EMDR has shown us that the brain takes experiences and processes them, much as the digestive system processes food. That is, if an experience is properly digested, it is integrated into the system and supports healthful growth. If a traumatic experience is not integrated because of the way it is stored in the brain, the child can suffer both psychologically and physically. In fact, physical symptoms with no obvious medical explanation may stem from earlier events that have been stored, with their accompanying disturbing sensations and emotions. Neither parent nor child can change the symptoms through an effort of will, but EMDR appears to tap into the physiological substrates of the information-processing system to rid the body and mind of the disturbance, leading to the resumption of healthful growth.

Dr. Lovett's detailed case examples and sensitive descriptions, combined with her expertise as a pediatrician and therapist, elucidate the striking complexity and beauty of the child's mind and guide both clinician and parent through a profound understanding of the child's experience. This book traverses the universe of childhood from one-and-a-half years of age through adolescence. It reveals how unhealed childhood experiences can haunt even the most intelligent and outwardly accomplished adult. Only through therapy that can release the client from the legacy of a negative past can he or she be provided with a healthful and happy present. Through all of these journeys Dr. Lovett is exquisitely careful to remind clients (of any age) that the "power" to heal is within themselves. This is why the children described in her book generally proclaim EMDR to be *their* "magic." For as importantly as anything else, this book shows its unbounded respect and concern for the children who suffered so valiantly and for the parents who had the courage to recognize the need for an intervention they could not personally supply. I believe that is why one of the children spontaneously calls Dr. Lovett by a name she has most certainly earned—Dr. Love-it-all.

Francine Shapiro, Ph.D.
Senior Research Fellow
Mental Research Institute
Palo Alto, CA
July 5, 1998

PART I

UNDERSTANDING TRAUMA

"WHY AM I AFRAID OF THE SOUND OF CARROTS CRUNCHING?"

Why would a bright 5-year-old boy suddenly become withdrawn and stop learning in preschool? Why would an athletic and confident 12-year-old have so much trouble falling asleep at night that she feared spending the night at a friend's house or going to camp? Why would an 11-year-old boy feel guilty about a death he didn't cause? And why would a successful, high-functioning doctor and parent suddenly become acutely sensitive to the sound of her children crunching carrots and chips?

As a behavioral pediatrician, I work to shed light on mysteries like these every day, to find the cause of behavioral problems that seem to come out of the blue. In my work I am continually amazed by my "small wonders," children who are able to reclaim their own innate power and heal from the traumatic events that abruptly knocked them off their smooth developmental track.

Some of the events that precipitate these developmental disruptions are clearly upsetting—a robbery, a car accident, a death in the family. But many initially appear to be minor occurrences, so that parents never notice them, or discount them automatically as too inconsequential to mention. Yet these everyday incidents—a news report on TV, a child's game of "Doctor," a chance comment overheard—can be enormous and life-changing to a child. And that is where the mystery begins.

When one parent gave me permission to include her family's story in my book, she said, "When my daughter had these problems, we couldn't find any information that helped us. We went to the bookstore and the library, but we couldn't find any book that explained what was going on with our child or how to help her. We thought she must have some unusual, weird problem or that we were doing something terribly wrong as parents. We wish we had known what we know now." Her words resonated strongly with me. Some years ago, like the little girl, I had experienced a similar terror of unknowing; and, like her parents, I had also experienced the frustration and isolation of being unable to convince medical professionals that something was really wrong.

AN ACCIDENTAL ENCOUNTER WITH POSTTRAUMATIC STRESS

In 1991 my life changed forever when I suffered serious physical injuries and almost died in an automobile accident. It was just after midnight, and I was driving home from a late call at a hospital, where I had admitted and treated one of my patients, an infant who needed emergency help. I was feeling very good about myself and the kind of work I was doing, and what I had accomplished earlier that evening. With my work complete, I was eager to get home to my husband and two young children. As I started the drive home on that dark night, I was glad it wasn't raining and that the roads were relatively clear.

As I approached a curve in the freeway, not far from home, in the distance I noticed a car stopped on the shoulder. As I rounded the curve, the car in front of me suddenly swerved out of the way to reveal that the car I had thought was on the shoulder was actually in my lane, dead ahead. Unable to stop in time, I crashed into the car at 60 miles an hour and changed my life forever.

Waiting alone in the car before help arrived, I was certain I would die. I was in tremendous pain, my heart was beating erratically, and I knew my injuries were serious. In fact, I felt like a living crash-test dummy. I had sustained cardiac contusions, severe whiplash, soft-tissue tearing, and more.

For the first few weeks of my recovery, I was too busy dealing with my physical trauma to give any thought to my future. But several months after the accident, my extensive injuries forced me to realize that I would not be able to return to work as a pediatrician because the work was physically demanding. In addition to physical pain and disability, I struggled with psychological suffering I couldn't understand. I had prided myself on being a hardworking, successful, "normal" woman; now I was plagued by nightmares, intrusive thoughts about the accident, panic attacks, and growing fears related to driving and disability.

In my medical practice I had dealt with all kinds of illness and injury that happened to other people, but after my accident I began to appreciate what "trauma" really means. As my body tried to normalize, I no longer felt like "myself." I told a friend that I felt as if I were seeing the world through prescription lenses that were just a few diopters off—the world looked at once familiar and extremely distorted. My entire sense of identity was disturbed.

Nonetheless, I struggled to get back into daily life. Six weeks after the accident, I still wanted nothing to do with cars, but I was ready to take an easy walk around my quiet residential neighborhood with a friend. We were discussing the pleasures of walking, admiring the trees and gardens, when a car filled with birthday balloons suddenly zoomed up the street, veered in our direction, jumped the curb, snapped the tall, slim tree in its path, and missed hitting me by inches as instinctively I leaped out of harm's way. It continued its crash course until finally it smashed into a house, tearing off a column of the porch. I was badly shaken. My theory that I would be safer walking than riding in a car had just been shattered.

As the weeks went by, my strange reactions seemed to multiply. I couldn't bear the sound of balls bouncing against walls when my children and their friends played handball. I still didn't want to drive on curvy roads. One symptom in particular confused and alarmed me. I had become unable to tolerate any cracking noises, including the sounds of people eating carrots, chips, or crackers. This was a real problem because my son and daughter were at an age when they loved crunchy foods, and while they were eating I felt inexplicably irritated and anxious. The feeling was comparable to hearing chalk screech on a blackboard while having a pop gun go off in my face. I found that I couldn't be in the room with them while they ate.

After 4 months I was feeling depressed and terrified. These symptoms were extraordinary. Before this accident I had felt good about myself. I had been a pediatrician and parent who was calm and focused in the midst of boisterous children and all sorts of environmental distractions. Now I was a wreck, and I didn't like it. At the time I didn't know that new posttraumatic symptoms can proliferate *months* after an upsetting event. I thought surely I should be over it by now. I was shocked that my symptoms seemed to be getting worse.

My intolerance for sudden, unexpected noises challenged my view of myself as a patient parent, to say the least. I now began to avoid children, walks outside, and noise of any kind. My internist, who had never heard of such symptoms, dismissed me with a pat prescription: "It just takes time and patience." The psychotherapist I consulted encouraged me to search my memory for times in the past when noises of people eating had bothered me. The only memory I could retrieve was that my mother had been annoyed by the sound of my father eating with his mouth open. As the therapist encouraged me to explore my feelings about my parents, I truly began to question my sanity. Could my parents' small dispute have caused me to avoid my own children, whom I adore? What did my childhood have to do with this?

I earnestly wanted to feel normal again, but I didn't know who to trust or what to do. Focusing on my deceased parents' relationship only made me worry about past history. "Insight" did not relieve any of my current symptoms. I knew my parents had loved me and cared for me. Their petty irritation at the dinner table could not be fueling my current anxiety, could it?

This was new territory for me. I was surprised to realize that during my medical training at three of the best medical centers in the world, I had not been taught useful information about the psychological aftermath of trauma. I had learned how to save lives, and to recognize symptoms dangerous to health; but in 20 years of practicing medicine, I had never heard of a patient who suddenly couldn't tolerate the sounds of her children eating.

"Time and patience" did not help. After three return visits to the internist, I realized that she had no help to offer me. She refused my request for a referral to a doctor who specialized in rehabilitation medicine with a now-familiar refrain: "Nothing more needs to be done. You just need time and patience." I was deeply disappointed in this doctor who dismissed my suffering even though I was not a complainer. She knew that I had never before called for any complaint. I had even endured childbirth and tooth fillings without anesthesia. She did not comprehend that it was her role to try to find appropriate help for me. It was shocking to me that even as a physician I could not persuade my doctor to give me a referral to a specialist. I have since learned that physicians often are unaware of the effects of trauma, and are uneducated in the resources available for relieving posttraumatic suffering.

EMDR: A METHOD TO LESSEN TRAUMA

Finally, 8 months after the accident, I consulted a psychiatrist because I desperately wanted relief from unrelenting anxiety, "flashbacks" and intrusive thoughts about the accident, and nightmares. The psychiatrist asked whether I had heard of EMDR, a method for treating posttraumatic stress. I hadn't, but at this point I was willing to try anything that might help me to function normally again. She referred me to a woman I'll call "Marianne," a therapist trained in the EMDR method. Hopeful but dubious, I went to see her.

After relating yet again the story of my accident and subsequent losses, I felt anxious and exhausted. Marianne explained that EMDR was a method she would use to help me lessen my traumatic symptoms. She explained that EMDR stands for eye movement desensitization and reprocessing, and told me the story of how Dr. Francine Shapiro had developed the method after discovering that eye movement helped to erase her excess fears when she had upsetting thoughts. "Desensitization" refers to the process of becoming comfortable with a memory of an event that was scary, but is currently over and now harmless. "Reprocessing" is a psychological term that means to work on understanding a memory so that the memory becomes useful instead of just scary.

WHAT IS EMDR?

EMDR developed from an observation of a natural behavior. Psychologist Francine Shapiro happened on the healing power of eye movement quite accidentally one day in 1987 as she was walking outdoors, thinking about some disturbing events in her life. A while later, when she reviewed her memories of the events again, she found that they were no longer disturbing. In thinking about what she was doing at the time, she realized that while she was thinking she had unconsciously been flicking her eyes back and forth. Could that have been a key? Intrigued, she worked on this theory some more, and eventually tried out her newly forming method with some of her clients, including Vietnam veterans and rape victims who were suffering from posttraumatic stress disorder. Over the years, Dr. Shapiro developed the method, which includes elements of cognitive-behavioral therapy; body-oriented therapy; psychoanalytic theory; the family-systems approach; as well as alternately stimulating the right and left hemispheres of the brain with eye movement, tapping, or auditory tones. As she refined the method, she had more and more success with adults suffering from all sorts of trauma. Eventually she developed a complete eight-part method. Today, more than 25,000 therapists worldwide are trained in this method.

We don't know exactly how eye movement helps us desensitize and reprocess traumatic memories. Initially, it was thought that the eye-movement component of EMDR worked to metabolize painful memories, much the way rapid-eye-movement sleep (REM sleep) works as the "night janitor" to clean up (or metabolize) some disturbing memories. Alternate tapping or auditory tones seem to be as effective as eye movement in effecting a change, however. Perhaps the shifting of attention from one hemisphere of the brain to the other recruits the memory fragments to form a coherent, consolidated memory in a more stable state.

Dr. Bessel van der Kolk, trauma specialist at Boston University, has postulated that eye movement or other alternating right-to-left stimulation promotes the movement of information from one hemisphere of the brain to the other through the corpus callosum. The right side of the brain is responsible for emotions and nonverbal experience. The left side of the brain contains the capacity to orient events in time, to use language to gain distance from the source of distress, and to assign meaning to experiences.

Intriguing research seems to give clues about the way EMDR may work. Researcher Martin Teicher and his associates have analyzed brain functioning in subjects with and without histories of childhood sexual abuse. They learned that subjects without a history of abuse used both hemispheres of the brain when they recalled a painful childhood memory. Subjects with a history of childhood sexual abuse only showed activation of functioning in the right hemisphere of the brain when they remembered a painful childhood memory. Apparently, EMDR nonverbally stimulates communication between the two hemispheres of the brain (van der Kolk, 1997), allowing traumatized people to use both right- and left-hemisphere resources in resolving painful memories.

Is EMDR hypnosis? No. During hypnosis, electroencephalographic readings indicate that there is an increase in alpha, beta, or theta waves that are associated with an increase in suggestibility. During EMDR, brain-wave tracings show brain waves that are within normal waking parameters. In EMDR, the person is actually less suggestible than usual to information that is not correct.

Although exactly how EMDR works on a biochemical level is still a mystery, research has demonstrated that people usually have fewer unnecessary fears or anxieties and feel better after they use it. The four most recent rigorously controlled studies have shown that 84–100% of the participants who had suffered a single trauma no longer had a diagnosis of posttraumatic stress disorder (PTSD) after only three 90-minute treatment sessions. Other treatment methods have been able to achieve success only after 25–100 hours of treatment, if at all. The first study of children treated with EMDR was presented by Dr. Claude Chemtob at the International Society for Traumatic Stress Studies in 1996. This study indicated that children with posttraumatic symptoms persisting 3 years after Hurricane Iniki showed significant improvement following EMDR treatment. Other studies of the effects of EMDR treatment on children are underway.

MY FIRST EXPERIENCES WITH EMDR

After taking a complete history, Marianne explained that when we began to desensitize and reprocess painful memories of the accident, she would ask me to hold in mind an image representing the worst part of the accident, to think the self-deprecating thoughts associated with the memory, and to notice the anxiety in my body. Then she would guide me to follow her hand with my eyes as she moved it back and forth horizontally through the air. I almost didn't go back. EMDR sounded weird, and I felt sure that I didn't want to revisit the horrendous experience of the accident or its aftermath while watching a waving hand that might magnify my terror.

Fortunately, this therapist was experienced and confident. She was encouraging and supportive while I tried the new method. She decided to address my most disturbing symptom first: noise intolerance. She explained the simple principle that posttraumatic symptoms arise from the traumatic incident. "Since noise makes you anxious," she reasoned, "some sound must have frightened you at the time of the trauma." (I was relieved to learn that my noise intolerance was related to the accident and not caused by my father's noisy eating.) Marianne encouraged me to remember the story of the first automobile accident once again, this time following her horizontal hand movements and listening internally to the sounds of the automobile accident to notice any cracking noises. As I followed her moving hand with my eyes and focused on the accident, I was amazed to find that I heard the sounds of screeching tires, of metal colliding with metal, and glass shattering. But I heard no distinctly "cracking" sounds.

Then she asked me to focus on the sounds of the second accident, which had upset me just when I was beginning to recover from my near-death encounter. Again I followed her hand movements. I heard the sounds of my friend and myself walking, the sounds of a car speeding toward us, the tire bumping the curb, and the CRACK of the tree beside me splitting and crashing down as I leaped out of the way to escape the out-of-control car. I realized suddenly that my quick reaction to the sound of the cracking tree probably saved my life.

Until that moment I had not consciously realized that the cracking of the tree breaking apart had programmed my nervous system to react to *any* cracking sound, even the harmless sound of a child crunching a carrot, as if it were life-threatening. Continuing to follow her hand movements with my eyes, I mentally viewed the second accident until it no longer terrified me and began to look like an old movie that had little relevance to my current life. I paused in between sets of eye movement to tell Marianne that the memory of the second accident no longer felt upsetting.

Then Marianne asked me to move my eyes while I imagined hearing the sounds of my children eating carrots and crackers. At first this was a painful task. Feelings of danger and extreme annoyance rushed through me. But, strangely, with a few more sets of eye movement, my anxiety subsided. The snapping of carrots and crunching of crackers no longer felt dangerous. Finally, she guided me in moving my eyes while I associated the cracking sounds of eating crunchy foods with healthy living and pleasure. I felt such relief! After weeks of avoiding children, eating, and noise, an important part of myself had suddenly been restored. The thought of my children eating no longer aroused anxiety comparable to the surge of fear that had propelled me out of harm's way when I was about to be hit by the car or the falling tree.

The very next day my family and I went to a busy street fair. My children were concerned that I would be "freaked out" by all the firecrackers exploding around us. All of us were astonished to discover that I had not even noticed the firecrackers or the many other "cracking" noises that surrounded me. That evening, I joined my family for dinner and felt calm and comfortable. The power of EMDR impressed all of us. I couldn't explain how EMDR had worked, but it was clear that it had.

I went back to the therapist for more EMDR to help me get over my feelings of helplessness and anxiety and the agonizing memories from the serious automobile accident that had crippled my life so abruptly. Speaking to friends later, I likened some of my EMDR sessions to open-heart surgery without anesthesia. It was excruciatingly painful to revisit the traumatic accident and my brush with death, but it was worth it. I noticed that although EMDR quickly cleared some of my most debilitating symptoms, like intolerance for noise and fear of driving, it did not seem to touch other symptoms, like my continuing nerve pain, which no doubt had an organic and structural basis. Gradually, EMDR, combined with expert psychotherapy, helped me tolerate the healing process. Later, my own training and clinical experience with EMDR confirmed that the procedure can not instill any beliefs that are false or erase any feelings of pain or anxiety that are appropriate danger signals.

A NEW DIRECTION

After my accident, my lifelong belief that I had to be self-sufficient and try hard became a hindrance rather than an asset. For a while at least, I was no longer able to take care of children, either as a pediatrician or a mother. I had to depend on others for help, which caused me enormous distress. "Trying hard" to overcome problems, a trait that had taken me so far for 40 years, now impeded the healing of injuries that required rest, and all of my strategies for dealing with stress failed.

Events are sometimes traumatic because they smash the carefully constructed beliefs that have kept us feeling safe for some portion of our lives. We cling to these beliefs even though they may have outlived their usefulness. In this wasteland of loss and unknowing, lacking my familiar structures and supports, therapy with EMDR gradually helped me understand that if I wanted to recover from my injuries, "easy does it" would be a more useful philosophy than "try hard."

Eventually, I accepted the fact that my new physical limitations meant that I wouldn't be able to return soon to work doing primary-care pediatrics. I decided to refocus my career on behavioral pediatrics, the area of pediatrics I loved best and for which I had already done specialty training. I sought additional training in child therapy, and I took the EMDR training as well. I wanted this valuable method as one of my treatment options for helping children. I became especially interested in helping children who had suffered from trauma.

WHAT IS TRAUMA?

The word "trauma," derived from the Greek word for wound, usually evokes thoughts of devastating events such as earthquakes, sexual abuse, or violent crime. But a trauma can also be an event that wounds our sense of safety and well-being and leaves us with false or destructive beliefs about ourselves and the world. For a child, a failed test, a fight with a friend, a playground accident, a chance comment by a trusted adult, and the loss of a grandparent can also be traumatic, continuing to undermine confidence long after the precipitating event has been forgotten.

Understanding how our bodies respond to trauma can give some insight into why this happens. Physiologically, our bodies are pro-grammed to ensure our safety and survival through the "fight-or-flight" response. We can flee, fight, or—when physical escape seems impossible—shift into a state of physical immobility and psycho-logical escape or surrender.

When we sense danger we become hyperalert. Blood circulation is redirected to our vital organs and away from our periphery to minimize blood loss, our hearts beat more quickly, we breathe faster, our muscles tense and ready for action, and a surge of adrenaline gives us the energy we need either to stay and fight the threat or run for our lives. If these reactions are thwarted we freeze, like the proverbial deer caught in the headlights. The unprocessed sensory and cognitive information relating to the event seems to be stored in an excitatory, state-dependent way in the nervous sys-tem. When the system for metabolizing traumatic memories has been overwhelmed, the information processing stops. This lingering immobilizing response keeps us simultaneously in a state of height-ened awareness of danger and inhibited ability to regain normal neurophysiologic balance.

These neurophysiological changes kick in not only when we are threatened physically, but also in response to emotional distress. Information encoded at the time of a threatening event is "hard-wired" into our complex memory network so that we will avoid or respond quickly to any similarly threatening situation in the future.

This elegant and useful system is designed to work in the moment and return to normal when the danger has passed. But when our danger-recognition system is overwhelmed—a situation that is not uncommon in the immature nervous system of chil-dren—we can get stuck in emergency mode. The slightest reminder of the traumatic event triggers high-amplitude anxiety, as if ready-ing us to respond to an attack. My reaction to the harmless sound of children crunching carrots is a good example.

CHILDREN'S RESPONSE TO TRAUMA

As my experience illustrates, trauma can shake an adult's life to its core. So what does it do to children, who have less experience in being self-sufficient and less of a context in which to make sense of events?

Children are extremely vulnerable to traumatic events, and they experience as life threatening many events that are ordinary for adults. For example, if you are hungry you can go to the refrigerator or the store and get yourself something to eat. At no time do you feel that your life is in danger. By adolescence, children can do these things for themselves. They may be annoyed to discover that their parents didn't stock the house with their favorite snack foods, but they don't feel threatened.

For infants and small children, however, the world is very different. When an infant is hungry, she is hungry *now*. She feels the lack of immediate gratification as life threatening. Without words, her only recourse is to cry and hope that someone understands her needs. A young child left alone, hungry, and crying in an empty room for a long time may feel as if no one cares, no one understands, she can't make her needs known, she's not good enough, and ultimately that she is not worthy of sustenance. For her, the lack of attention is a trauma that can affect her future development.

Children are naturally resilient. Developmental imperatives, the drive to accomplish tasks such as learning to use the toilet, walk alone, talk, and even sleep through the night propel children through the arduous process of growing up. Early childhood is filled with repeated attempts and failures and ultimately successes as we struggle to learn to walk, talk, relate to others, and negotiate our way through a potentially dangerous world. Children are normally equipped with a strong sense of their own power, an egocentricity and healthy narcissism that sustains them through this hero's journey.

In order to achieve developmental milestones young children must believe, "I am lovable. I have worth. I deserve care. I am safe." These beliefs give them the courage to dare, to risk the perils inherent in their growth toward independence. Trauma, even a small event like a playground accident or momentarily choking on a piece of food, can sometimes deprive children of these self-sustaining beliefs, rupturing the sense of safety and security that normally envelops and protects the maturation process. Especially when a series of traumatic events seems to give a repeated message about vulnerability, the child might begin to believe that he or she deserves punishment. As a result, the traumatized child behaves as if he or she is not safe, worthy, or lovable.

Parents can be confused and concerned when children who were developing at a steady pace suddenly develop unacceptable or disturbing symptoms for "no reason": they begin fighting with other children or become withdrawn, they become excessively fearful, or they develop puzzling fears and anxieties. Then we have to ask, "What happened?"

HOW I BEGAN USING EMDR WITH CHILDREN

A fter completing EMDR training, I felt confident that I could treat adults for symptoms of posttraumatic stress, but how could I modify the method to meet the needs of young children? Perhaps a 10-year-old would cooperate with the standard adult protocols, but I didn't expect a 4-year-old child to be able to "hold in mind the picture representing the worst part of the accident, think the negative thought about yourself that still seems true about you today, and notice the feelings in your body while you move your eyes back and forth." Before using EMDR with children, I asked myself how treating children is different from treating adults, and how I could modify the method to be developmentally appropriate for children.

I am naturally conservative about trying new therapies with children, and I was extremely cautious about introducing EMDR into my work. I thought about how EMDR might affect a young child, and carefully considered similarities between EMDR and other methods I have used to calm infants and children. Repetitive alternating side-to-side movements are a natural part of soothing an upset baby. Crying babies respond well to rhythmic stimulation such as rocking, being bounced up and down on a parent's shoulder, swinging, or being cradled over the parent's forearm and being rocked from side to side. Distressed toddlers can frequently be comforted by engaging in games like "patty-cake," which involves some alternate hand tapping.

Children under the age of about 5 often cannot repeatedly move their eyes horizontally past the midline to follow a moving object. With young children, or anyone who finds the eye movements uncomfortable, the alternating-stimulation aspect of EMDR is often done by gently and repetitively tapping first one hand and then the other, or by using auditory tones to draw attention alternately to the left and then to the right side.

It seemed to me that it would be safe to begin by thinking of EMDR as an extension of natural soothing methods that parents use every day. As with adults, I stop tapping when I notice a change in facial expression, a change in breathing patterns, or a change in the child's position. These shifts tell me that processing of the traumatic memory is progressing. I then ask, "What's coming up for you now?" or "What's happening now?" or simply, "How do you feel?"

USING EMDR TO ENHANCE POSITIVE FEELINGS

The calming effect I noticed after using EMDR techniques to soothe encouraged me to incorporate EMDR into play therapy whenever I saw an opportunity. Initially, I only used eye movement and alternate-tapping techniques for soothing or enhancing feelings of well-being and as natural extension of play. I found that the children liked imagining a safe place or a favorite place or a time when they had fun. Then they were willing to play tapping games to strengthen their feelings of safety and well-being.

Sometimes I asked a child to remember an experience of success and to concentrate on the associated physical sensation. Then we used rapid alternating stimulation, like eye movement or alternate hand tapping, to augment the feelings of accomplishment. EMDR, unlike most other psychotherapeutic methods, dissolves physical tension and reinforces physical sensations of relaxation and well-being. Every child has had some experiences of success, such as toilet training and learning to do various things: tie shoes, read, ride a bike, make a friend, or play a sport. I asked the child where he or she felt the physical sensation of success in the body. Almost every child was able to identify a body location associated with a positive feeling. Meredith, a young soccer player, felt power in her legs as she remembered kicking a goal; Mario felt pride in his chest as he recalled learning to read; and Regina felt beauty flowing from her hands as she imagined playing a favorite piece on the piano.

In EMDR terminology, using alternating stimulation to reinforce or instill positive thoughts and feelings is called "installation." We used EMDR to strengthen or "install" the self-affirmations and natural feelings of confidence and pride associated with competence, and the result was stronger self-esteem. EMDR seemed to enhance learning, and most important, I did not see any ill effects from adding eye movement or alternate tapping to play.

ALAN: USING EMDR TO TREAT CRITICAL-INCIDENT TRAUMA

EMDR is most likely to work quickly and completely in a healthy, well-adjusted child who experiences a single, time-limited, traumatic event. There have been more controlled studies confirming the effectiveness of EMDR in treating traumatized adults than for any other treatment method. The first research supporting the efficacy of EMDR with children who have suffered critical-incident trauma was presented in 1996. The study included 32 elementary school children who still had posttraumatic stress disorder $3\frac{1}{2}$ years after Hurricane Andrew, despite receiving postdisaster counseling that had been effective for the majority of children in Kauai. Following three EMDR sessions, most children reported significant reductions of trauma-related symptoms, and these gains remained at 6 months follow-up (Chemtob, 1996).

A healthy child who develops posttraumatic stress disorder following a critical-incident trauma may develop intrusive thoughts about the incident, nightmares, fears, and disturbed behavior. For example, 6-year-old Alan was startled awake one night by the sound of burglars breaking into the house, he saw two men stealing the television, and was left unharmed.

Two years later, Alan began to develop posttraumatic symptoms relating to safety. He suffered from excessive fears about strange men, intrusive memories about the break-in, nightmares, and had difficulty falling asleep. He became anxious whenever he heard the front door open. Alan startled and became anxious whenever he heard banging noises, even the sound of ice cubes dropping into the refrigerator tray. He developed ritualistic behaviors involving checking the front door repeatedly before he went to bed. By the time he came to me, the family had moved to another city, and their front door had been secured with a dead-bolt system. Even though Alan was safe, he suffered from these symptoms for years.

We used EMDR to desensitize and reprocess his memory of the break-in, so that he was able to fully believe, "It's over. Now, I'm safe in my house." Then we used EMDR to target and desensitize his fears about abrupt noises, like the sound of ice cubes dropping into a container. This work soon restored his sense of well-being and confidence, with complete resolution of the posttraumatic symptoms.

DANITRA AND RYAN: INTEGRATING EMDR WITH PLAY THERAPY

EMDR is also useful for addressing symptoms. When working with an adult, targeting a symptom (such as my inability to tolerate cracking noises) often spontaneously opens up earlier memories of a trauma that are in some way related to the current symptom. Using EMDR to target a memory of a *template experience,* or similar, earlier experience, usually reduces the anxiety associated with that memory, and also reduces the anxiety that fuels current posttraumatic symptoms.

I wondered whether targeting children's posttraumatic symptoms with EMDR would be as effective as targeting template experiences. I decided to begin by focusing on posttraumatic material that young children presented to me during our therapy sessions, rather than stimulating memories of the traumatic event itself. Children usually bring as much traumatic material to their play as they can tolerate.

For example, I thought about Danitra, a 4-year-old who was terrified of closed doors and had prolonged temper tantrums whenever her mother went out on the porch to bring in the mail. Marcia, her young mother, was in despair. "I don't know what to do," she told me. What could possibly be behind Danitra's mysterious behavior?

At first, Marcia could think of no reason for it. But careful questioning revealed a singular event. When Danitra was 18 months old, she had lifted her arms to her father—who turned away from her, left the house, and slammed the door, leaving the family forever. No wonder this child was terrified of closing doors!

I wondered whether EMDR could help Danitra feel more comfortable when doors were closed, but I didn't expect a 4-year-old to be able to follow the EMDR protocol for treating critical-incident trauma in a way that would be suitable for an adult or adolescent. It also didn't seem appropriate to tell her to remember the day her father abandoned her, as she did not mention that event.

Children play, and children usually get over upsetting events by playing. Their imagination usually works the magic of healing. This child played repetitively and grimly, however, which is typical of posttraumatic play. It does not lead to resolution of the trauma, but repeats endlessly. Danitra wasn't just afraid of closing doors, she was terrified. Any closing door precipitated a full-scale meltdown, as if she were being abandoned—as she was at the age of 18 months.

One day when Danitra entered my play room, she swung the door back and forth for a while, then settled herself under a table. I reasoned that she had "closing doors" on her mind, so I knew I had an opportunity. It occurred to me to adapt the children's song "Open, Shut Them" so that it would apply to doors instead of hands. Then I moved a pillow back and forth in front of her, singing, "Open, shut them, open, shut them, *you are safe inside*." I sang it several times, continued moving the pillow, and watched her relax.

When she returned the next week, I could hardly wait to ask her mother if she had noticed any changes over the past week. "No," Marcia said slowly, thinking over events of the past week. "No changes." I asked specifically, "Did you notice any changes in the way she responded to the door closing?" "Now that you mention it," she replied, "she did go into the bathroom this morning and shut the door. That's a first. And now that I think about it, she hasn't had to come with me or make a fuss when I go out to the front porch to get the mail." The child's behavior had changed without addressing the template experience.

Marcia was a very observant person, but she didn't remember this significant improvement in her daughter's behavior until I asked a specific question about her response to closed doors. Why? I have seen many children, as well as adults "not notice" improvements after EMDR until they are pointed out to them. It seems that once EMDR has stimulated the self-healing process and behavior has "righted itself," the change feels so natural that we just take it for granted that we feel fine in that aspect of our lives. Like having an annoying cold clear up, we may not focus on how good it feels to breathe easily for more than a few breaths.

Inspired by success with closing doors, I integrated more EMDR reprocessing techniques into play therapy, again as a natural extension of play. For example, I was working with Ryan, a child who had moved from foster home to foster home, and whose play consisted of driving toy trucks around and around the playroom. When he finally paused to rest, I picked up the truck and moved it back and forth, saying, "That's right, you can rest and feel safe now, the moving is over for now." I stopped moving the truck back and forth when I saw Ryan sigh and then relax, indicating a shift in his attitude about moving. I guessed that Ryan relaxed when he realized that moving was not only associated with danger; moving had finally brought him to safety. The theme of Ryan's play changed after that, and his foster mother said he seemed more relaxed at home. Was the change a result of EMDR? I had no way to be sure, but so far, it wasn't doing any apparent harm.

JAKE: USING EMDR TO TREAT NIGHTMARES

Next I was called on to treat Jake, a 5-year-old in foster care. He had been having terrible nightmares for 2 weeks, and everyone in the family was tired and irritable from being awake at night. "Do something!" they pleaded. Jake's regular therapist had referred the family to me because, as pediatrician, I could prescribe a sedative. I don't like prescribing medication for children if there is another alternative. The foster mother had already tried soothing baths and warm milk at bedtime, quiet, comfortable bedtime stories, and lots of reassurance. Again, I wondered whether EMDR might help reduce this child's anxiety.

I asked what had been happening in Jake's life around the time when the nightmares began. I learned that the day before the first nightmare, a social worker had come to the home, where Jake had lived since infancy. There were four other children in the home, but the social worker directed his attention to this child. A distant relative of the boy had expressed an interest in adopting him. Although the social worker had spoken only with the foster mother about the possibility of adoption, Jake must have picked up on his foster mother's anxiety. He certainly noticed that the social worker was only interested in him, not his "brothers and sister." The foster mother was very attached to this boy, who she had raised "like her own." Although she was not prepared to adopt, she would have been heartbroken if the child had been removed from her care. She couldn't tell Jake what was troubling her, because she didn't want to alarm him unnecessarily about a change that might never occur.

I saw Jake alone, and he looked me straight in the eyes as he anxiously told me, "I have nightmares every night. The nightmares are always the same. A tiger jumps out of the moon, runs in through the kitchen window, and chases me around the house. Then I wake up screaming and crying and calling for my mom." In every dream, he explained, the tiger was only chasing him, never his brothers and sister, even though they were there too. He looked at me expectantly.

The dream seemed to represent the experience of having the social worker (the tiger in the dream) jump out of the moon (an unlikely event indeed, just as unlikely to this child as having an unknown social worker with an unspoken mission enter his life) and chase only the boy and not his siblings (the "why me?" associated with the social worker taking an interest in him and not his siblings). The strange visit aroused the foster mother's extreme anxiety, which she transmitted to the child. The anxiety was so enormous that Jake was unable to process it, and awoke from the nightmares in a panic.

I glanced to the shelf holding sand-tray toys and noticed a miniature tiger. I asked Jake if he would be willing to try something to see if we could make the nightmare less scary. "Sure," he said. I asked him to think about his dream as if it were a movie and to watch the toy tiger as I waved it back and forth. He steadily moved his eyes with the tiger, back and forth. I watched his face for a shift in expression, and then, when he swallowed and blinked, I stopped moving the tiger. "What happened?" I asked. He responded calmly, "The tiger jumped out of the moon the way it always does, and it chased me around the house and not my brothers and sister, but then the tiger licked my hand and went to sleep on the floor." Then he picked out some toy trucks and began building roads in the sand.

The dream had begun the same, but instead of Jake being devoured or waking in terror, the ending of the dream had changed to something less frightening. The tiger (like the social worker) tried to make friends and, though tamer, it stayed as a dormant risk to safety. Jake's EMDR experience seemed to allow him to have a more appropriate level of worry about his encounter with the social worker, even though he didn't have any additional information to help him make sense of the event.

His foster mother happily reported back to me that the sleep disturbance had stopped. No more nightmares. Eventually, the "threat" of adoption by a distant relative passed. I've never seen Jake again, but I've often wondered what made it possible for his excessive fear to dissipate, and how EMDR allowed him to have an amount of fear that was appropriate to the situation. It was intriguing to me that the tiger stayed on the floor near the boy and didn't go away in his EMDR-stimulated dream. EMDR seemed to allow him to validate that there was indeed some threat, though dormant, to his current well-being. This experience with moderation of anxiety in a young child encouraged me to trust that although EMDR changed a child's nightmare, it did not alter his very accurate perception of some kind of potential threat to his security.

USING EMDR TO TREAT ANXIETY-CHARGED PLAY

I continued to have success using EMDR to treat children, adolescents, and adults for critical-incident trauma, and I began to use the method to ameliorate the anxiety-charged play of children who were in long-term therapy to treat the effects of chronic abuse or neglect. I ask for the children's permission before doing EMDR, and I always tell them that they are in control, that they can tell me to stop at any time, and I will. I frequently offered EMDR to several children with histories of chronic abuse who had been in therapy with me for over a year. I knew their issues well, I had experience in judging their responses, and we had the kind of trusting relationship that is an essential foundation for doing trauma therapy. Initially, they accepted EMDR very well, when I used it to enhance positive feelings or to reinforce positive cognitions as they came up in play.

I began to present EMDR while 5-year-old Jana was doing highly charged, posttraumatic play (for example, having dolls reenact a scene of physical violence). I picked up the fighting dolls, moved them back and forth to guide the child's eye movements and asked her to remember the fighting and notice the feelings in her body. After a few minutes, Jana relaxed and said she felt better. With some children, this kind of intervention clearly reduced anxiety. Sometimes children told me to stop doing EMDR, however. I complied, of course, and postulated that the EMDR had opened up memories of the actual violence, and that they were flooded with anxiety (although there were few physical indicators of anxiety, as there seldom are in children during EMDR). Taylor had finally exclaimed, "I would rather die than do EMDR again!" and fell off his chair in mock collapse. He immediately got up and played, looking pleased that he had dramatized his point. I never attempted EMDR with him again. Since then, I use EMDR cautiously during play with children with chronic, complex PTSD who are in a tenuous living situation. I offer eye movement or alternate tapping for relaxation, for enhancement of self-esteem, for reinforcing positive cognitions that arise out of play, and for reprocessing upsetting material related to specific critical incidents.

WHEN EMDR WITH CHILDREN DOESN'T WORK

Although I have had great success using EMDR with children, there are some situations for which it seems neither suitable nor effective. EMDR may not reduce a child's anxiety when there is an underlying organic pathology, when there is unresolved trauma in the family and an unstable environment, or when the parents are what I call "too good," or when "health" appears to threaten the child or family.

ORGANIC PATHOLOGY

In my experience EMDR does not work for treating organically based disorders such as psychosis, bipolar disorder or manic-depressive illness, and learning disabilities. It does not change underlying conditions like attention-deficit hyperactivity disorder (ADHD), unless the child is actually suffering from PTSD that was misdiagnosed as ADHD. Both PTSD and ADHD can present with symptoms of anxiety, difficulty concentrating, impulsivity, low self-esteem, poor school performance, and difficulty in personal relationships.

EMDR can sometimes reduce the anxiety resulting from organic conditions, however, and can modify the beliefs the child has adopted as a result of the secondary trauma associated with having a handicapping condition. For example, a child with ADHD and learning disabilities may believe, "I'm stupid. I can't learn." EMDR might help to shift this child's self-assessment so that he believes, "I can learn in my own way" or "I can learn one step at a time." EMDR can have limited benefit for children with developmental disabilities that affect their cognitive processing. EMDR can treat their critical-incident trauma or anxiety-based symptoms, but the results may not generalize to other situations.

UNRESOLVED TRAUMA IN THE FAMILY AND AN UNSTABLE ENVIRONMENT

For adults, childhood trauma is in the past. Abusive, abandoning, or disturbed parents no longer have substantial power over adult children. Adults have choices about where they will live and whom they choose for friends and associates; children are truly dependent on their parents for their well-being.

In doing EMDR with adults whose high level of distress does not diminish while processing a traumatic memory, clinicians are trained to use a "cognitive interweave" to access information that would allow them to feel safe from their abuser, to alleviate self-blame, and to affirm that the adult has choices. Dr. Shapiro (1995), the originator of the EMDR method, coined the phrase "cognitive interweave" to refer to techniques that might help the adult client gain perspective on a situation that is no longer dangerous. For example, to facilitate processing of a memory of childhood abuse that continues to cause intense anxiety despite numerous sets of eye movements, she trains clinicians to pose questions such as "Whose responsibility was it?" or "Do you have choices now?" or

"Are you safe now?" An adult might respond with a sigh of relief, "It was my father's responsibility. He was the adult. He should not have humiliated me and used abusive language with any child. I am safe now. I have choices about how I live my life and how I will treat my children."

For the child, however, the question, "Whose responsibility is it?" imposes an insoluble dilemma. If the child acknowledges that his parents are responsible for their mean actions, the child is a subordinate, doomed to a powerless position. If the child perceives himself as responsible for the parents' punishments, he views himself as bad or unlovable.

The question "What choices do you have?" is merely rhetorical. Children do not have choices about where they live, where they go to school, or who their parents are. Children may indeed be powerless over the safety of their environment. EMDR cannot change the reality of their situation, nor can it make them perceive harmful treatment as benign. The best the clinician can do may be to use EMDR to install "educational interweaves," or developmentally appropriate information, to teach children. For example, an abused child might need to know that children can never make an adult harm them (therefore children are not to blame for abuse), that all children deserve safety, and that they can go to a trusted adult when they need protection. EMDR can be used to reinforce the learning of these principles and to rehearse strategies for coping with difficult situations.

It is not only abusive parents who make it impossible for a child to feel safe. Often, attentive, caring parents carry feelings that make it difficult for a child to get over a traumatic event. For example, Sheena was injured at preschool, and her posttraumatic nightmares and fear of returning to school were initially resolved with EMDR. But her anxiety mounted again as her parents became increasingly upset about the inadequate supervision that permitted the accident to occur. The parents were reluctant to have Sheena return to school because they no longer trusted the school staff to protect their child. By the time her parents decided to sue the school for negligence, Sheena was understandably fearful about returning to school. She began clinging to her mother and her nightmares resumed. For Sheena, and other children in this position, EMDR does not clear out anxiety that belongs to other family members. If a parent continues to be anxious, that anxiety is continuously registered by the child.

The problem here is not that EMDR failed, but that the environment, both at school and at home, is not yet safe. In this situation the safety of the school environment must be secured first, the parents' own limiting beliefs—such as "I can only keep my child safe if I am the sole caregiver, or I cannot protect my child"—must be reprocessed, and all legal action must be settled before the child's anxiety level can return to normal. EMDR with the child alone will not usually be sufficient to restore his or her sense of well-being, unless resolution of the child's symptoms alone completely reassure the parents that all is well again.

"TOO GOOD" PARENTS

Another example of well-meaning parents "getting in the way" of their children's trauma resolution can be seen in what I call "too good" parents. These are parents who are determined to be sensitive to their perception of their child's needs, when in fact they are taking care of the needs they themselves had as children. For example, as a child, Jeff repeatedly felt invalidated by his father, who ignored his fears. When Jeff became a parent, he decided that he would always take his child's fears seriously.

Unfortunately, as a result, he proudly responded to his 5-year-old son Dylan's fears by validating Dylan's intense, frightened response to new or mildly scary situations with overly protective responses: "Oh, it is scary to go play at a friend's house without me. I'll stay with you or you don't have to go. . . . I can see you're afraid to speak at circle time. I'll ask the teacher not to call on you. . . . I know the dark is scary. You can have the light on, and I'll stay with you all night." In the name of being parents who are respectful of their child's feelings, "too good" parents like Jeff are actually depriving their child of the opportunity to develop his own courage.

Similarly, parents who suffered abuse or severe, restrictive criticism as children often "bend over backwards" not to coerce their children in any way. They may equate any discipline or limit setting with punishment. Although this philosophy is well-intentioned, it may result in parents who refuse to set important limits for their children or teach them about appropriate behaviors.

Parents must teach a child valuable life skills by advocating cooperation or encouraging a child to take on an age-appropriate task to promote independence. For example, Jeff could encourage Dylan to attend kindergarten, to practice taking a turn speaking at circle time, or to try some strategies for keeping himself company, in bed alone, after story time. Appropriate parenting is essential for sustaining the new confidence EMDR may promote.

WHEN "HEALTH" THREATENS THE CHILD OR THE FAMILY

Appreciating young children's profound dependency on their parents helps us to understand some of the variables that determine whether EMDR can work for a particular child. As we have seen, a hungry baby not only wants to be fed, he *needs* to be fed, for his very survival depends on it. If he isn't fed, he isn't merely disappointed, he is desperate. Children are exquisitely attuned to their parents' cues. They learn the nuances of their caregivers' emotions because being able to please, enchant, predict, and persuade the bonded caregiver means life itself for a vulnerable infant.

Trauma returns children to their most vulnerable state, and activates their most primitive survival instincts. Children's loyalty to their parents is of utmost importance in the hierarchy of the psyche's priorities for protection. EMDR only clears excessive anxiety when the ecology of the system permits. Sometimes a child's psyche appears to prefer disabling symptoms to "health," if health means that the child or the child's parents would be in jeopardy. Lack of motivation or disinterest in getting rid of fears and anxiety may appear to prevent trauma resolution, when in fact a child may be attempting to protect her family.

For example, EMDR initially did not seem to work for 13-year-old Jamie. Jamie's mother wanted her daughter treated successfully for increasingly severe phobias before she left on an assignment to Africa, where she would report on the effects of the devastating Ebola virus. Jamie believed that if she got well, her mother would go to Africa, contract Ebola virus, and die. Although her mother tried to persuade her daughter to move her eyes and think about her phobias, the girl repeatedly asserted that EMDR wouldn't help her, and, despite her mother's observations to the contrary, denied that there were any changes following EMDR. When her mother returned from Africa, the child's phobias cleared quickly with one EMDR session. Motivation to feel healthy and free of excess anxiety and interest in using the EMDR method are both important factors in the success of this approach to relieving stress.

USING EMDR TO TREAT "CASCADES OF TRAUMA"

Sometimes a series of traumatic events occur within a relatively short period of time or traumas are followed by a deluge of secondary traumatic losses. Some children live in a traumatic environment (for example, with an alcoholic or psychotic parent) in which upsetting events occur frequently and at unpredictable times. I call these overwhelming traumas "cascades of trauma" because they remind me of the cumulative force of a waterfall gathering power as it pours over rocky cliffs. Children and families who experience cascades of trauma never have a chance to recover fully from one crisis before they have to deal with the next. When EMDR is used in the treatment of cascades of trauma, it typically takes longer to achieve a significant reduction of anxiety, and treatment effects are less predictable and may be less complete than when treating a critical incident.

The hallmark of cascades of trauma is that the child or the family feels fearful and powerless for a prolonged period of time. Three-year-old Darius experienced the deaths of his grandfather and two uncles over a 3-month period, repeated school failures, and placement in a class for severely emotionally disturbed children, as well as his parents' ensuing alienation. Nine-year-old Eliza lived with her alcoholic father and never knew when she would be the subject of verbal abuse, so she fearfully anticipated her father's outbursts. Eleven-year-old Gordon had already been abandoned by his mother, expelled from school for fighting, and exposed to his father's drug-dealing friends when he was molested by a man at his uncle's house. Neither EMDR, therapy, nor medication can completely make up for lost years of childhood development. Nevertheless, EMDR helped each of these children achieve significant relief from fear and reduced many of their distressed and distressing behaviors.

SMALL WONDERS

Many of the cases you will read about in this book required only brief intervention for trauma resolution. In every case, in addition to play therapy, I used eye movement desensitization and reprocessing as a therapeutic tool. I have selected cases that present the drama of daily living and illustrate the effects on children of common upsetting events, from breaking a bone in a playground accident to having repeated bouts with head lice.

Most of these children are basically healthy and growing up in a stable environment with caregivers who are concerned about their well-being. Their cases look tidy, fairly straightforward, and simple compared with the cases of children who have suffered chronic abuse and neglect, or those who are victims or witnesses to violent crime or overwhelming accidents. Work with severely traumatized children offers a chance to learn about the devastating psychopathology that destroys children's health and distorts their future. So-called minor trauma offers an opportunity to examine determinants of self-confidence, personality, and identity formation.

Although the aggressive, difficult-to-control child is likely to receive some kind of therapy, the quiet, fearful child's underlying problems often go unnoticed. Parents sometimes attribute their child's difficulties to temperament. They explain the child's lack of confidence and self-esteem as a personality characteristic: "He's shy" or "sensitive." "She's cautious." It seems to me that these adjectives to describe temperament sometimes became excuses for posttraumatic symptoms.

It is not always easy for parents to bring a child into treatment. Some parents are dissuaded by the time involved, the cost, the vague goal, and the stigma of having a child in traditional psychotherapy. I find that parents are more likely to accept EMDR as treatment for a traumatized child because it often can work faster than other treatments, it can make medication unnecessary, and the goals of treatment are clear: to relieve the anxiety that remains from the trauma so the child can get on with his or her normal development.

EMDR may sound simple, and some parents or clinicians may feel tempted to try it. It is important not to use EMDR without training, however. EMDR is more complex than it first appears, and it takes a trained, experienced professional to keep processing safe and successful. It is essential that EMDR for children is always guided by a clinician who has expertise in working with children as well as EMDR training that has been approved by the EMDR International Association.

The children in these stories exemplify a wide range of ages and developmental stages, and the cases present a variety of problems and demonstrate a range of therapeutic approaches. Always, I try to get to the heart of the mystery: What is causing this behavior and what can we do about it? EMDR acts as the lens that reveals each layer of posttraumatic beliefs, feelings, and behaviors, while it peels away the excess anxiety and facilitates trauma resolution.

I have written this book for parents, clinicians, and readers curious about the workings of trauma in childhood, therapies that can facilitate trauma resolution, and the remarkable ability of children to heal from traumatic experiences. EMDR cannot treat every child and every problem, nor is it a therapy I use exclusively in my work. It should never be used by someone who has not been trained in the method, nor should anyone expect it to be a panacea.

I have done my best to stay close to the facts of the histories and the therapeutic process, while maintaining the confidentiality of families and protecting the sensibilities of children who may someday read this book and recognize their personal story. I have obtained permission from parents and children whose stories you will read in the following chapters. Details of name, address, occupation, and physical appearance have been changed in every case. Gender, number of family members, and family configuration have been altered in some cases. The children come from a wide socioeconomic spectrum and a variety of families: some live with both parents, some have been raised by single parents, foster families, adoptive parents, or a grandparent. They are Caucasian, African American, Asian, Hispanic, and from diverse socioeconomic backgrounds.

They all have one thing in common: Through therapy and EMDR, these children were able to use their own special, inner "magic," to reclaim their power and sense of self, and to get back on a healthy developmental track. These children, and many more like them, continue to amaze and inspire me with their courage, strength, creativity, and uniqueness. I call this book *Small Wonders* in their honor.

PART II

SMALL
WONDERS

THE CASES

3

WHO'S AFRAID OF A TOILET?
CRITICAL-INCIDENT TRAUMA

T hree-year-old Tanya screamed relentlessly as her parents tried to persuade her to enter the kitchen of their newly remodeled home. Eyes wide, lips trembling, digging her fingernails into her mother's neck, she looked as if she were entering a torture chamber.

That wasn't all that was worrisome about Tanya these days. She was fearful about many things and seemed to be developing new fears daily. She insisted on riding with the car windows closed. She anxiously asked "Fire?" whenever she heard sizzling noises of food cooking. She backed away—far away—from anything hot, like a bowl of soup. Even clouds high in the sky upset her. "Smoke?" she worried. The toilet had become another cause for alarm. Confidently toilet trained by age two, Tanya now ran screaming from the bathroom whenever the toilet flushed. If she was in another room when she heard the toilet flush, she covered her ears.

Tanya's parents knew that she had been upset by seeing fire destroy their kitchen 3 months earlier. They were grateful that no one was hurt, but they were concerned because Tanya's new fears were popping up so fast. Before the fire Tanya had been a playful, bright, outgoing, feisty 3-year-old, and they assumed she would be her cheerful self again within a few weeks of the fire.

At first, they thought that Tanya's reactions to the fire were normal. Tanya was quieter and more irritable than usual, but her parents were stressed too. There were insurance people to talk with, the search for a temporary apartment, concern about time missed from work, and endless discussions about how to remodel the house. Tanya and her 8-year-old sister spent a lot of time together that summer. Her sister cut flames out of paper and both girls ran through them over and over. For her older sister, this was mastery play. She had triumphantly escaped the flames. Tanya, on the other hand, screamed in terror at this game. By the end of summer, Tanya became so anxious that she constantly worried that a fire would break out.

Tanya's parents did their best to soothe and reassure their daughter about her fears. As they approached the day for moving back into their newly remodeled home, they took her to the front porch of the house and talked to her about how pretty their house looked, all fixed up. They tried to coax her to look at her bedroom, where a new toy was waiting. Tanya started screaming as soon as she saw the house. She calmed a little on the front porch, but closed her eyes as her mother carried her inside and no amount of encouragement persuaded Tanya to open her eyes. She held tight to her mother's arms and her lips trembled.

Tanya's parents decided to ask for professional help. They had tried everything they knew to reassure their child, and they were concerned that forcing her to stay in the house she dreaded so much might make things worse. They called their pediatrician who referred the family to me.

CRITICAL-INCIDENT TRAUMA AND CHILDREN

A critical incident is a single event that is perceived as threatening to one's life or sense of safety. It can leave a child feeling helpless, powerless, and fearful. Sometimes, a parent can help a young child get over a critical incident by reassuring her that she is safe now (if that is true), by listening to and acknowledging the scary feelings, by being comforting, and by explaining what happened and pointing out that they know the incident is over now and that everyone is safe. Sometimes, the event is so threatening that parents, too, are very upset, and children read their parents' unspoken, profound fears. After all, children are highly sensitive to emotional cues, and the well-being of very young children truly rests on their ability to detect nonverbal, emotional signals of safety or danger. Sometimes the child experiences such fright in a critical-incident trauma that even the calmest, most competent, and appropriately reassuring parent cannot prevent posttraumatic stress.

When a child is traumatized there may be an identifiable moment when he appears "like a deer in the headlights," that is, too stunned to move, perceiving that death is nearly certain, and he doesn't have time to escape. Perhaps at that time there is a change instantaneously activated in the brain's biochemistry, so that the brain begins to process information differently. When this "emergency mode" is activated, the brain sorts all incoming information related to the traumatic event into one of two categories: safe and unsafe. The child or adult in a similar situation has no time to consider, "The sound of food cooking isn't dangerous unless it's accompanied by smoke and flames. Even that could be safe if someone is cooking over a camp fire." The emergency mode helps the threatened individual bypass time-consuming thinking that might waste lifesaving moments for escape.

Furthermore, this special biochemical configuration is designed to protect the individual from future harm by stimulating the anxiety response any time anything happens that remotely resembles the trauma. After a child has experienced a critical incident, like a fire, anything that looks, smells, sounds, or feels like the trauma will signal an alert and will stimulate the anxiety response.

So it is not surprising that everything that looked like smoke, sounded like steam hissing or food cooking, felt hot, or in any way reminded her of the traumatic incident caused anxiety for Tanya. Initially, it was not apparent why she had become afraid of toilets, but I suspected that something about a toilet was connected to the traumatic event.

The practitioner has to approach recent critical incidents differently from more distant critical incidents (those occurring more than 3 months previously). Recent critical incidents have to be processed frame by frame—that is, EMDR must target every component of the trauma. In adults, memories of long-past critical incidents seem to consolidate, so that if the practitioner uses EMDR to target the worst part of the trauma, the benefit of EMDR generalizes to decrease anxiety related to the entire trauma. For young children, however, traumas seem to be stored in fragments, regardless of when the trauma occurred. For best results, the practitioner must use EMDR to target every aspect of the traumatic memory. Storytelling is an effective way to do this, and one I felt would work with Tanya.

STORYTELLING

When I first started treating young children using the EMDR method, I used eye movement to enhance feelings of safety and mastery or to diminish feelings of helplessness and anxiety that came up during play therapy. EMDR in conjunction with play therapy seemed to help children feel better more quickly than play therapy alone.

I was challenged to develop another way to apply EMDR when I met Hue (pronounced "Way"), a 20-month-old Vietnamese boy who spoke no English, but understood the expression, "good boy." Hue had been sitting comfortably in a child-safety seat in the back of his family car when all of a sudden his calm life changed to terror with a big jolt and bang as another car smashed into the side of the family car and sent it spinning out of control. The accident had left easygoing Hue irritable, angry, and disturbed by nightmares several times each night.

Because I was unable to communicate verbally with Hue, it occurred to me that Hue's parents could tell him the story of the accident, in Vietnamese, while I used EMDR tapping techniques to desensitize the memory of the frightening experience. I asked Hue's parents to tell me what they imagined his experience of the accident to have been, using language that Hue would understand if they were speaking Vietnamese. The story was brief and simple: "Riding in the car. Everybody happy. Big boom! Everybody scared and crying! Go to hospital. Everybody fine. Everybody go home. Go to sleep." I asked them to tell Hue the story of the accident while I tapped his knees alternately.

I wanted to make some connection with Hue before I tried to use alternating movements to desensitize frightening memories of the accident. Usually, I start my preparation for treatment with children by playing with them or having them imagine a favorite place or a safe place. Young children often identify a parent's lap as a safe place. Some children enjoy a favorite song as fun and relaxing. The idea is simply to practice EMDR tapping while enhancing a good feeling and teaching the child how to participate by tapping or being tapped. I decided that my verbal affirmation "Good boy" would have to be Hue's safe-place equivalent as well as his good thought about himself (in EMDR lingo, his *positive cognition*).

First, I taught Hue to tap my hands repetitively. (Although there has been no research to date to determine the relative effectiveness of tapping the child's hands or knees or having the child tap the clinician's hands, it seems that these methods are equally effective.) Then I tapped his hands. I said, "Good boy," and watched him smile.

I prompted Hue's parents to tell him their story about the day of the car accident. Hue sat on his mother's lap while his father related the story in Vietnamese. I sat in front of Hue and expended my hands for him to tap alternately. As soon as the story became upsetting, Hue stopped tapping my hands. I gave him a toy car to hold, and I tapped his knees alternately while his father continued relating the story in a dramatic way. In less than a minute, when the storytelling and rapid-alternating stimulation were over, Hue sat peacefully on his mother's lap. I tapped Hue's knees alternately as I repeated "Good boy," and Hue smiled. Our session was over.

Follow-up calls to his parents and pediatrician revealed that after only one session, Hue's symptoms cleared completely. His cheerful disposition had returned and he was sleeping soundly through the night. Hue didn't need to come back. When I called his pediatrician several years later, I found that Hue had continued to grow and develop well, without any notable behavioral problems.

My rewarding experience with Hue prompted me to try a similar approach with other young children in which parents create and tell a story about the traumatic event. This approach has many advantages. Storytelling, in conjunction with EMDR techniques, is well suited to satisfying the developmental needs of young children. Children love stories, especially if the story is about them. Young children usually have difficulty verbalizing their fears or retelling the details of a trauma that has happened to them; because the parent tells the story, the child isn't required to speak, but may if she likes. The therapist has the opportunity to observe and evaluate the child's response to the story.

Children live in a family: Whenever a child has been traumatized, the parents have also been affected. Furthermore, the parents often feel inadequate or ashamed because they have not been able to protect their child from suffering. The storytelling approach gives the parents an opportunity to help their child feel better and can be an effective way of resolving some of their own issues about parenting and about the traumatic event.

Let us return to Tanya. I thought that Tanya sounded like an ideal candidate for my storytelling approach. The traumatic event that affected her was a discrete critical incident with a beginning, a middle, and an end. Her symptoms were traceable to the trauma itself and not in any way a result of her parents' attitudes or handling of the situation. Her parents were willing to be partners with me in her treatment, they were able to write a story about the event for their child, and their treatment goals for their daughter were realistic and appropriate.

PREPARING FOR THE STORY: THE FIRST VISIT

Tanya's parents came alone to their first visit, as I had requested. Tyrone and Roberta were both tall and gave an impression of strength and stability. They presented their concerns clearly. They wanted to handle things as well as possible so their young daughter could get over her fears and move back into their house comfortably. They enumerated Tanya's symptoms: She was fearful and covered her ears whenever she heard popping sounds, traffic noises, fire-engine sirens, cooking sounds, and hissing steam. She was afraid of being burned whenever she felt heat, and appeared terrified when the toilet flushed. She was almost constantly worried that a fire would break out again.

Aside from witnessing the fire, Tanya had had a calm life. She had no history of hospitalization, injuries, or significant illness. She was the 7-pound product of a normal pregnancy, labor, and delivery. She was breast-fed for 2 years and her developmental milestones were appropriate.

Tanya's mother started recounting the story of the night the house burned. "I was at work, as usual. I got home from work at 8 P.M., and when I turned onto our street I could see the fire engines and the smoke but at first I didn't even realize that it was our house that was on fire. As soon as I realized it was our house, I saw my husband coming down the driveway to meet me. Right away, my husband told me that our girls were safe at our neighbor's house, so I didn't have time to wonder whether anyone was hurt. We went over to the neighbor's house to get the children. Tanya was real glad to see us. She had just been quiet, sitting there watching TV. Tyrone will have to tell you what actually happened before I came home."

Tanya's father continued, "That night I fed the children dinner first, the way I usually do. I gave them some soup and sandwiches they wanted. They ate, then they went in the family room, behind the kitchen, to watch TV. I decided to fry up some chicken so Roberta and I could have it when she came home from work. I heated the grease. It started bubbling and smoking and before I knew it the grease caught on fire and the flames leaped up and started to race across the ceiling to the other side of the room. I grabbed the phone with one hand and called 911 while I turned off the stove and threw the lid over the flaming pot. By that time the room was filling with smoke and flames. I grabbed a dishtowel to cover my nose and looked up to see my older daughter run by the kitchen door to the front door to go outside.

"Then I saw Tanya. She stood in the kitchen doorway, frozen. Then she screamed, a long scream, still standing frozen. I rushed over and scooped her up and took her outside where I handed her over to our neighbor, who had come running over to see what was going on. I ran to get the garden hose and pulled it into the kitchen to start putting out the fire. By then the fire had destroyed the kitchen and was moving into the family room.

"I was pretty calm and level headed," Tyrone told me, "I guess because I was in Vietnam and had to deal with a lot worse stuff than this. I knew that the children were both safe. I only got a little burned on my arms. I went outside when the fire fighters started getting things under control. Just as I went down the driveway, I saw my wife and told her the girls were okay. We were both relieved that nobody was hurt.

"We went to get the girls. I knew they were upset, but Tanya seemed like she was in shock for a while. We were all a little disoriented, I guess. We went to a motel to spend the night. Then we had to start dealing with the insurance company in the morning. It's been pretty hectic since then."

I asked Tyrone and Roberta what beliefs Tanya might have about herself as a result of the fire. In EMDR terms these posttraumatic beliefs are called *negative cognitions*. Traumatic memories are also stored as beliefs about the helplessness, powerlessness, or worthlessness of the victim. Although the victim may have been helpless to stop the traumatic event, this belief is followed by a profound loss of self-confidence that does not serve the individual well after the critical incident has passed. Negative cognitions do not seem to change without intervention, and the untreated trauma survivor can continue to view herself as devalued and can continue to feel unsafe.

Roberta said, "I think Tanya feels, 'I'm not safe. It's going to happen to me again. I'm overwhelmed. I can't deal with it.'" I find that parents and young children are usually so close psychologically that the parents' perceptions about their child's beliefs are generally accurate. I asked what positive cognitions, or true and useful beliefs, they wanted their daughter to have about herself in relation to the fire. They talked for a few minutes and then Tyrone read me the list of beliefs they wanted Tanya to have: "I'm safe now. It's over. I can take care of myself by expressing myself and screaming or running when I need help."

I told Tyrone and Roberta that we could work together to help Tanya get over the fire and to regain her confidence. I explained EMDR and asked permission to use this new method to resolve the trauma. They agreed that it was worth a try. I asked whether they would write a story about the fire for Tanya. They nodded. I instructed them to begin the story with everyone being safe, to include any details leading up to the fire, to describe the fire as they imagined it appeared to Tanya, and to end the story with the fire over and everyone safe again. I suggested that they write the story about "a little girl," without mentioning Tanya's name. Some children can deal with the memory of something scary happening to someone else, but might be too upset to hear a story about their own trauma. Other children immediately claim the story as their own, and then the parents can personalize the story as much as they like. We would adjust the story later to meet Tanya's preference.

I asked Tanya's parents to tell her that she would be coming to see a doctor who helps families get over being upset and helps make things easier for children. Children may need reassurance that I am the kind of doctor who plays with them, not the kind who gives shots. I explained that the main goal of the first visit would be for Tanya to feel safe and to know that my office is a place where problems get better. Children love to hear their parents say good things about them, and I prepared Tanya's parents to expect me to ask questions such as, "What do you like best about Tanya? What are her favorite ways to play? Tell me about her imaginative power—what does she like to pretend?" We set up an appointment for me to meet Tanya.

TANYA'S FIRST VISIT

Later that week Tanya's parents returned with their petite 3-year-old daughter. She held both of their hands as she entered my office, then let go when she spotted the doll house. I sat on the floor beside her to meet her at eye level, and said, "This room is a special place where problems have a way of getting worked out. We have only two rules in my playroom: One, the sand stays in the sand tray and two, you may play whatever you like but no thing and no one ever gets hurt for real." She nodded solemnly. I told her that she could choose to join her parents and me while we talked, or she could play. Tanya looked at me with big brown eyes and then turned to my playhouse with its castle-like air. Her choice was made. She sat on the floor and immediately started playing, putting dolls in the kitchen and intoning, "The day it burned up."

Then Tyrone handed me the story he had written for his daughter. I quickly read the story to myself while Tanya's parents hung up their coats and settled themselves on the sofa. The one-page story would do just fine. I tucked it in Tanya's chart. While Tanya played, I asked her parents to tell me about her special qualities. "Tanya loves to sing and dance," Roberta told me, clearly pleased, "and she's very creative. She loves to play imaginative games." I said that I am always interested to know how children meet developmental challenges, that is, to do really hard things like learn to use the toilet. Tanya glanced up. Of course, I already knew that she had learned to use the toilet fairly easily and with her parents' patient encouragement. Tanya listened as she played, and her parents praised the way she had mastered that skill.

Every child I have ever met in my office enjoys hearing the positive things her parents say about her. Even a child who appears to be deep in play is registering those words of appreciation. If the parent mentions that her child's favorite color is pink, the child might snap to attention and assert "No, purple!" Some children will check in by asking "Who? Are you talking about me?" Conversations in my office rarely escape young children, especially if they are the topic of interest. It's also important to remember that young children absorb and remember the emotional tone of everything they hear, even if the vocabulary is beyond their understanding.

When I ask questions about how a child met a particular developmental challenge, I hope to tap into the knowledge that if she has accomplished other hard things, she can master this difficult task, too. Toilet training is one of my favorite early-developmental milestones, because I figure that if a tiny child can use a toilet, she has a lot of courage. Imagine going up to a toilet that comes up to your chest, being lifted, naked, onto a cold seat, balancing so you won't fall into the water, emptying your contents into this bowl, then being wiped and lifted off just before the toilet flushing results in a big roar, and your contents are swirled away. Recalling these acts of bravery can be used to bolster the courage of a young child.

Tanya's parents surprised and intrigued me by telling me that Tanya has "magic" and that she knows it. I noted their choice of words with recognition: It is this feeling of power, of magic, that I work to elicit and enhance for every child I see. Tanya's mother explained, "Tanya can feel whether her magic is high or low. When Tanya feels her magic is low, I give her an extra special hug or kiss. When her magic is low, Tanya also tells her godmother, who rubs Tanya's hands and wrists to increase her magic or help her feel stronger." I decided to use their concept of magic, already familiar to Tanya, to strengthen her self-esteem.

I asked Tanya whether she would like to choose a doll to help her get her own magic so strong that the memory of the fire would not be scary any more. Adults usually watch my hand or a "wand" guide their eyes through EMDR movements. I find that most children and many adolescents like to choose a doll or sand-tray figure or wand to help them, rather than simply following the movement of my hand during EMDR. I then hold the chosen object in my hand, and they can follow that with their eyes as I move my hand back and forth. Young children who are unable to do EMDR with their eyes sometimes like to be tapped on their hands or knees by their chosen figure. The figure may bestow its powers of comfort, strength, or companionship on the child.

Tanya selected a "mother" doll and came to sit on her mother's lap. I asked whether the doll had a name and Tanya's mother prompted her daughter, "You can call her Magic Lady." I asked Tanya whether she would like Magic Lady to help her get her own magic strong. She nodded. I asked where in her own body Tanya could feel her magic. She pointed to her wrists. Probably the rubbing of Tanya's hands by her godmother worked to place the physical sensation of magic in her hands.

I asked Tanya if Magic Lady could dance from hand to hand to get her magic strong. She nodded. I asked Tanya if she would let Magic Lady know when her magic felt very strong. She nodded again. Whenever I work with a traumatized child, I give her many opportunities to be in control. After all, one of the hallmarks of trauma is a feeling of not having any control, and my job is to restore the child's appropriate feelings of control in the world. With her permission, I used Magic Lady to perform EMDR by tapping Tanya's hands, and in less than a minute, Tanya smiled and agreed that her own magic was getting stronger already. One of the benefits of EMDR is that it enhances positive states and strengthens a child's feelings of strength and well-being.

Then I handed the story back to Tanya's father. I explained that I would interrupt his reading to ask Tanya questions that would focus her on certain emotional experiences and physical sensations that would be either enhanced, like the feelings of being safe, loved, and secure, or direct her attention to erase the fears that were no longer justified. EMDR can only instill true beliefs and can only remove false beliefs.

I used Magic Lady to alternately tap Tanya's hands while

Tanya's father began reading the story he had written. The story-telling session went like this (my interjections are written in italics, Tanya's responses are in parentheses, and sets of EMDR movements or tapping are represented by three dots: . . .).

TANYA'S FIRE STORY

Once upon a time there was this family composed of Father, Mother, and two sisters. Dad and Mom were very much in tune with their children. They loved both girls very much. The big sister was clever and pretty. The little girl of the family was smart and pretty and also very sensitive.

Can the little girl feel her dad and mom loving her? . . . (Tanya nodded).

Can the little girl feel herself loving her mom and dad? . . . (Tanya nodded again and snuggled close to her mother.)

On one of the many evenings that the children and Dad are home together, there occurred an accident that would get the little girl's attention. This evening after Dad had fed the children and put on their pajamas to get them ready for bed, then it happened. Dad was heating grease to cook him some dinner when it (grease) went poof!

Can you hear the sounds the grease makes? Let Magic Lady know when it sounds better. . . . (I want Tanya to remember the scary feeling associated with the sound of the grease sizzling, and I wait for an indication that she has processed the memory. I tap Tanya's hands alternately for about 10 seconds until she says "Better." When she says "better," I know that some of the scary feeling has dissipated.)

Before you knew it, the kitchen was full of flames and smoke.

Can you feel the heat? Let Magic Lady know when it feels better. (. . . "Better.")

Can you see the flames and smoke? (. . . "Better.")

The Big Sister ran past the flames and went out the door as her Dad had told her to do. The little girl was afraid to pass by the door because of the flames and the smoke. It turned out that the little girl was afraid and she also thought her father, who was fighting the flames, was on fire and would melt.

Can you see the father? . . . (Tanya looked at her father and nodded.)

Is Father safe now? . . . (Tanya examined her father. He nodded, and she nodded in response.)

She was also scared that she would melt too.

Is the little girl safe now? . . . Are you safe now? . . . (Tanya looked relieved as she nodded again.)

Where in your body do you feel that safe feeling? Point and show me. . . .

(Tanya arched her back off her mother's lap and patted her buttocks.)

The little girl screamed.

Show me how she screamed. . . . (Tanya opened her mouth and let out a scream of terror.)

What a smart girl to scream to get the help she needed. . . . Think about how the girl got the help she needed by scream- ing. Can you feel how smart she is? . . . (Nods.)

Her father recognized what was happening so he stopped fighting the fire, picked up his little girl and carried her out- side to safety. One of the neighbors held her while her dad returned to fight the fire. This action frightened the little girl again, and she cried. Then the firefighters came.

Can you hear the sounds of the fire truck? . . . Can you hear the sirens? . . . Can you see the lights flashing? . . . (She nods.)

The firefighters came and began to fight the fire. The lit- tle girl was taken to the neighbor's house so she could rest. After the fire was put out, Mom arrived, then Dad and Mother went to get their children. We didn't know it then but the lit- tle girl was very happy to see her dad not melted. The little girl and her family are all safe now. Their house has been remodeled and her family likes the new kitchen.

Can you see the new kitchen? . . . Can you imagine the sounds of yummy foods cooking? . . . (Tanya began to lick her lips.)

The storytelling was over for this session. I asked Tanya what helps to keep her safe. She spoke carefully, "Mommy, Daddy, Big Sister, friends, and . . . Magic Lady," and she leaned over to give Magic Lady a kiss. I asked Tanya where she felt the safe feeling, and she arched her back and patted her buttocks area again. It was time to stop our first session. Tanya's parents agreed that in the coming week they would notice Tanya's fearful behaviors and the situations that seemed to trigger them.

Tanya lifted her arms to her father. When he picked her up so that she was sitting on his arm, it became apparent that the safe feeling was literally seated in her buttocks area, the part of her that felt her father's arms carrying her away from the fire to safety.

"BETTER"

When they returned a week later, Tanya's parents reported that Tanya was much more relaxed and they had been able to move into their newly remodeled house. Tanya still responded to cooking noises by leaving the room or covering her ears and asking anxiously, "What is that?" She also became anxious and covered her ears whenever water faucets were turned on or the toilet was flushed. We agreed that the phobias about the sound of water running and the toilet flushing probably stemmed from the sound of water rushing through the fire hoses.

During the week since our last visit, there had been another upsetting incident. Smoke filled their newly remodeled kitchen while they were cooking, setting off the smoke detector and causing the parents to rush around anxiously, trying to open tight new windows. Understandably, this was upsetting to Tanya. Roberta told me that she had evoked the image of Magic Lady, and Tanya calmed down as her mother reminded her that Magic Lady was there to help her. For a few days, Tanya had talked about Magic Lady when she needed to calm herself. Tanya's parents were pleased that despite these difficulties, Tanya had begun to sleep throughout the night again without diapers.

Both of Tanya's parents noticed that Tanya had become bolder—she had touched a hot coffee cup even after her mother warned her not to touch because it was "hot." She would appropriately warn her parents to "be careful" when she saw steam, however. They remarked that although Tanya was still anxious when she saw a fire engine, she was able to ask questions, such as, "What is it? What are they doing? Where are they going?" She was able to ride in a car with the windows down, and traffic noises no longer bothered her.

Some of Tanya's fears had cleared in a single session, but some symptoms, such as worries about cooking sounds and steam, were probably rekindled by the incident that activated the smoke detector. The symptoms related to the sound of water going through the fire hoses had not yet been addressed. I decided to target the current symptoms this time, as well as targeting their precipitating traumatic origins. I asked Tyrone and Roberta to help me simulate the sounds of food sizzling, the smoke detector, fire-engine sirens, and water rushing through a hose to put out the fire. Tanya listened intently while Magic Lady danced back and forth between her palms until Tanya signaled "better." Then I asked Tanya to imagine she could see her new kitchen. She nodded. I asked if she could hear the sounds of yummy food cooking. She nodded again and licked her lips.

The following week Tanya returned for her third session. Her parents reported significant changes. They were surprised that she had calmly watched a TV show about forest fires. Tanya had become so comfortable in the kitchen that her parents had to make sure that she did not get too close while they were cooking. They thought that she was fearless, just as she had been before the fire. Tanya thought otherwise. I asked her whether she wanted Magic Lady to help her with anything. She looked up from her play in the sand tray and said, "Flashing lights and toilets."

I took my small flashlight from the cupboard and picked up the toy fire engine. Tanya sat on her father's lap while I held the light and the fire engine in one hand and waved them in front of Tanya's eyes. With my other hand, I guided Magic Lady back and forth between Tanya's hands. Tanya's teeth began to chatter. I remembered that Tanya had been outside in the cool night air when she watched the flashing lights of the fire engines. Within a minute, Tanya's face relaxed and she said, "Better."

Finally, it was time to work on reducing Tanya's anxiety about toilet flushing. I asked Tanya if she would come to the bathroom with me so she could practice flushing the toilet. Tanya took my hand and together we approached the toilet, while her parents waited in the playroom. Tanya agreed to flush the toilet. She pushed the lever, then covered her ears as the noisy toilet flushed. Meanwhile, I stood behind Tanya and used EMDR tapping, first on one shoulder and then the other. I asked Tanya whether she wanted to practice again or whether she wanted to ask her parents to watch. Tanya knew she was ready. She went back to the office, returned to the bathroom with both of her parents, and marched confidently up to the toilet. She flushed, watched, and proudly strutted out of the room. When we returned to the office I asked Tanya, "Is there anything else we need to do?" She picked up Magic Lady and kissed her good-bye.

Tanya and her mother returned a week later. Tanya had had a good week with no evident fears and no mention of Magic Lady, and she was definitely feeling confident. Every once in a while she reported, "I'm okay, I'm not afraid." Proudly, she told me she had invented a chant: "I am Tanya, it is true, I can do what I want to do!"

"I GET REAL NERVOUS"

A CAR ACCIDENT

"I just eat and eat," said 13-year-old Rosa. "I can't seem to stop eating. Ever since I was in the car accident 6 months ago, I've been real nervous. I can't stop thinking about the accident. I eat too much, I'm scared to ride in a car, I can't go on the street where we were rear-ended, and I wake up nervous at night whenever anyone opens or closes a door and my room shakes a little."

Rosa had been a passenger in the car her grandmother was driving when a truck suddenly and forcefully rear-ended their car while stopped at a traffic signal, while they were just waiting to turn. Rosa hurt all over and suffered minor whiplash, but her physical injuries were not serious. Both Rosa and her grandmother were very upset at the time of the accident. Their car had been badly damaged. They were frightened, confused about what had happened, unsure about the extent of their injuries, and worried about their damaged car. An ambulance took Rosa's grandmother, Graciella, to the emergency room to be checked, but Rosa refused to go and called her cousin to take her home.

Since that time, Rosa had become very reluctant to get in a car, especially when her grandmother was driving. When she did ride, she shook with fear and constantly worried that there would be another accident. Rosa pointed out that her hands trembled even as we talked about it. She refused to ride on the street where the accident had occurred, a main intersection near her home. Avoiding that intersection added a twenty-minute detour to many trips, an inconvenience that often got in the way of traveling.

Notice the power of the posttraumatic fears. Rosa understood that it was totally irrational to avoid that particular intersection. It was safely designed, with a traffic light, clearly marked signs, good visibility, and a left-turn lane. Yet her fear of a similar accident was so strong that it convinced her to avoid that site, even at the cost of greatly increased travel time. She acted *as if* her life depended on avoiding circumstances that reminded her of the accident. Her grandmother, who was driving, complied with Rosa's fears.

Rosa had heard that I could help her get over her fears of riding, but she was dubious. Fears can sometimes become so powerful that they manage to convince their owner that anything that might reduce fear should also be avoided. Rosa was distressed, but she was also rational, and she was willing to explore the possibility that I could help.

FEARS: A FALSE SECURITY SYSTEM

I explained to Rosa that fears are our psyche's way of trying to protect us, and that her psyche was working really hard to keep her away from perceived danger. Rationally, she understood that another accident could occur, but that neither fear, nor avoiding that intersection, could prevent it. She recognized that her fear was a false security system, yet she was not consciously able to discard it. Because there was no protective lesson to be gained by studying the trauma, I silently predicted that the most useful beliefs Rosa could attain would be "It's over. I'm fine now. I can calmly take the normal risk of riding in a car." As it turned out, Rosa had stronger healing power than I had imagined.

Rosa told me again that she used to like to ride in a car, and that she used to ride comfortably. She was distressed that she had become so nervous about riding. She volunteered that she was also terrified of earthquakes, "When someone closes a door at my house, and my bed shakes a little, I wake up scared and think it's an earthquake." She had also noticed that after the big San Francisco–Bay Area earthquake in 1989, she had started eating more and gained weight. "Since the wreck happened," she told me, "I eat even more."

MORE SOOTHING, MORE EATING

Not only do fears become extremely powerful after a trauma, but soothing methods and coping strategies are amplified as well. Many people, like Rosa, soothe themselves by eating when they are upset.

The more upset they become, the more soothing they need, and the more they eat. Rosa was so upset that it seemed she couldn't stop eating. This is a situation in which too much of a good thing becomes a problem. Rosa's constant eating gave her some comfort, but eventually caused even more distress. Now she was not only excessively fearful, she was becoming excessively overweight, and she began to worry about her weight, compounding the heavy load of problems she already carried.

MEMORIES OF TRAUMATIC EVENTS

I explained to Rosa that there are similarities in the way that everyone responds to a traumatic event. Usually we have a visual image or mental picture of the traumatic incident. When we view that picture or remember the unavoidable trauma, we often have a negative thought about ourselves, like "I'm helpless" or "I'm powerless." That negative self-assessment can circulate in the subconscious and appear at odd times. For example, for Rosa, that annoying thought might resurface whenever she paused at a stop sign or noticed an intersection, or perhaps whenever she considered going somewhere in a car. It is not helpful for a young woman, or anyone else for that matter, to mentally replay a version of "I'm powerless" as she goes about making life decisions.

The memory of the trauma is also stored in the body as an *affect* or feeling, a physical sensation, and sometimes as a behavior. Often, people who have experienced a serious trauma feel shame. They sometimes feel abnormal, as if just being who they are caused the problem. They sometimes feel guilty, regardless of whether they did anything wrong or not. Perhaps the discomfort of shame and guilt is preferable to the terrifying realization that neither being different nor doing something different could prevent a tragic occurrence.

USING IMAGINATION

After I explained EMDR, Rosa agreed to try it. I proposed that we start by doing some imagination exercises and using eye movement to help her strengthen feelings of being safe and relaxed. I told Rosa that she was in charge and urged her to practice giving me a signal to stop moving my hand whenever she wanted to stop moving her eyes. "You can always stop by closing your eyes or turning your head," I reminded her. "Let me know the speed of eye movement that is comfortable for you and the distance from your eyes that you want me to move my hand." It's important for people—adults and children—to be in control of their own EMDR process, especially if the trauma left them feeling powerless.

I asked Rosa to hold in her mind the image of a safe place or a favorite place, either real or imagined, where she could feel safe, relaxed, and comfortable. Rosa shared that she pictured herself in her bedroom with her friends and stuffed-animal collection. Then I instructed her to watch my fingers moving back and forth, and asked her to imagine she was pushing my fingers with her eyes. I asked where she felt the safe feeling in her body. She pointed to her chest. I elicited her eye movements by moving my hand, while she was thinking about the safe place and feeling the safe feelings in her body. After about 20 sweeps of my arm, I stopped. "How are you doing?" I asked. Rosa told me she felt "really relaxed."

Next, I asked Rosa to bring to mind her safe place again, and when she felt the safe feeling, to begin moving her eyes, this time in a different direction. I wanted Rosa to choose the direction of eye movement that was most comfortable for her. After a minute, Rosa took a big breath and stopped moving her eyes. She surprised me by saying, "I can feel the earthquake getting less scary already." She had switched her attention from the safe place to the earthquake, which was clearly on her mind. I had intended to start our work by focusing on the car accident, but Rosa's psyche had a different agenda.

Usually, when a person is concentrating on her safe place, memories of a frightening experience do not intrude. Perhaps in this situation, the memory of the earthquake surfaced because Rosa may have been focusing her attention on the earthquake instead of the safe place. Perhaps the two experiences were linked because Rosa had been in a bedroom with her friend when a safe place turned into a terrifying experience. This is a good example of why only trained professionals should be using EMDR. Even guided eye movement to reinforce feelings of safety can quickly turn into feelings of terror. In that situation, an untrained person can be faced with a terrified person who is rapidly being retraumatized, whereas a skilled clinician can steer the client toward successful resolution of the trauma.

MAKING CONNECTIONS

I began to help Rosa focus on her memories of the earthquake. At age 13, Rosa was able to handle the EMDR process much the way an adult does. That is, she was able to describe the visual image representing the scariest part of the traumatic incident, articulate her negative cognition and her desired positive cognition, and locate her feelings in her body. She was able to rate the severity of the upset using the Subjective Units of Distress Scale, or SUDS (developed by Joseph Wolpe in the 1950s), in which 0 represents calm and neutral, and 10 represents the most upset imaginable. She was able to judge how true the positive cognition felt in her body (using the VoC or Validity of Cognition scale developed by Shapiro in the 1980s) to ascertain how true the positive cognition felt before desensitization of the painful memory, after desensitization, and after installation of the positive cognition.

She could also process information like an adult. Her memory network extended back from the car accident that "shook her up" to the earthquake that "shook her up." Her coping strategy of eating for comfort had become a secondary pleasure, but her overeating had also become linked to the earthquake in another way. Rosa said that when she remembered the earthquake, the negative belief she had about herself was, "I lost everything." Now she wanted to "regain" what she had lost. Her psyche had associated "gaining" with eating to gain weight. So, her memories were linked through the common experience of "shaking her up" and in increasing her eating to help her gain, when she perceived that she had lost. This complex memory network is typical of an adult mind.

Younger children do not make these links spontaneously during EMDR. Although a 6-year-old might come in and talk about the pictures he has in his mind and his beliefs about himself and where he feels his feelings in his body, he would not spontaneously link memories and reprocess related memories while doing EMDR. It is the job of the clinician to prompt the young child to remember "other times you felt like that." Rosa's processing system was mature enough to spontaneously link memories of events that seemed related.

"What is the picture representing the scariest part of the earthquake?" I asked. Rosa described being at her friend's house and seeing the wall "going back and forth." Perhaps watching my hand moving back and forth had reminded her of the swaying motion of the wall. I asked Rosa what negative thoughts she had about herself as she looked back at that memory. She replied, "I'm gaining too much weight. I lost everything," and, with some prompting, "I can't deal with it."

HOW TRUE DOES IT FEEL?
HOW UPSETTING DOES IT FEEL?

I asked Rosa to consider what she would prefer to think about herself when she remembered the earthquake. She decided that she would like to believe, "I can deal with it as well as other people." Given a VoC scale of 0 to 7, with 0 being false and 7 being completely true, Rosa estimated that her positive cognition felt about 3 or 4, half true. The Validity of Cognition scale, formulated by Dr. Shapiro, is a convenient way of measuring how true the positive cognition feels. Rosa said that she felt a "scary feeling" when she remembered the earthquake. Given a Subjective Units of Distress Scale (SUDS) of 0 to 10, with 0 representing a calm, neutral feeling and 10 being the scariest she could imagine, Rosa said that her memory of the earthquake rated a 7. (The Subjective Units of Distress Scale measures how upsetting the memory feels.) I asked where she felt the scary feelings, and she responded, "My hands." (I remembered that her hands were shaking when she first told me about the automobile accident.)

Then I asked Rosa to do three things at once: to visualize her image of the earthquake; to think "I can't deal with it, I've lost everything"; and to feel the scary feeling in her body. I then began to guide Rosa's eyes with my fingers. I watched her facial expressions and breathing for clues that she was processing information, and after each "set," or group of eye movements (represented here by three dots: . . .), she paused and made a comment. Rosa's comments indicate rapid desensitization and reprocessing of her memory of the earthquake.

As she moved her eyes, Rosa volunteered these comments: "Why is it happening? . . . Why is it happening to me? . . . Why is the house shaking? . . . Jesus is sending a message we're doing something wrong, and I'm doing something wrong. . . . I didn't do anything. . . . I didn't do anything. I'm okay again. . . . I'm happy. I feel fine now."

I asked Rosa how scary her picture of the earthquake looked now. "Not scary at all," she replied matter-of-factly. Her positive cognition, or desired thought about herself, "I can deal with it," now felt completely true. Rosa had done all of the processing by herself. Within 5 minutes, she had "gotten over" her scary memory about the earthquake, and she had a more realistic view of her own coping skills. We used eye movement to "install" or strengthen the positive self-assessment and the feeling of well-being that Rosa was experiencing.

"I'D LIKE TO BELIEVE I CAN DEAL WITH IT"

Next, Rosa launched into her memories of the automobile accident. She had a picture of "us being hit." When she viewed that picture, the thought she held about herself was, "I cry too much." I asked Rosa what she would prefer to think about herself as she viewed the incident. She responded quickly, "I'd like to believe I can deal with it." She was pensive for several moments, and then talked about reasons why she could not deal with her grandmother's driving. "Since the accident, her driving has gotten worse and worse. She drives so slow that I'm afraid someone will rear-end us again. Not only that, but if someone passes us, she starts crying and praying, and I'm afraid she won't even be able to see where she's driving, and she might actually cause an accident."

I agreed with Rosa that she shouldn't try to convince herself to "deal with it" when someone wasn't driving safely. I assured her that EMDR cannot make her believe anything that is not true. We talked about how she could use her judgment about whether it was reasonably safe to drive with someone. If someone is an unsafe driver, or drives under the influence of alcohol, or drives without a driver's permit, she should not "deal with it." She should not ride with them at all.

On the other hand, if someone is a safe driver, she could "deal with" the consequences of taking a risk of daily living, and she could relax and enjoy her ride. Rosa decided that she would like to believe about herself, "I can relax when my judgment tells me everything is reasonably safe." I agreed that Rosa had chosen a positive cognition, or belief, that was healthy, workable, and appropriate for her. The positive cognition only felt half true before desensitization and reprocessing the memory of the accident.

The EMDR protocol for critical-incident trauma could help 13-year-old Rosa process memories of her car accident. She required age-appropriate information necessary for formulating new, workable, personal-safety rules, however. Children and adolescents often need developmentally appropriate information to be able to arrive at an understanding and resolution of the traumatic situation. An adult probably would not have needed that discussion clarifying elements of good judgment about when it's reasonably "safe" to ride in a car before arriving at a valid positive cognition.

Although her processing was very much like an adults' processing, Rosa was an adolescent who was too young to drive, and she had never needed to exercise judgment about safe riding conditions. The accident was unrelated to her grandmother's driving skills, and Graciella had been a fine driver at the time of the accident. Even so, now that her grandmother was an insecure driver, I knew that Rosa could not and should not feel safe again when she was not. Her exaggerated fear of riding had become somewhat appropriate because of the current situation. EMDR would not take away the appropriate fear, thankfully. It would, however, allow her to have a new set of beliefs that could actually contribute to her safety, though no belief or understanding could assure her complete safety in a car.

Rosa told me more about her feelings about the accident. Although she said, "The car wreck shook me up, but not as bad as the earthquake," she rated her anxiety level as 10 on a scale of 0 to 10, with 10 being the most anxious she could imagine. I asked Rosa to bring to mind the picture of the accident, the thought, "I cry too much," and the feelings of being scared. When she was ready, I started guiding her eye movements. Sets of EMDR stimulated a rapid succession of comments: "Maybe this time if someone hit us someone could die. . . . I don't feel scared. . . . I feel anxious. . . . It happened. . . . It's over. . . . If it happens again I'll deal with it. . . . I'm not afraid to go places. . . . I'm safe. . . . I'm happy. . . . I can do whatever I want to do. . . . I can do what I have to do to get over it."

Looking back on the car accident, Rosa didn't feel any anxiety at all. Our work on the car accident had taken about 10 minutes. She now felt that it was completely true that "I can relax when my judgment tells me that everything is reasonably safe."

"I CAN PAY ATTENTION TO MY BODY"

Rosa proceeded to tell me that she wanted to stop eating so much. I asked her how much she wanted to eat. Rosa answered, "As much as my body needs, but not so much that I just keep stuffing myself even when I'm not hungry." We talked about recognizing the cues her body gives to let her know when she's hungry and needs to eat and when she feels full and it's time to stop eating. We discussed how she could trust her appetite to be her guide. If she was hungry, her body was telling her to eat. If she felt full, her body was telling her to stop eating. Rosa offered her own positive cognition, "I can pay attention to my body and decide how much to eat." She chose to picture herself eating while she thought about her negative cognition, "I eat too much. I'm gaining too much weight" and felt the "stuffed" feeling in her body.

These are the observations she spontaneously shared between sets of eye movement: "I just eat food, food, food. . . . I don't need that much. . . . When I'd get nervous, I'd just eat—pray and eat. . . . I can pray when I'm nervous. . . . I feel good about myself. . . . I feel happier with myself. . . . I feel stupid I ever did that. . . . I forgive myself. . . . I feel happy and not worried about what people will say about me. . . . I feel positive about myself now. . . . I feel self-confident. . . . I can eat and not stuff." Rosa no longer felt nervous when she thought about her eating. She said that it felt completely true now that she could pay attention to her body and decide how much to eat.

I recognized that eating had probably been a lifelong method of self-soothing for Rosa. She had indicated that praying also helped her to feel calmer when she was in a tense situation. Although she had obviously cleared a lot of her anxiety and appeared to need less self-soothing currently, we had not done any work to increase her use of prayer instead of eating to comfort herself when stressful situations arose in the future.

GOING HOME

My work with Rosa reminded me that children and teens need to be taught more than adults about assessing conditions of safety and danger. Optimally, their good judgment can develop as a result of experience, education, and opportunities to make choices. Sometimes traumas occur when children are too young to have the resources necessary for making sense of what has happened to them or how they can keep themselves safe in the future. EMDR with children and adolescents requires age-appropriate and developmentally sensitive educational interweaves.

Furthermore, a child can never feel safe unless other family members feel safe. Although treating children for the effects of trauma may progress more quickly than treating adults, the child's improvement will only be partial or temporary unless the significant adults in the child's life also feel that they and their child are safe. One of the biggest challenges in treating children is convincing related adults to address their own fears and anxieties so that the child can return to a more secure environment.

I could hardly believe the results we had achieved in a 45-minute session. Rosa now felt that the earthquake and the car accident were over. She felt that she could be more in control of her eating. When Graciella came into the office to set up Rosa's next appointment, I recommended that she make an appointment to help her get over her anxiety about driving. She reflected, "I know I should."

I asked Rosa whether her grandmother could drive her home the most direct way, through the intersection where the accident had happened. Rosa nodded, "Sure." Her grandmother looked doubtful. I asked her whether she would give it a try and call me when she arrived home to tell me about the car ride. That evening there was a phone message from Rosa's grandmother. "She rode home past the place where the accident happened. It didn't bother her."

Rosa came back to see me 2 weeks later. She said that the earthquake felt over for her. She said that she was more comfortable riding in a car, but that she couldn't be really comfortable riding with her grandmother, who was "a nervous wreck" in the car. She added that the accident couldn't feel completely over because her family felt financially stressed about having to pay so much to fix the car. Then Rosa smiled proudly and said, "I'm eating less. Now I only eat when I feel hungry, and then I stop when I'm full. I'm happy."

I asked Rosa to look back at her memory of the earthquake. "Do you still think Jesus is punishing you for doing something wrong?" "No," she beamed, "Jesus is proud of me."

5

"I HAVE TO GET THEM OUT!"
HEAD LICE

"We call them 'The Dreaded' at our house," Jenny's mother told me. "I start itching just thinking about them. Do you know what it's like to find lots of little bugs crawling in your child's hair? Head lice is a plague, and the treatment is almost as bad as just having the lice. What a way to ruin a day!" How can a common childhood experience, like head-lice infestation and treatment, be merely a nuisance for one child, whereas for another child, a very similar experience results in posttraumatic symptoms that interfere with basic healthy functioning?

This was the case for Jenny, an 11-year-old girl who came to me with a disturbing case of trichotillomania—that is, she pulled her hair out to such an extent that she was balding. The traumatic element is best understood by looking at the situation from three perspectives: one is offered by Jenny's mother; one by Jenny; and that of myself, the clinician.

THE MOTHER'S STORY

Jenny's mother, Nancy, punctuated her story with grimaces and rolling eyes, "First there was the call from school to pick up Jenny. When I arrived at school, my 5-year-old daughter was sitting in the office, looking forlorn while everyone walked wide circles around her like she was a leper. I felt repulsed at the thought of the lice on my child's head, but I acted as calm and matter-of-factly as I could. I explained to her that she had some little bugs in her hair that we would wash out. We stopped at the drug store to buy the medicated, over-the-counter shampoo and spray and a special comb for removing nits.

"At home, we did the shampoo. Then we had to do nit picking. I didn't understand the true meaning of the expression 'nitpicker' until I had been one. There I was with a magnifying glass trying to see something that is smaller than a pin head. I used the nit comb, but my daughter's hair is so fine that the smallest nits slid between the teeth. She must have nine million hairs in her head! I didn't want to shave her head, but I was tempted. After 2 hours of combing, I had probably only gotten through about half her hair, and I had a new appreciation for the term 'nitwit.'"

"That was only the beginning," Nancy lamented. "Then we had to attack the invisible lice and nits that might be lurking in our home. We had to wash all of the bedclothes and all of her clothes, vacuum the floors, take sweaters and jackets to the dry cleaners, put stuffed animals in sealed plastic bags for 3 weeks. Our house started looking like a mortuary with all the body bags. Then we had to spray the car and the backs of chairs and sofas with toxic-smelling insecticide. One family I know ironed all their fabric-covered furniture instead of spraying. Next we had to notify everyone—the other families in our car pool, my child's friends, and our neighbors, to let them know they had been exposed to lice.

"Just when I thought I was getting things under control, my daughter reminded me that I had put my head next to hers, on her pillow, when I read to her the evening before. I had to treat myself too. When my husband came home from work I told him the story and asked him to look for nits in my hair. I combed through our daughter's hair to show him what to do and found yet another nit that I had overlooked. My husband claimed that he couldn't see it. We added the magnifying glass, and he reluctantly agreed that it was a nit. He browsed through my hair and proclaimed that I didn't have lice or nits, but I wasn't totally convinced, especially since by now, my scalp felt like it was crawling with little bugs. I itched all over. I added my clothes and bedding to the wash and dry-clean piles. My husband used the medicated shampoo, too, just to be on the safe side." But the saga had only just begun.

"A week later, we had to shampoo and vacuum and launder again because any remaining nits would have hatched. Two days after that, a louse crawled out of my daughter's bangs while she was talking to her teacher, and she was sent home again. We went through the whole routine again. She was either reinfected or a nearly invisible nit had hatched. By the time we had treated Jenny three times, I was convinced that the lice had become immune to the shampoo. I shampooed her hair with the special medicated shampoo, but after I rinsed it out, a live louse crawled out of her hair. We went through this louse-eradication ordeal at least a dozen times.

"I got to the point where I wouldn't let Jenny invite a friend to our house to spend the night, and I wouldn't let her sleep over at a friend's house because I was afraid we would get reinfested. I reminded her not to lean back and rest her head on sofas or seats in movie theaters. I vacuumed the house diligently, every day. Nothing we did seemed to deter the lice. I took the lice, and my daughter's feelings, seriously. My husband tried to make light of the whole thing so that she would be less obsessed with lice, but his casual attitude seemed to infuriate her."

Nancy continued the tale of the family nightmare. "Jenny got head lice every year from kindergarten through sixth grade, while we had her in private school. Our pediatrician advised us not to use the prescription product for treating lice because it is neurotoxic and might cause brain damage. I figured that my daughter and I were already losing our minds over the lice, so it would be worth it to risk a few more IQ points if we could really eradicate the lice. My pediatrician thought I was joking (I wasn't). He said that head lice don't carry diseases, and I shouldn't expose my daughter to a toxin unless she had cancer and needed chemotherapy.

"So we spent hundreds of dollars on ineffective medicated shampoo and dry cleaning, not to mention the expense of time lost from work. We went through the treatment ordeal six or more times every year. Last year, when Jenny was in sixth grade, she had a terrible case of lice despite all of our precautions. It was very discouraging. I found more than a dozen live lice crawling in her hair. I picked out countless nits. Jenny was very upset.

"Even though she hasn't had lice since then, she still worries about them a lot. Our whole family has been disrupted by dealing with lice. About 6 months ago, Jenny started pulling out her hair, and says she just can't help it. I reassure her that we haven't had lice for a year, and we probably won't get them again. I've tried to help her not pull out her hair by getting her a nice pony-tail holder. I took her to a hairdresser to get a hairstyle she likes. I taught her to crochet so she'd have something to keep her hands busy. I made a positive reinforcement chart and rewarded her for days when she didn't pull hair. None of that really worked because the hair pulling was beyond her conscious control. She even pulled out her hair in her sleep.

"I knew we had to get professional help when she started avoiding friends because she was concerned they'd ask why she was balding. I heard her explain her thinning hair to a friend by claiming that she had an allergy. I didn't want her to turn into a liar, but I did understand her embarrassment. She worries every time we go somewhere, and especially if she has to sit in a high-backed seat, like in cars, buses, airplanes, the dentist's chair, or friend's houses. She vacuums after friends have visited. She has nightmares about lice infesting her again. Her confidence and self-esteem seem to be sinking lower and lower." As Nancy ended her story, it was clear that this resourceful woman had reached the end of her rope.

THE CLINICIAN'S PERSPECTIVE

Every year, more than 10 million children develop head lice, and judging by pediculicide sales, the number is rapidly increasing. According to Lennie Copeland's (1995) *Lice Buster Book*, girls are more likely to get head lice than boys because the density of girls' hair makes it harder to find and remove nits. (My guess is that girls are also more likely to share hair ribbons, headbands, hats, and to have tête-à-tête conversations.) Caucasian children, ages 5 to 12 are most likely to get lice, regardless of socioeconomic status. African Americans rarely get head lice.

POSTTRAUMATIC STRESS DISORDER VS. OBSESSIVE-COMPULSIVE DISORDER

With so many children exposed to the "trauma" of head lice, I wonder how many suffer from posttraumatic, lice-related symptoms. How many of these children have been misdiagnosed as having obsessive-compulsive disorder (OCD), rather than posttraumatic stress disorder?

OCD is an organically based disorder that is treated most effec-tively with medication. Other kinds of therapy, like cognitive-behavioral therapy, can also be useful for managing the behaviors and anxiety associated with OCD. A diagnosis of OCD can com-mit a child to years of psychotherapy and medication for symp-tom relief. Trichotillomania, Jenny's diagnosis, usually requires treatment with psychotherapy and medication. Posttraumatic obsessions and compulsions are often removed completely with a few sessions of EMDR-facilitated therapy.

WHAT MADE LICE TRAUMATIZING?

Human beings learn from repeated experience. Repeated exposure can sometimes desensitize people to events that seem scary but are not dangerous. So why were Jenny, and several other adolescents I've treated, traumatized by repeated experiences with head lice?

These children were not merely upset about lice, they had devel-oped symptoms that interfered with their basic healthy functioning. They were no longer able to sleep peacefully, to relate to peers com-fortably, to clear their minds of troubling thoughts about lice or their symptoms, or to concentrate fully on school work. They had developed odd and sometimes disabling symptoms like trichotillo-mania, frequent hand washing, obsessive house cleaning, or aver-sion to any contact with their hair. Probably most troubling, their self-esteem plummeted so that they felt embarrassed and miserable much of the time. You might expect that after a dozen exposures to the "lousy routine" of dealing with lice, they would understand that lice are annoying but not dangerous, that lice-control proce-dures are tedious but not threatening.

I puzzled over the power of a seemingly innocuous and nearly ubiquitous experience. In my practice I was beginning to see bright, beautiful, competent girls who were suffering from serious effects of an essentially benign condition. Not only that, none of these girls had been infested with lice during the year prior to seeking therapy. Lice were not only harmless, they were history. The girls all had parents who were diligent in their attempts to minimize the impact of the lice experience for their daughters. Rationally, they all under-stand that lice are a nuisance but not a serious threat to health or safety. Nevertheless, as a parent and a pediatrician, I know well the frenzy and panic that often accompanies a lice outbreak. Was this community anxiety enough to traumatize a child?

Reviewing my notes from my sessions with each of these girls, I discovered that in each case, there was a point at which the girl got "stuck" in her anxiety as she processed her experiences with head lice. At these junctures, I asked the same question, "How are head lice dangerous to your life?" At first, I expected that the girl would access her fund of knowledge about the harmless little critters, realize that head lice are indeed not dangerous to her life, that she would then feel some relief, and would continue to reprocess her memories of her experiences to a satisfactory resolution. Not so. After a set of eye movements while focusing on my question, each girl gave an irrational, yet totally convincing affirmative response to my question about head lice being a threat to life.

These responses prompted me to think more about what makes a common occurrence traumatic for a particular child. Jenny believed that the lice were a threat to her *social* life, and indeed they were. To an adolescent, relationships with peers are of utmost importance. There is a hard-wired developmental directive making friendship, social activities, and peer-approved appearance synonymous with life itself at some time during adolescence. I have witnessed adolescents earnestly claiming that they will die unless they are allowed to see, be with, or talk to their friends. They may not simply think that their relationships are essential for their social life. They may believe that their relationships are a prerequisite for their very existence.

One of the girls had been plagued by lice infestation repeatedly for 7 years. Finally, a family friend told the girl's parents that in Europe, malathion spray is used to eradicate head lice because it kills the nits as well as the lice. The family took a vacation in Europe, where they purchased malathion and jubilantly sprayed the whole family. The 11-year-old girl was terrified by being "fumigated" and thought that she was being poisoned by the pesticide. Although the lice were eradicated, her fear was that someone would look in her hair, see a louse or a nit, and kill her with a toxin.

Another adolescent client had parents who became extremely angry every time there was another outbreak of head lice, and she felt she was responsible. She became hypervigilant about preventing head lice and found herself trying to "stay clean of lice" by washing her hands five or six times an hour, as well as showering and changing clothes several times a day. When we used EMDR to work on her memories of lice infestation, she became "stuck" in her anxiety until I asked how lice were threatening to her life. Unconsciously, she believed that her family would be better off if she were dead because she caused the family so much distress with her head lice. EMDR uncovered the problem, but EMDR alone could not have solved it. We had a session in which both of the girls' parents affirmed that they were angry with the head lice but not angry with her.

JENNY'S STORY

The following account of my session with Jenny illustrates the traumatic potential of events that interfere with a child's developmental directives and demonstrate how EMDR can expedite the resolution of posttraumatic beliefs and behaviors. Jenny and her mother came to my office looking understandably distressed: Jenny was noticeably balding. My attention first went to her fine blond hair and visible scalp, but settled on her sad eyes and grim expression. I suspected she wasn't happy about having to share her troubles with me, and that only her feeling of desperation was worse than the prospect of risking my scrutiny. I gently asked her to tell me what was going on.

Jenny reluctantly told me, "I can't stop pulling out my hair." Her eyes downcast, she continued with a voice that was full of shame, "I don't know why but I just keep finding myself pulling out hair, when I'm bored in school, when I'm talking on the phone, or whenever I'm not using all of my attention to stop myself from pulling. I even find a lot of hair on my pillow in the morning, so I know I pull out hair in my sleep."

A PROCESS PHOBIA

Jenny grimaced as she recounted the saga of her repeated bouts with head lice. In response to my questioning, she recounted the first time, the last time, and the worst time she had struggled with lice. I decided to approach the problem as I would a process phobia.

A process phobia—like the fear of public speaking, or the fear of flying in a plane—is a fear that is triggered by a recurring situation that the person would like to handle comfortably. The EMDR method for treating a process phobia involves targeting the first time the traumatic experience happened, the most recent time, and the worst time, and then to use EMDR to practice handling the situation comfortably in the future.

I decided not to approach Jenny's head-lice experience like a critical-incident trauma that was over and was very unlikely to occur again. I based my decision on several factors. Jenny had not been infested by lice for over a year, she was exquisitely careful not to expose herself to lice, and she was approaching an age group in which infestation is much less likely. Nevertheless, she could contract the pest again. Even if she avoided head lice during adolescence, she might encounter them again as a parent. I wanted to make sure that she felt confident that she could handle "The Dreaded" if they reoccurred. I chose to focus on the underlying stressors initially, rather than target the troublesome hair-pulling behavior. My goal was to clear out any traumatic residue that may have been left by her experiences with lice. If the symptoms didn't clear, I could always target the hair-pulling directly.

EVALUATING THE EFFECT OF THE SYMPTOMS

I asked Jenny how the hair-pulling affected her life. I wanted to explore whether there would be any other losses if she no longer had that behavior. Sometimes a behavior requiring lots of attention can bring an adolescent the connections she craves but may not know how to attain on her own. Not so for Jenny. It was evident that she had a healthy relationship with her parents and that she was able to make friends and maintain friendships despite her difficulties. She said she hated the hair problem because people noticed the thin spots in her hair and asked her what caused it. She felt uncomfortable lying and saying that she had an allergy, but she was ashamed to admit that she had pulled out her own hair.

I invited Jenny to imagine how her life would be if she no longer pulled out her hair or worried about head lice. She smiled at me for the first time. "Things would be fine. My hair would start growing back, and not everything would be covered with hair anymore."

I probed a bit more, "How would your relationships be different if this were no longer a problem?" Jenny responded quickly, "I'd feel better about my friends because I wouldn't have to lie to them, and I wouldn't have to worry about my hair looking weird and ugly."

FAILED REMEDIES

Jenny told me that she had attempted a lot of things to help herself not pull her hair. She had tried to train herself to use touching her hair as a cue to put her hand down, but that took too much concentration. She tried wearing her hair in a bun, but she still pulled out hair from the sides and front of her scalp. She tried wearing a hat or scarf to cover her head completely, but she continued to pull out hair while she was asleep. I was convinced that Jenny's unconscious hair-pulling was causing her nothing but trouble.

BEGINNING EMDR

I introduced Jenny to eye-movement work by asking her to imagine a safe place. She readily imagined her bedroom with her family and friends and pet beside her. I asked her to hold that relaxing image while she followed my fingers with her eyes. I asked her to practice giving me the "stop" signal. She stopped me after a few sweeps of my hand, saying that she didn't like moving her eyes and that it made her feel dizzy. We tried eye movement in several different directions, with the same results. I suggested that we try alternate hand tapping instead, and Jenny found that less annoying.

First, we desensitized Jenny's memory of getting head lice when she was in kindergarten. She remembered that her friends were told to leave class, one after the other, and she wondered what was happening to them. Her confusion caused anxiety. "Why are all the kids disappearing?" she wondered. Desensitization and reprocessing of that first memory proceeded rapidly.

THE MOST RECENT AND WORST TIME

When it was time for Jenny to work on the most recent and worst time she remembered having head lice, she had an image of herself sitting in her living room, with her mother picking out nits. Jenny's negative cognition was "I'm never going to get rid of the lice." She wanted to believe, "It's over now. I can deal with it." The validity of that self-affirming belief only registered a 3 on the VoC scale with 0 feeling false and 7 feeling completely true. When she viewed that scene, with her mother picking nits out of her hair, Jenny felt nervous. Her nervousness rated a 7 on the SUD scale, with 0 being calm and relaxed, and 10 being the most nervous she could imagine. She located the nervous feeling in her stomach. With Jenny holding in mind the image of nit picking, the negative beliefs—"I'll never get rid of the lice. I can't deal with it"—and the nervous feeling in her stomach, I started tapping her hands alternately.

Whenever I saw a shift in Jenny's facial expression, I stopped tapping to ask what she was noticing. The following are Jenny's spontaneous comments following sets of EMDR, indicated by. . . . "I see myself trying things to get rid of the lice. . . . People were noticing the bugs in my hair. . . . I feel the nervous feeling in my throat and chest. . . . I see myself brushing my hair. . . . Lice are biting me. . . . Itching. . . . Itching. . . ."

During most of the desensitizing and reprocessing of these lice-related memories, Jenny squirmed and grimaced. She and the other people I've seen who were working on posttraumatic sequellae of lice infestation are among the most distressed of the clients with whom I've done EMDR. Revisiting the sensation of having lice crawling in their hair was extremely anxiety provoking and uncomfortable.

Jenny continued, and there was a change in her facial expression. She began to look angry. . . . "I'm killing them. . . . I'm killing them with a sword. (Smiles) I'm shooting them. . . . I'm hitting and kicking them. . . . They're gone and my hair looks nice." . . .

We only had 5 minutes left in our first session. I asked Jenny to look back at the original picture and to rate how nervous she felt as she viewed that scene now. Her SUDS number was 3 to 4 (down from 7 when we started). Jenny said she was ready to stop for the day because she had too much homework. I thought she had also had enough "lice work" for one day. I suggested that we end our session by imagining that her hair looked nice, and she was doing something she enjoyed. Jenny said she imagined that her hair looked nice, and she was not pulling it out. She imagined that she was playing a game.

SECOND AND FINAL EMDR SESSION: JENNY RESOLVES HER TRAUMA

When Jenny returned for her second and final session, she looked dejected as she told me that she was still pulling out her hair. I asked her what image came to her now when she thought about the lice problem. Sometimes, between sessions, processing continues on its own. Jenny's visual image was similar to the image she had near the end of our first session, however. She imagined the lice, with her killing them. She described the feeling associated with the picture as a "bad feeling" which she located in her stomach. Her distress rated a 3 on the SUD scale, with 0 indicating relaxed and 10 indicating the worst feeling she could imagine.

Jenny agreed to try eye movement that day, instead of tapping, and this time it didn't bother her. As she began to move her eyes, she looked distressed. . . . "My hair looks scraggly. . . . I see myself washing the lice out of my hair. . . . I'm picking the lice out. . . . The lice are gone. My hair is nice. . . ."

I asked Jenny to look back at the original incident and checked the SUDS rating. Her distress was up to a 4 on the SUD scale. I asked Jenny to concentrate once again on the upsetting memory.

Jenny concentrated and moved her eyes. . . . "The lice are gone. . . . I forgot about them. . . . I was killing them. . . . I was pulling them out. . . . I remember the whole process—trying to get rid of them again and again. I remember we tried washing my hair in vinegar. My hair was really nice again. . . . It was really bad, but the lice are gone."

I checked Jenny's SUDS level again. Back to 3. The processing hadn't stopped, but Jenny's anxiety level was not decreasing. I guessed that a significant part of her trauma was the repeated experience of thinking that the lice were gone, only to discover a new infestation.

I asked Jenny to see the picture, think the thought about never getting rid of the lice, and notice the feeling in her body. . . . "I found one in bed and it was scary. I killed it. . . . I have to wear hats when I do homework."

Because Jenny's processing seemed to be changing tracks from lice to hair-pulling, I decided to steer her attention back to the original mental image of the lice to see whether her anxiety about the memory had diminished. It hadn't. The SUDS was still 4. I wasn't certain that we were making progress. I decided that Jenny might benefit from some additional information about head lice. What information might reduce her anxiety?

An event is traumatic when it is threatening to one's life. An event may also be traumatic when it is perceived as threatening to one's safety or sense of well-being. Jenny was behaving as if lice were a serious threat to her safety. I wanted to understand why she perceived lice as more than a nuisance. Maybe when Jenny realized that lice could not threaten her life, she could let go of her hyper-vigilance.

I decided to ask Jenny directly, "Are the lice dangerous?" Jenny focused intently as she followed my fingers with her eyes and considered my question. . . . "Lice are dangerous. They're dangerous because they bite and cause pain. . . ."

Jenny looked distressed as I posed my next question and began to guide her eye movement. "Are they dangerous to your life?" I asked. . . . She responded thoughtfully, "Yes, they're dangerous . . . to my social life." . . . Jenny continued. "I see myself shampooing and pulling my hair back in a rubber band. . . . The lice are gone. . . . Now I can take a regular shower with regular shampoo, without having to worry about lice. . . . I see myself taking all of my stuffed animals and pillows out of the sealed plastic bags. . . . I'm throwing away the lice combs. . . ."

USING THE IMAGINATION TO RESOLVE TRAUMA: IMAGINAL INTERWEAVES

I checked Jenny's distress level, looking back at the original memory. It was still a 3 on the SUD scale. I decided to try an imaginal interweave. I thought that Jenny might gain more control of the situation by imagining herself in a position of authority, teaching a family who had head lice for the first time. I asked Jenny whether she would be willing to imagine giving advice to someone dealing with head lice for the first time. She nodded. She imagined telling someone about using the medicated shampoo, pesticide spray, and a nit comb. She told about cleaning the house and the bedding and laundering or dry cleaning clothes. She would remind them to repeat the procedure after a week. I asked if she had any other advice. She added, "They shouldn't worry!"

I asked Jenny whether she had done everything she could do to prevent the head lice. Yes, she had. (One girl with a lice phobia admitted that she had continued trading hair barrettes with a friend in kindergarten. I helped her accept that as a 5-year-old she really didn't understand the importance of not sharing. When her guilty feelings cleared, so did her anxiety.) I asked Jenny whether she had done everything she needed to do to take care of herself. . . . "Yes. I was telling someone lice isn't that bad. . . ."

I checked the SUDS level. Looking back at the original memory, Jenny's anxiety level was down to a 2. We were on the right track! I asked Jenny to notice the anxious feeling in her body, and I began to guide her eyes again. . . . "I hate the idea of bugs living in my hair. . . . One day I found a louse in my fingernail. . . . My scalp feels nice now. It doesn't itch. . . . The lice are gone and I don't need to worry." Jenny's SUDS was down to 1. . . . "I don't like insects. . . . I really didn't like seeing that louse in my fingernail."

I've found that another method that often helps a person master her fear of a perpetrator (in this case, a louse) is to imagine telling the louse what she thinks of him. I invited Jenny to tell the louse whatever she wanted. . . . "Leave me alone!" (she shouted while continuing to move her eyes.) Jenny looked considerably more relaxed, but she continued moving her eyes without a change in expression. After about a minute of tracking with her eyes, she announced, "That was the last one. They're all gone. I don't have to deal with it anymore."

I asked Jenny to review the original memory and notice whether it still made her anxious at all. "A little," she replied. I directed her to pay attention to that anxiety and notice what was holding it in place. . . . Jenny looked startled by the memory that came to her. "About a week after I had head lice for the last time, a year ago, I went over to my friend's house, and they made me wear a plastic bag to cover my hair while I was at their house." . . .

Jenny's mother had been watching silently through the whole procedure. When she heard about the plastic bag on her daughter's hair, she gasped. I don't know whether she hadn't remembered or had never known about the offensive incident. It's not at all unusual for the child and the parents to be totally unaware of an event that has had an enormous impact on the psyche.

I encouraged Jenny to stay with that memory until she finished desensitizing and reprocessing it. Jenny shared her stream of thoughts as she moved her eyes. . . . "I don't have lice. I don't need this. I don't have lice. I see myself pulling off the plastic bag and saying to them, 'I don't have lice. I don't need this.'" Jenny lifted her arm, moved her hand over her hair as if she were removing the odious plastic bag, and began to smile. "I really don't have lice. I don't need this."

Finally, the mystery of the hair-pulling was solved. Jenny's social life certainly had been threatened when she was made to wear a plastic lice bag on her hair. For a long time, she had been pulling out her hair in a subconscious effort to remove lice, nits, and perhaps most insulting of all, a plastic bag, from her hair.

When Jenny reviewed her memory of the head-lice episode, she no longer felt any anxiety. Then I asked Jenny to evaluate the validity of the cognition, "It's over now." She said this statement felt completely true to her, and we used EMDR to install that cognition. The positive cognition, "I can deal with it," also felt completely true. Finally, I asked Jenny to focus on the statement, "I can deal with it even if it happens again." I asked her to imagine herself dealing with it again. She sighed, and moved her eyes.

When she blinked and looked directly into my eyes, Jenny said, "I can go on with my normal life. I can see myself in class, bored, and doodling on my paper. I am not pulling my hair!" We set up an appointment for Jenny to return in a week so that we could see whether there was any residual anxiety about the head lice and to target the hair-pulling if necessary.

Two days before the scheduled return, Jenny's mother called to cancel the appointment. "Jenny says she doesn't want to come back. She said she doesn't have a problem anymore, and she wants to try out for the volleyball team instead of wasting any more time on head lice. I think the treatment really worked. She hasn't pulled out any hair since we saw you. I'll call you if she pulls out any more hair."

A year later, when I called Jenny to follow up, her mother told me that all was well. No more lice. No more hair-pulling. Lots of confidence and friends and volleyball games. Nancy summed it up, "Our lousy ordeal is over."

6

"WHAT IF . . . ? WHAT IF . . . ?"
CONVERGING STRESSES

Allison's parents were frantic. Their 7-year-old daughter had changed from a happy, well-adjusted child to an extremely worried, clingy child in less than 3 weeks. Allison's mother, Helaine, lamented, "She used to be so confident and independent. Now she worries about everything and doesn't want to let me out of her sight." Helaine shook her head.

"She won't take the mail from the mailbox anymore because she frets, 'What if the Unabomber sends us a bomb?' When she saw a milk carton with the picture of a missing child, she asked, 'What if I get kidnapped?' At bedtime, she worries that she might be taken from her home and killed, like Polly Klaas. She's been reading at bedtime then putting herself to sleep for years, but now she insists that I keep her company when she goes to bed. Sometimes it takes her as long as 4 hours to fall asleep. I keep reassuring her that she's safe, but nothing I say or do seems to help her." Helaine looked sadder and sadder as she told me the story.

"For the past several weeks," she continued, "Allison keeps saying, 'What will I do if my mommy and my daddy die at the same time?' One day, while she was saying this, she began to have trouble breathing. She became frantic. George and I were terrified too, watching her gasp for breath, so we took her to the emergency room. We were concerned that she might have asthma. The doctor checked her heart and lungs and assured us that Allison was fine." George added, "He said that it was probably just a panic attack." "Just!" Helaine repeated indignantly. She had had panic attacks of her own, and knew how frightening they could be.

Although her parents were reassured that Allison was physically "fine," they didn't know what caused her panic attacks or how to stop them. Fear of having panic attacks interfered with Allison's normal life and made Allison reluctant to go to school or to play with friends. Helaine and George were mystified and bewildered by the sudden changes in their child.

Allison's parents had presented me with a real mystery. What had caused these overwhelming fears that threatened to erode completely Allison's confidence and sense of safety? Allison's prenatal history, birth, infancy, and medical and developmental history didn't provide any clues. She had not had any notable illnesses, injuries, losses, or recognizable traumatic events. Allison got along well in her family, which was stable and loving. Seven-year-old Allison liked school and had friends.

I thought that several seemingly minor events may have contributed to this eruption of fears. Two years earlier, when Allison was 5 years old, she had heard about the Polly Klaas kidnapping. For weeks the local and national news were filled with stories of the 12-year-old girl who was kidnapped from her own room during a slumber party while her mother and sister slept nearby. Allison was sad and matter-of-fact when she talked about it, but she hadn't shown excessive distress at the time. Occasionally, Allison watched the TV news with her parents. Then, after watching a TV news report on the Unabomber, Allison had reassured her parents that she would be especially careful when she took the mail from the mailbox.

Stories of death and danger began appearing closer to home. Helaine recalled that when Allison heard that a distant relative, who lived in another state, was dying, she had wanted to know, "What is death?" Helaine had responded, "When someone dies, their body dies and their spirit lives." Recently, Allison had overheard her neighbor and her parents talking about someone who had choked on a hot dog. That night she had had her first difficulty breathing. Probably, Allison's developmentally appropriate comprehension that death happens and is irreversible contributed to her sense of vulnerability as she became aware of real-life dangers.

Several other factors may have contributed to Allison's anxiety. Allison had always been an imaginative child who was eager to please. Her natural ability to sense the needs and feelings of others made her lovable, compassionate, and perhaps vulnerable. Some children are born with a propensity to "take to heart" and to personalize everything that happens around them. Her parents' experiences may also have contributed to her susceptibility. Allison's mother had a history of panic attacks, which she had mastered through self-hypnosis and biofeedback. Knowing how terrible panic attacks can feel, Helaine had empathized with her daughter and took her fears very seriously. Allison's father had gone through a divorce many years previously, and his son's mother had retained custody of their child, cutting off George's visitation rights. Allison's fears that she would be kidnapped triggered George's fears that this child too could be taken from him.

It seemed to me that a complex constellation of factors was contributing to Allison's difficulties. Her sensitive nature, her genetic predisposition, her parents' histories, and her exposure to the media's reports of tragedies were evident. There may have been other more subtle stressors that predisposed highly sensitive Allison to anxiety. Was Allison's anxiety her parents' fault? No. Could Allison's parents have done anything to prevent Allison's anxiety? No.

Could Allison's parents have done anything to help Allison? Yes, and they had already done their best. They had taken Allison to their pediatrician as well as the emergency-room doctor to determine whether Allison's difficulty breathing was caused by asthma or any other medical condition. Helaine had taught her daughter deep breathing, muscle-relaxation exercises, and the visual imagery that had helped her master her own anxiety response. These methods for inducing relaxation soothed Allison temporarily, and are valuable skills. Before long, however, her worried thoughts and anxious feelings overwhelmed her again. Both of Allison's parents reassured their daughter that she was safe and that it would be very unlikely that anything bad would happen to her or her family. Now her parents were taking the next step by consulting me. Unfortunately, many parents already feel like "bad parents" by the time they consult me, although they have done everything that a "good parent" can do.

ALLISON'S FIRST MEETING

I could see at once that Allison was a child who liked to please. Despite her distress, she came into my office and noticed my "pretty vase with pretty flowers." She listened attentively while her mother described her as a bright kid with a great sense of humor and a kind soul. I asked Allison what she would like to have easier in her life. She said that she wanted to feel safe when she was in her own bedroom. Allison explained that one night she had looked out the window and had seen what looked like a knife. "Maybe it was my imagination," she mused, "but it was really scary."

ALLISON'S SAFE PLACE

I asked Allison to imagine a safe place. "A safe place is where a princess would meet a prince and marry him and live happily ever after," 7-year-old Allison responded. She continued, "The beach we visited last summer could be a safe place. I like that one. There are pretty oceans, pretty palm trees, pretty hotels, pretty lands, and pretty fishes under the water. There are pretty butterflies. The pretty sand at the beach sparkles like glitter in the sun. There are tasty drinks and tasty food. I like everything on the menu! Everyone is wearing pretty short dresses." I asked Allison where she could feel the safe feeling in her body. She pointed to her forehead and her arms and said, "I feel it in my mind and also where I put suntan lotion."

DEFINING GOALS AND IDENTIFYING TREATMENT TARGETS

I asked Allison what she would like to believe about herself, and was impressed by her strongly positive self-description. "I'm kind. I am a good friend. I like pretty things and beautiful things. I am a good reader. I am a good writer. I'm good at baking cookies." Allison paused, and I posed another question, "What would you like to think about yourself and your fears?" She answered confidently, "I'm safe even when I think about or imagine scary things. I'm as safe as I can be."

Allison confided that she felt extremely scared when she thought about Polly Klaas at night and when she remembered the "thing that looked like a knife" glimmering in her window. I decided to treat these two frightening memories much as I would treat a critical incident with EMDR. For Allison, these two memories *were* events that were threatening to her sense of safety and well-being, and branded her with the self-limiting belief, "I'm not safe, even in my own house."

I explained EMDR as a way Allison could feel as safe as she really was. Allison chose the toy figure "Strawberry Shortcake" to help guide her while she moved her eyes. She focused on her recollections about Polly Klaas while I held Strawberry Shortcake and guided her eye movement. Allison had not had any direct connection with Polly Klaas and had not even seen any newspaper pictures or news stories about her on TV. All of her images had been produced by her own vivid imagination as she overheard discussion of the tragedy when she was in kindergarten.

Allison began her dramatic commentary as she moved her eyes: "I see Polly Klaas. He choked her. I am safe. He threw Polly out on the grass. Polly Klaas was with her friend, and Polly opened the door, and the mean man came in and took her. Her Mom was down the hall with the baby."

USING IMAGINATIVE POWER

I decided to enlist Allison's animated imagination to empower her. I asked, "What would you tell the mean man?" Allison spoke firmly and continued to move her eyes, "You shouldn't steal people and choke them!" I asked, "What would you tell Polly?" Allison advised, "If that happens, wake your Mom up, and tell her to come help you!" I asked, "What happens now when you think about Polly Klaas?" Allison sounded worried, "Maybe that man is in jail or dead, but maybe one of his brothers will come!" Allison's fears were persistent, but so was I. I asked, "What would you tell the brothers?" Allison's voice steadied, "I told that man if he had brothers they had better not bother me!" I asked Allison to think about Polly Klaas again. "It's not scary anymore," she said triumphantly. I asked Allison to imagine Polly and to move her eyes while thinking, "I'm safe even when I think or imagine scary things."

Next, I asked Allison to think about the image of the knife. Allison told the story of how the image of the knife came to her. "I was sleeping, and I woke up. I saw a shiny thing in the window. I thought it was a knife. I feel that I'm not safe when I am alone." I encouraged Allison to remember how she had felt when she had that experience. She felt very frightened. I guided her eye movement while she remembered the experience. "I woke up and called, 'Mommy! Daddy! I saw a knife.'"

I directed Allison's attention to her physical sensations. Allison said, "I feel it in my teeth," and then she clenched her jaws again. Soon, her jaws relaxed a little. "Mom and Dad let me in their bed," she remembered. "What do you see in the window?" I prodded. Allison answered anxiously, "A big, dirty knife. In the window I didn't see any person. I see the knife, and I'm scared." Allison continued to watch the Strawberry Shortcake figure I moved back and forth in front of her. Her tone softened, "Now I remember being safe and cozy and comfy in Mommy and Daddy's bed."

I brought Allison's attention back to the image of the knife. She said that it was just a little scary. I asked what was keeping it looking scary. Allison concentrated on following Strawberry Shortcake with her eyes while she said, "I think it's going to bother other children. . . . I told the knife not to do it on other people either. The knife came alive, but now it's gone. It's not scary anymore."

We talked about how sometimes the light from the moon can make a shiny reflection in a window, and your imagination might make you believe that it was a knife. I asked Allison to thank her strong imagination for helping her to feel safe again. I also asked Allison whether she could imagine feeling very safe alone in her own room at night. Allison considered these suggestions while she moved her eyes. When she had finished, she said, "My Mom can go out when I go to sleep tonight."

"MY BODY CAN KEEP ME ALIVE AUTOMATICALLY . . ."

When Allison returned for her next visit, her anxiety had decreased, but she was still having the problem with her breathing. We devoted the next two sessions to helping Allison feel confident that her body would keep her alive even when she wasn't "breathing hard to keep her lungs working." Allison explained the problem, "It seems that I don't get it into my lungs. The first time it happened was when my parents and our neighbors were talking about choking. I think about my insides and my heart and my lungs. I think they're not going fast enough." Allison wanted to believe, "My heart and lungs do their job to keep me working."

Allison chose Strawberry Shortcake again as her point of focus during eye movement. As she moved her eyes, Allison remembered overhearing a conversation about choking. "The man next door was talking about choking. My dad was talking about the woman who choked and died. I told my mom, 'It feels like I'm going to die.' When they were talking about choking I felt scared all over, but mostly in my head. I remember eating a hot dog and almost choking once. I coughed and coughed."

I thought that Allison could benefit from some information that would help her realize that her body's response of coughing was appropriate and protective. I offered this educational interweave to give age-relevant information, to reduce Allison's anxiety, and to increase her confidence in her body's ability to protect her without any conscious effort on her part. I encouraged Allison, "Think about your body knowing what to do to protect you when the piece of hot dog started going toward your lungs instead of to your stomach. Your body did a good job of coughing to get the hot-dog piece out of the wrong place." Allison considered my comments as she moved her eyes. She said, "I told my body, 'Thank you for taking care of me. You're very right for me.'"

I asked Allison, "When you think about your heart and lungs what do you think about now?" She responded, "I think about my heart beating and my lungs working." I asked, "When is it normal for your heart and your breathing to go fast?" Observant Allison had the answer, "When I run."

THE "GLUE-AND-TAPE" PROBLEM

When Allison and Helaine returned in a week, Helaine was exasperated. "Allison still complains about trouble breathing at night, and I can't leave her alone because I know how scary panic attacks are. I keep her company, and she wants me to keep talking. I pick a topic that's pleasant for her, like her upcoming birthday party, and I just keep talking. Last night I talked until midnight when she fell asleep."

I asked Allison what she would call the problem her mom was

describing. Allison named it "the glue-and-tape problem" because she felt stuck to her mother. Together we decided that we were now going to undo the "glue-and-tape problem" and to work toward "back to normal." At this point in Allison's transition back to feeling *and* behaving in normal ways, I thought that some positive reinforcement might give Allison an incentive for giving up her mother's company at night. I suggested a star chart to acknowledge every night that Allison put herself to sleep after her mother read her a bedtime story.

Then we used EMDR to reinforce Allison's desired cognitions: "I'm normally close to Mommy. I can love my mom without the 'glue-and-tape problem.' I'm safe and feel close to Mommy even when she's not with me. I'm safe alone in my bed at night."

When Allison returned in 2 weeks, she proudly showed me her star chart. She beamed, "I've put myself to bed for 14 days, and when I've done it for 21 days, I get to pick out a doll I want." Helaine was relieved that Allison felt safe alone in her room at night. She reported that Allison occasionally worried about her breathing.

When Helaine told me that two elderly relatives had died in the past month, I thought it was understandable that Allison had been thinking about death again. Helaine and I talked some about death as a natural part of life, and I encouraged Helaine to share her beliefs and feelings about death with Allison. Allison explained her concern, "Sometimes it seems like I'm running out of breath. I'm afraid I'm dying." We discussed how feeling like you are out of breath when you are running is very different from dying. Together we formulated some preferable beliefs, "I'm alive right now. I'm healthy. I'm safe. My breathing is fine. My body knows how to keep me alive." A brief EMDR session cleared the remainder of Allison's anxiety. Phone reports confirmed that Allison's life was "back to normal."

MORE SCARY POSSIBILITIES

Five months later, Allison came to see me again. Two recent events had frightened Allison, and her parents were concerned that she might start having panic attacks again. Both of these incidents point out the need to teach children to speak out to protect themselves and the need to establish safety in the child's environment. Fears tend to proliferate when children feel helpless and don't know how to assert their rights.

Allison had overheard a "bad boy" in her class saying that he was going to get a Swiss Army knife. Allison was worried that he might bring the knife to class and stab someone. Allison and Helaine and I talked about the rules at school that help to keep children safe. I suggested that Helaine go with Allison to talk with the teacher about the situation. While discussing safety rules with the class, the teacher could mention that no knives are allowed in school. Allison seemed satisfied that she could protect herself and other children by talking to the teacher.

The second situation had been more difficult. A firefighter had come to class to demonstrate first aid. By chance, he chose Allison to play the part of the victim who was choking. Allison complied, but she felt tense in her abdomen. Afterward she kept thinking, "I'm scared. I'm dying."

We discussed ways that Allison could have handled the situation. She practiced saying, "I don't want to play the victim." She also thought of things she could have said to herself. Allison thought she could have helped herself by thinking, "I'm fine because he's just showing us how to take care of an emergency." We used EMDR to reinforce the fact that Allison could protect herself by speaking up for herself. We discussed the importance of Allison learning to control situations and prevent scary feelings by asserting herself.

THE BLUE FAIRY TRIUMPHS OVER THE WICKED QUEEN

When Allison returned for her follow-up visit 2 weeks later, she was doing fine. She had joined a drama class and was enjoying playing the roles of powerful characters. Drama programs are a great way for children to develop skills for self-expression and self-protection. Mastery comes with practicing the skills, not simply learning them.

Allison chose to spend her last session with me making a sand-tray picture. Her miniature drama in the sand tray illustrated the triumph of good over evil—the power of the helping forces to gather

strength and stand united. She arranged Strawberry Shortcake and
the Wicked Queen facing each other from opposite ends of the sand
tray, and she placed animals all around them. Allison explained
that the Wicked Queen had cast an evil spell so all the animals were
stuck in the sand. The Blue Fairy arrived and knocked over the
Wicked Queen. Then the Blue Fairy cast a good spell on the animals so that one by one they were able to pull each other out of the
sand. Finally, all of the animals could stand again. Allison arranged
all of the animals in an orderly way, facing the center of the sand
tray from the four corners. Allison concluded her story, "Everything
is the way it should be now."

Allison thrived. She no longer experienced undue anxiety, she
put herself to bed after reading to herself at night, she did well in
school, enjoyed flute lessons, 4-H activities, ice-skating, friends,
and family.

AN INSIGHT

Sometimes an insight into a situation comes after the crisis is
resolved. This is what happened in Allison's case. Two years later,
Helaine phoned to make an appointment for Allison, now 9 years
old. Allison's teacher had told the class a cautionary tale about a
boy who chewed on his pencil and choked on the eraser and turned
purple. Allison was worried that she might choke and was beginning to show signs of anxiety. Once again she was afraid to leave
her mother.

I met with Allison and EMDR quickly helped her clear all signs
of anxiety. When Helaine and I met alone for our concluding session, the story she told about a traumatic incident in her own life
helped me understand why she became so frantic whenever her
daughter was anxious.

When Helaine was a young teen, her older brother and her parents often argued heatedly about his friends, his school work, and
his habits. One night, after a particularly stressful argument, everyone was anxious, and her brother slammed the door as he retreated
to his room. Impulsively, Helaine opened the door to his room, and
saw him holding a gun. She was terrified. She didn't know whether
he intended to shoot himself or the whole family. He didn't shoot

anybody, but after that, any anxiety felt like a life-and-death situation to Helaine. So when her own daughter started having symptoms of anxiety, Helaine was extremely alarmed, no doubt fueling Allison's own fears about safety.

Helaine's posttraumatic mind-set and George's worries about the loss of a child certainly didn't cause Allison's problems with anxiety, but they probably contributed to her vulnerability. Parents' fears resonate in their children's hearts, and children's fears have the power to stir their parents' deepest apprehension.

7

"WASITZ?"

CASCADES OF TRAUMA

S ome clinicians who work with children have begun to use EMDR in more complex situations than critical-incident trauma or converging stresses. These complex cascades of trauma consist of a cluster of traumatic incidents that occur within a relatively short period of time, traumas followed by secondary traumas, or a traumatic environment in which upsetting events occur frequently and at unpredictable times. Cascades of trauma are more difficult to treat than critical incidents, particularly in very young children who are losing crucial developmental time while they are trying to recover from an overwhelming series of events.

Fear and a sense of helplessness are two of the most debilitating aspects of trauma, making it difficult to act effectively in the face of a new threat. A person who suffers repeated traumatic assaults faces profound difficulties. As described in *Waking the Tiger,* a look at an animal model makes this very clear: If you quietly approach a bird from behind, firmly and gently trapping it in your hand, it freezes. The bird stays frozen for a few minutes, even if you turn it upside down. When you release the bird, it comes out of its state of shock and flies away as if nothing happened. If, however, you frighten the bird before you capture it, the bird will struggle to escape. This time, the frightened bird freezes and remains frozen much longer. When it finally comes out of its state of shock, it is in a state of frantic excitability. It may thrash about wildly, pecking frantically or flying in an uncoordinated way. Clearly, fear potentiates the freezing response to trauma. This cycle of fear, rage, and immobility is followed by violent activity aimed at escape or a fight to the death. In the same way, a cascade of traumas incapacitates people and renders them more vulnerable to a deeper state of shock.

EMDR is not a panacea in these complex cases, but may be

helpful in facilitating some aspects of therapy. The following cases demonstrate the significant contribution of EMDR in treating cascades of trauma in children. I could not have predicted the resilience of Carl, a 2-year-old boy for whom surgery had abruptly halted development during his "oral stage," and Eliza, a 10-year-old girl with an emotionally abusive, alcoholic father and a fearful mother.

CARL

Rhonda and Curt seemed very reserved as they greeted me on their first visit. Rhonda's quiet voice certainly didn't convey how worried she was about her 2½-year-old son. "Today a preschool teacher told us that Carl wouldn't fit in at preschool. The teacher told us that Carl was constantly running around the playground wildly, shrieking when the other children came near him. And, of course, no one could understand anything Carl was saying. We just want to know whether Carl just has a problem with articulation, whether he is on track developmentally, and whether we should be doing anything else to help him." Curt added, "We're both high school teachers. We don't care whether he gets A's in school, we just want him to be the most he can be."

A ROUGH START

Carl had had a rough start in life. Conceived after his mother had had a series of three miscarriages, this pregnancy was also tenuous. Rhonda received terbutaline to stall premature labor. When labor did proceed, there were signs of fetal distress and Carl was delivered by cesarean section. Not only did Carl have the umbilical cord wrapped around his neck four times, he was born with a cleft lip and palate.

When he was 4 months old, Carl underwent his first surgery to have his lip repaired. Curt remembered, "He had his operation, and we took him home the same day. It was painful for Carl when we had to clean his lip where it was sewn together."

When Carl was 10 months old, he had surgery to repair his cleft palate. Rhonda's eyes focused on the floor as she sadly recalled that experience. "At that time, my mother was also in the hospital—for treatment of a respiratory condition. Both Carl and my mother had pulse oximeters attached to their fingers to monitor their oxygen saturation. I went back and forth between the two hospitals so I could spend some time with both of them. I noticed that my mother looked pale—and kind of gray—and my mother's monitor showed that her oxygen level was dropping. Then I drove back to visit Carl and examined his monitor for any indication of low oxygen. I was really worried that Carl's oxygen might drop too." Rhonda paused, then sighed, "My mother died that day, the same day Carl had his second surgery."

Carl's father stayed by his side after his surgery. He was particularly pained by seeing his baby restrained with a "No-No," a tube-like restraint used to keep Carl's elbows from bending, devised so that he would be unable to touch the surgical repair in his mouth. Carl had to wear the "No-No" for 2 weeks. Even after the "No-No" was removed, Carl no longer put his hands or his toys in his mouth. His oral-exploration phase of development had halted abruptly.

Before he was 2 years old, Carl started weekly speech therapy. As expected after cleft-lip-and-palate repair, he had difficulty with articulation. The speech therapist also noticed that Carl would not let her touch the area around his mouth. Even after several months of speech therapy, Carl didn't speak like other children his age, and he didn't act like other boys his age.

Rhonda and Curt admitted that they were afraid to find out that Carl might have more problems, but they needed to know whether he could go to a preschool or whether they should be doing something more to help him. I agreed to meet Carl.

CARL'S FIRST VISIT

Rhonda and Curt returned with their son. Carl apparently didn't want to leave the waiting room. He hid his head on the couch and put pillows over his head. Finally, his parents persuaded him to enter my office. Carl never made eye contact with me. He ran toward my shelf with toys and backed away. He pushed his father toward the shelf and pointed. Curt handed him the toy he designated. Carl fingered the toy and made some noises. Then he gave his mother a hug and a kiss. After a minute, he pointed to another toy and pushed his mother toward it. He clearly wanted toys, but he seemed reluctant to take them, despite much encouragement.

When Carl spoke, I couldn't understand anything he said. His noises were like babbling, without distinctive words. Even though his parents modeled appropriate speech and language for him, he didn't make any attempts to imitate them. I observed that Carl had a habit of sticking his tongue out of his mouth a little and flipping it over. I also noticed that Carl didn't move his upper lip, even when he made sounds. I thought that the unusual movement of his tongue and the immobility of his lip must be impeding his progress in forming words. More concerning, Carl's articulation difficulty didn't explain his inability to use language or his reluctance to imitate. Children with cleft lip and palate do routinely have difficulty with articulation, but they do not necessarily have language problems.

I also noticed that Carl didn't play like other children his age. He seemed attracted to toys, but when he had them, he just fingered them or put them in and out of a small toy chest. Even after he had visited my office several times, there didn't seem to be any recognizable organization or theme to his activity. He often put his hands in his father's mouth, although he never put his hands in his own mouth. He occasionally played peek-a-boo with me, but I noticed that he covered his mouth instead of his eyes when it was his turn to "hide."

I referred Carl to the Regional Center for the Developmentally Disabled for evaluation of his language and development so that he would be eligible for a special state-financed preschool for children with communication problems. I set about the work of beginning to build a relationship with Carl, of understanding his behavior, and of guiding his parents in promoting his development.

WOULD EMDR HELP?

I knew that most of Carl's difficulties had not stemmed from trauma, but I imagined that his experiences at the time of his surgery must have been traumatic. Experts who work exclusively with children with cleft-lip-and-palate repair tell me that those children have no more anxiety or psychological problems than other children. The day Carl had his surgery at age 10 months, however, his grandmother died and his mother and father were extremely distressed. Carl's pain and immobility, and the sense of anxiety in his family, must have impressed him. I thought about how fear and anxiety potentiate the depth of trauma.

I didn't know whether EMDR could help Carl, but I introduced the possibility to Rhonda and Curt, and they were willing to try. We decided that our goal was to help Carl tolerate having his mouth touched so that he would allow his parents to brush his teeth and his speech therapist would be able to show him how to move his mouth to form words. I reasoned that Carl's painful experience with his mouth surgery may have caused him to believe something like, "It's not safe for me to let anyone touch my mouth." Perhaps he had abruptly stopped his oral exploration at the time of the surgery because he associated pain with anything having to do with his mouth.

Initially, I had no idea how I could integrate EMDR into our sessions. One day, while Carl was putting Mickey Mouse into the small toy chest, I was talking with Rhonda about activities Carl enjoyed at home. Rhonda told me that she had made chocolate cupcakes the day before, and that Carl had enjoyed eating them. Carl smiled. I saw my first chance for introducing EMDR. I tapped Carl's shoulders alternately while I said "chocolate cupcakes." Then I talked about how chocolate cupcakes taste good and feel good in his mouth. My intention was simply to have Carl experience a strengthening of a pleasant oral sensation. Next I picked up Mickey Mouse and pointed to his mouth. I said, "Mickey Mouse's mouth hurts. His mouth and lips hurt." I tapped Carl's hands with the toy as I talked. In a few seconds, when Carl changed positions, I said, "His mouth and lips feel better now. Now he can play and have fun and eat chocolate cupcakes."

Carl returned the next week with his father. When he entered the room, he began his weekly routine of approaching the toys and then backing away. When I asked Curt how the week had gone, he reported that Carl would sometimes sit restrained in his safety seat and pull at his arms (*not* the straps of the safety seat), saying "Aw, aw," which was Carl's way of saying "Off, off." When I see repetitive behaviors that puzzle me, I try to think of a part of the traumatic event that might be related. An image of Carl with his arms held in extension with the "No-No" floated to mind. Unable to fulfill his developmental directive for oral exploration at age 10 months, maybe he formed the belief, "I can't have what I want," or the thought, "I want it, and I can't have it."

I shared my thoughts with Curt, and asked him to hold Carl's elbows for a few seconds to demonstrate how the "No-No" restraint had restricted Carl's movement. While Curt held Carl's elbows, Carl struggled to free himself, and I tapped Carl's hands alternately a few times. Then I signaled Curt to release his child. I continued to tap Carl and repeated, "It's off. You can play now." We spent the rest of the session with Carl climbing on the sofa or the table and his father following him to catch him when he jumped or to keep him from falling.

The next week Carl came with his mother. No changes to report from home, except that Carl had stopped saying "Aw, aw" and pulling on his arms. Now, he said "Aw, aw" and pulled on his index finger. Rhonda told me the story of the pulse oximeter and talked about how difficult it had been for her to see Carl and her mother in pain. While she expressed her sad memories, I alternately squeezed Carl's index fingers and repeated, "You're okay. You can play."

When Carl returned the next week, he went immediately to the cupboard and began to pull his favorite toys from the shelves. This was the first time in our 3 months of working together weekly that Carl had not gone through the ritual of getting one of his parents to hand the toys to him. I also noticed that Carl was putting his fingers and toys in his mouth, that his upper lip was more mobile, and that he was no longer flipping his tongue over. He now moved his tongue in and out smoothly. His play had changed, too. He now played "Broken-Fix It," during which he took apart the faucet on the toy sink and handed me the pieces, saying something like "Broken-Fix It." I fixed it and handed it back, and Carl started the game all over again. Rhonda told me that she had explained to Carl that his mouth was "broken" when he was a baby and that he had an operation to "fix" the "owie."

Then Carl pointed to a cat marionette hanging on the wall. I took it down. (Later, I realized that cats have cleft lips.) Carl grabbed the cat and started swinging it wildly back and forth. "It's a nice cat," he said. The sentence was unmistakable, but the words were still difficult to understand. I was so impressed by Carl's ability to put together his first sentence that I just held the marionette by its stiff wire frame, swinging it back and forth saying, "He's a nice cat." Carl moved his eyes back and forth as he watched the cat swing from side to side.

Carl started a special communication preschool and began to have speech therapy twice a week. During his next sessions with me, he always chose to play with the cat marionette. One day, the cat came apart. It was easy to fix. Carl loved playing "Broken-Fix It" with the cat. He would say, "Swing, swing" and I would swing the cat back and forth, saying "It was broken. Now it's fixed. You're all fixed too! You can play too."

Looking back, I think EMDR has helped to desensitize some of Carl's body sensations associated with his surgery. Following EMDR sessions, Carl stopped approaching then quickly withdrawing from toys. He was able to take toys and explore them with his mouth. His oral phase, which had halted abruptly at 10 months, resumed at age 2½ for about 3 weeks. He began to move from infantile play (his hands in his dad's mouth and peek-a-boo) to using toys in a symbolic way. He stopped flipping his tongue and his upper lip became more flexible. He has begun to imitate, but not yet with the persistence of a toddler. His speech is barely understandable, but he points to everything asking, "Wasitz?" (His way of saying "What is this?")

EMDR seemed to have jump-started Carl's stymied development, but his continuing development will require years of speech therapy, play therapy, and socialization experiences in preschool, and all the love and patience I know his parents are prepared to give him.

ELIZA

Sandy was used to her 11-year-old daughter Eliza being a "shy, fearful child," but she called me for a consultation the day Eliza told her what she was thinking. Sandy sighed and explained, "I knew we needed help when Eliza told me that she was afraid she would stab herself in the eye, that she would cut herself with scissors, that she would drown a baby, and that the family would be killed in an accident."

Sandy dabbed her eyes and then continued, "Not only that, but I'm also worried that Eliza doesn't have friends, she's overweight, she cries a lot, she has panic attacks, and she refuses to sleep without me in bed with her." Sandy pushed her blond hair back from her face and poured out the rest of her concerns, "Eliza has daily headaches and asthma. She whines about pains from small scratches or bumps. Maybe she's trying to get attention, but when I give her extra attention she still complains a lot." Sandy paused for a moment, then added, "Something odd that I don't understand is that Eliza loves listening to instrumental music, but she cries at *any* song with words and refuses to listen."

Sandy had fears too. She had been in therapy for years to help her deal with her own childhood trauma and recently had started using EMDR. Sandy had grown up in an abusive, alcoholic household. She confided her fears. "I was always determined to protect my children from the kinds of pain I suffered. I was afraid that my children might be molested, so I never took any chances. I didn't want to let them out of my sight, so I never let my children go to camp or spend the night at a friend's house. I usually sleep with Eliza, and I check on her three brothers several times a night to make sure they're safe."

Sandy admitted, "I used drugs before the boys were born when Eliza was a baby, but one day I woke up and found her climbing up to the stove. I knew I had to stop using so I'd be able to take care of her. After that I started going to meetings to take a hold of my life, and I made up my mind to be the best parent possible." Sandy was so afraid that she might traumatize her children by making them unhappy that she never insisted that they do anything. She even allowed them to miss school when they really wanted to stay home.

Eliza's father, Lester, was prone to drinking when he was stressed. He would become very critical of his wife and children. He frequently berated Eliza for being fat and sensitive. Sandy apologized for Lester. "He had a hard childhood. His father left home when he was really little, so he never had a model for how to be a parent. His mother was always working to support the family, so you could say that Lester had to raise himself. He does love our children. He's never physically abusive with me or the children, and I know he would never sexually molest a child." Sandy did admit that she was sometimes scared when Lester began drinking and shouting. When Lester began erupting, she took all four children to her mother's house.

Eliza was afraid to say or do anything that would provoke her father. She learned to be "invisible" when Lester was drinking. Sandy threatened to leave Lester if he didn't stop drinking, but she could never bring herself to leave Lester for more than a few hours. She depended on him financially. More than that, she didn't want her children to blame her for taking them away from their father.

Eliza was drowning in a cascade of traumas. From her father's verbal attacks and her mother's overpowering fears, she had learned that she was bad and helpless. Her panic attacks were like thwarted urges at escape, but she had nowhere to go, and she felt powerless to say anything to protect herself.

ELIZA'S FIRST VISIT

Eliza refused to see me without her mother in the room. She huddled next to her mother on the sofa, occasionally whispering something in her mother's ear and nudging Sandy with her elbow until Sandy spoke for her. I encouraged Sandy to wait for Eliza to speak for herself, but Sandy seemed unable to refrain from "helping" her child.

In one of her sessions, I invited Eliza to use the sand tray to create a safe place while her mother sat beside her. Eliza stared at the empty sand tray. Finally, looking glum, she said in a barely audible voice, "The only way a place could be safe was if no one was there, because then nothing could happen."

Next, Eliza agreed to make a sand-tray picture representing "scary." She picked up a spider, a figure with a gun, and a car. "The spider might crawl over me. The man might shoot me. The car might run over me." "What could you do to them?" I inquired. Eliza looked blank.

"Would you like to pick a figure to help?" I asked. Eliza looked over my collection of toys and chose Garfield. She put him in the sand and made him run away from the car. "How does Garfield feel after he ran away?" I asked. Eliza replied hesitantly, "He feels scared but glad he didn't get run over. He feels good."

Next Eliza covered the spider, the shooting figure, and the car with sand. At least in the tiny sphere of the sand tray Eliza had some power to protect herself. I asked Eliza how she felt. "Better," she said. "Where do you feel that feeling?" I asked. Eliza pointed to her head. I invited her to watch Garfield guide her eye movement while she noticed that happy feeling. Eliza felt the happiness in her head and her heart.

Eliza volunteered, "I almost got run over once when a truck backed up. It was scary." (Eliza's mother could barely remember the incident because no one had been hurt, and she hadn't realized that Eliza had had a "close call.") I asked Eliza whether she would like to use the car to erase the scary feeling. She readily agreed. She pictured herself on a bike behind the truck as the truck began to move backward. On a scale of 0 to 10, Eliza rated the scary feeling as 100! Her negative cognition was "I'm going to get killed." Her positive cognition was "I'm fine." I moved the toy car back and forth, and Eliza watched. Her anxiety quickly dropped to 5. I asked Eliza what she had done to stay safe. She had moved. The truck had stopped. I surmised that Eliza had been "lucky." The anxiety dropped to 0. Eliza felt lucky and happy in her head and her heart.

LIFE GOES ON

After that session, Eliza showed some significant improvement. Her "scary thoughts" diminished, her panic attacks stopped, and she generally seemed more relaxed. Of course, it took many more months of therapy before Eliza began to feel confident about expressing herself. I wondered whether the incident with the truck had really been critical, or whether it represented her emotional experience of feeling trapped and nearly "run over." Interestingly, we never used EMDR to process any of Eliza's memories of encounters with her father. Nevertheless, she did begin to feel safer in his presence and may have realized that he would be threatening but not truly dangerous regardless of whether she was silent or outspoken.

Eliza's home situation didn't change at all, although I did meet with Lester a few times. He claimed that he drank because the children annoyed him so much. I tried to help him be more successful at encouraging his children to cooperate, rather than berating them until they did what he demanded. He was interested, but not enough to follow through on any referrals to help him stop drinking or to get any therapy or parenting education. Sandy was distressed by Lester's behavior, yet she knew she wasn't ready to leave him.

Every week, for over a year, Eliza played at the sand tray while her mother and I sat beside her. Initially, while Eliza played, her mother and I talked. We talked about how Eliza could feel safe, despite the difficulties at home. I encouraged Sandy to stop talking for Eliza both at home and in my office. Sandy laughed. She was beginning to get the idea that she could help Eliza more by doing less for her. Eliza needed to know that her mother had some confidence in her ability to express herself and that her mother believed that it was safe for Eliza to speak for herself. She also needed to see her mother model how she could stand up for herself and lead her life more confidently.

In the sand tray, Eliza used toy boats, pirates, and treasure chests to play out the themes of plunder, sinking, and rescue, searching for buried treasure, and sailing to a new country. I inferred that Eliza was showing me the drama of her own experience of feeling like a sinking ship, of her mother bringing her to a place where she could begin to acknowledge her own inner treasures, and the exciting, yet frightening prospect of exploring new territory. Eliza demonstrated her knowledge of geography by drawing countries in the sand and naming key cities, rivers, and other geographical features. Eliza enjoyed EMDR, so she usually accepted my offers to guide her eye movement when she demonstrated that she was smart, or creative, or bold, or strong through her play in the sand tray.

After several months, Eliza moved her play from the sand tray to the toy cupboard. She developed a scenario in which she owned injured puppies and I was the vet. I acknowledged all of her puppies' little injuries with great compassion, and Sandy and I tenderly cared for their wounds. Like many children who are constantly assaulted by little injuries to their feelings, Eliza demonstrated her emotional hurts by having strong emotional reactions to minor physical bumps. Gradually, as her mother and I acknowledged the extent of Eliza's traumas that derived from ridicule and fear, she began to feel better.

"I CAN TALK FOR MYSELF"

Eliza started fifth grade without her usual reluctance. She joined a soccer team. She began to make friends. She started to speak up for herself, and was surprised to find that her father picked on her less as she gained strength. Her play became more exuberant, and in her final session with me, she dressed up with a neon pink boa, a shiny black cape, sunglasses, and a crown. She drew pictures to cover my walls. When her decorations were ready, she turned up the volume on her boom box and sang song after song along with her favorite group.

Two years after Eliza stopped coming to see me, I called to ask how she was doing. Sandy said that Eliza had started junior high school and was doing well. Eliza had friends, did well in school, and argued heartily with her brothers. She continued to be overweight and had no interest in dieting, unlike some of her thin friends. Eliza asked to visit her grandmother or go to friends' houses when her father was drinking. She was outspoken and had developed a hilarious sense of humor. She no longer complained of invisible pains from minor bumps, and she no longer had headaches. Sandy said she had learned that Eliza obviously could take care of herself and that she didn't need to speak for her daughter. I could hear Eliza laughing and yelling in the background, "Yeah, I can talk for myself!"

8

"I'LL LOVE YOU FOREVER"
UNRESOLVED GRIEVING

The day 11-year-old Sam hurled his bat and helmet at the Little League umpire, his reputation as an angry bruiser was sealed. For the past several years, Sam's incessant angry outbursts had exhausted his family and alienated his peers at school and on sports teams. His teacher was at a loss to explain why such a smart boy was repeatedly provoking her anger, especially as she was giving him so much positive reinforcement for his appropriate behaviors. His constant refrain was, "That's not fair!" and he complained that he never got enough attention. What was going on?

His parents felt it might have something to do with the loss of his grandmother. Even though 5 years had passed since her death from a stroke, Sam thought about his grandmother all the time. He adored her. She had always seemed to know what he needed and was able to give him time and attention, even in his busy household with five young children. Ever since she died, Sam felt guilty about her death. He didn't know why, but he felt responsible. It wasn't Sam's grief that brought him to therapy, it was his anger. But even with over a year of play therapy, Sam's behavior did not improve significantly.

Sam's therapist and his parents decided to request psychological testing to help them understand Sam's daily outbursts of anger, his overly aggressive behavior, and his extreme sensitivity to criticism. Testing showed Sam to have superior intelligence. The testing psychologist also observed Sam's low frustration tolerance and his tendency to "jump to conclusions." He described Sam as "oversensitive and overreactive, without sufficient emotional resources to handle the everyday stresses of life." He commented that Sam's paucity of emotional resources led to personal disorganization and vulnerability. He observed that Sam had a tendency to feel helpless, to feel isolated from his brothers and sisters, and to have a pervasive feeling of loss. On the Rorschach inkblot test, Sam had three times the number of morbid (that is, wounded, hurt) responses than is normal for his age.

The examining psychologist concluded that Sam's "weak ego strength" was responsible for letting mild irritations mushroom into intense anger. He recognized that Sam's depressed feelings were characterized by a sense that he is deprived. He reasoned, however, that Sam's longing for his grandmother highlighted Sam's present feeling of isolation and lack of support, rather than seeing Sam's sense of loss as continuing posttraumatic feelings stemming from unresolved grief.

The psychologist recommended that Sam's parents spend more time with him, give him more attention, and express their own feelings of vulnerability, frustration, and irritation to Sam in addition to explaining how he needed to change. But Sam's parents had four other children, two careers, and no more time or attention to give.

Sam's therapist had heard me speak about my work using EMDR with children. He was concerned that Sam seemed "stuck" in thinking about and talking about his grandmother, and that no amount of play therapy seemed to be helping him resolve his grief. He asked me whether I would see Sam for a few EMDR sessions, and I agreed to meet with Sam's parents.

THE HISTORY OF A CRITICAL LOSS

Joy and Cole came to see me about their son. Sam's father rolled his eyes in exasperation and sighed as he summed up their efforts to meet his son's needs. "We make every effort to play with him, I coach his baseball teams, we help with his homework and settle his constant arguments with his siblings. We give Sam 80% of our attention even though our other four children need us, too. He never seems to get enough attention to satisfy him."

Sam's parents had hoped to raise their boys as a cooperative team, but Sam never felt like or acted like a team member in his family. He constantly accused his parents of not caring. He loudly claimed unfair treatment whenever he ran out of his favorite cereal and there wasn't another box waiting, whenever one of his siblings got to sit in the front seat of the car, even when he was asked to feed the cat—the chore that earned his allowance. He argued loudly and often with his brothers. He never wanted the same TV station, even when the other four could agree on a program. Their music was always "too loud" or "too low" or the wrong choice for him. Cole and Joy told me that Sam often seemed miserable, and he made everyone else in the family miserable too. They were sad but not surprised when they realized that no one ever called to invite Sam anywhere.

I asked Sam's parents about their son's infancy, development, strengths, illnesses, injuries, and traumas. Joy and Cole smiled as they both remembered Sam as a sweet, lovable baby. They had enjoyed having such an affectionate, easygoing child. His developmental milestones had been "on target." He had always been physically strong, agile, and athletically inclined. He had never been hospitalized, and he had only had typical childhood illnesses. Sam had adjusted to the birth of his younger sibling reasonably well, probably because Joy's mother had given him a lot of attention during that transition. In the 4 years since his grandmother's death when he was in first grade, Sam seemed to become more and more needy and angry.

The main trauma Sam had experienced was the death of his beloved grandmother, whom he always called "Baba." Joy also missed the love and support her mother had showered on her large family. She recalled the day of her mother's stroke, which was clearly still very upsetting. "My mother was sitting next to Sam on the living-room couch, reading to him from *Green Eggs and Ham*. Suddenly, she stopped and she got pale. Then she just keeled over.

"I thought that she had had a heart attack. I stretched her out on the couch and went to call an ambulance, while Sam sat beside her. I opened the front door of the house so the paramedics could come in without ringing the bell, and explained to Sam that I had asked them not to turn on their sirens because I didn't want to make Baba nervous. I thought that it was important to keep a heart-attack victim as calm as possible. I told Sam to sit quietly so he wouldn't upset Baba. The paramedics arrived quickly and put my mother on the stretcher and carried her away. That was the last time Sam saw her. She died in the hospital the next day."

Joy and Cole realized that the death of Sam's grandmother was a critical incident in his life, and that his personality had changed in the ensuing 4 years. I wondered to myself whether the terrifying moment when Sam's grandmother stopped paying attention to him was still triggering Sam's urgent need for attention and his rage when he didn't get it. I explained to Joy and Cole that EMDR might be able to help reduce Sam's anxiety when he remembered his grandmother and that it might help him tolerate not being the center of attention. They readily agreed to bring Sam for two sessions.

SAM'S FIRST SESSION

Sam, wearing a baseball jersey and cap, came to my office ready to work. He knew that we only had two sessions together, that he would try EMDR, a new method for getting over upsetting events, and that our goal was to help him get over his grandmother's death. We chatted for a few minutes about Sam's favorite baseball team and Ken Griffey, Jr., his favorite player. Then I invited Sam to imagine a safe place, where he could feel relaxed and safe, knowing that everything was just as he wanted it. Sam imagined all of his friends and all of his family doing something fun together. I added eye movement to his daydream, and he chose the direction and speed of eye movement that felt most comfortable to him.

I asked Sam what he could remember about the day when his grandmother had a stroke. He recalled, "She was sitting beside me, reading me a story, when all of a sudden she stopped paying attention to me and stopped reading and looked funny." I asked Sam what negative thought he had about himself when he looked at that picture in his mind. Sam replied, "I feel like it was my fault. I could have done something to help her."

Once we had established his negative cognitions, I asked Sam what he would prefer to believe about himself when he remembered that event—his *positive cognitions*. He said that he'd like to believe that he had done everything he could to help her. He wanted to believe that everybody did everything they could to help her. Furthermore, he told me, "I want to believe that death can happen to anybody and I can accept that." I asked Sam to rate his positive cognitions on a scale of 1 to 7, and he said they felt "almost true."

But he was still very upset when he remembered the image of the scene.

Now I asked Sam to do something more difficult. I asked him to hold in mind the image of his grandmother having a stroke and the statements, "It's my fault. I could have done something to help her." I guided Sam to move his eyes and then waited for him to talk between sets of eye movement. "I'm sad," Sam began, "and I miss her. . . . It's upsetting. It's my fault. . . . It's in my mind. . . . It's like a mystery: What I did or what I didn't do."

Sam's face suddenly clouded. "I panicked. I overreacted. If I had been calm, she would have been all right. I made her nervous." He looked alert, remembering what had happened. "I feel that's what made me feel weird. . . . I'm shaky. . . . I have a cold feeling down to my spine. . . . I feel not so good. . . . I feel like it's my fault. . . . I still get the same thing—it's my fault. . . . It's still scary."

Sam seemed to be circling around and around with the erroneous belief that his grandmother's death was his fault because he had gotten nervous, and he thought he had made her nervous. His mother's well-intentioned cautions about being quiet so that Baba wouldn't be upset may have inadvertently caused 6-year-old Sam to believe that his anxiety had caused his grandmother's death. I wanted to help Sam realize that anyone would have felt nervous in that situation and that his anxiety did not cause his grandmother's death.

IMAGINAL INTERWEAVE: KEN GRIFFEY, JR. HELPS SAM

I chose an *imaginative interweave*, an intervention that I hoped would normalize Sam's anxiety at the time of his grandmother's stroke. "If Ken Griffey, Jr. had been there, would he have had that same anxious feeling?" Sam considered my question as he moved his eyes back and forth. He looked surprised. "Wow, Ken Griffey, Jr. would be scared too. Anybody would feel scared!" I guided Sam's eye movement again and noticed that his anxiety was visibly subsiding. He continued, "It looks a little less scary. . . . I feel better about it. . . . It feels like I panicked too much. . . . I panicked because I was so upset. . . . My body was shaking. Baba must have known. . . . I don't think it was my fault she got scared."

I asked Sam to pretend that he was standing in the doorway

watching what was happening instead of sitting next to his grand-mother. I hoped that Sam would realize that his grandmother would have had the stroke whether he was there or not. But Sam protested, "I'd really feel even more guilty if I *hadn't* been there with Baba." I asked Sam whether he would be willing to imagine that he was standing in the doorway watching while Ken Griffey, Jr. was sitting beside his grandmother. Sam nodded and began to move his eyes. He startled, "I can see that something was happening to her even though Ken Griffey, Jr. was there with her instead of me!"

I wondered whether anything besides Sam's understandable nervousness had contributed to his feelings of guilt, so I asked, "Do you have anything to feel guilty about?" Sam began to move his eyes and responded to my question, "I don't feel guilty. Not now. I helped. I tried at least. . . . I still feel I did something wrong. I tried my hardest. . . . It's a mixed feeling. . . . I'm starting to feel not guilty. It's not my fault."

Now Sam's voice began to sound stronger and more sure. "It's not my fault and I couldn't have caused it. *I couldn't have caused it.* I loved her and everything she did. She put me and my brothers together, and she never got angry with me, and that's how I know she loved me. I feel she knows I loved her."

FEELING THE LOVE

I encouraged Sam to find a special place in his heart to hold his memories of his Baba and to feel her loving him. Sam smiled quietly as he moved his eyes and said, "I have a special place in my heart for her if I ever need her." When Sam looked back at the original incident, he no longer felt upset. He concluded, "It's not my fault. I did everything humanly possible to save Baba. We all did everything humanly possible to save Baba." Sam moved his eyes again, and mused, "I feel Baba safe in my heart."

THE SECOND SESSION: BUILDING A TEAM

Sam returned the following week for his second and final session with me. "How have you felt since last time we met?" I asked eagerly. Sam responded matter-of-factly, "I don't feel guilty. No other changes." It seemed that one EMDR session had changed

Sam's view of himself in relation to his grandmother's death. We still needed to address the angry, irritating behaviors that interfered with Sam's relationships, however.

For the past 4 years, Sam had protected himself from the loss of intimacy by alienating people with his flaring temper. I speculated that Sam had developed a "protective" posttraumatic strategy of using anger to distance himself from people he cared about so that he wouldn't jeopardize their life with his caring or his anxiety. (Did 6-year-old Sam believe that his love and caring, as well as his anxiety, contributed to his grandmother's death? So far, it appeared that his life-insurance policy claiming "Distancing prevents death" had worked.) It made sense that Sam didn't want to risk losing another person who was dear to him, and if that meant Sam couldn't be close to anyone, so be it. Irrational posttraumatic beliefs are powerful, even if they are untrue and detrimental. Sam no longer felt guilty, but he still didn't feel safe, and he hadn't practiced having intimate relationships for 4 years.

I asked Sam what three things he would like to change for himself. He didn't have to think for long. "I just want to change my relationship with my family. I get in a lot of arguments with my brothers. My dad and I get in big arguments. If I'm fighting with my brothers, he jumps in and referees. I think the arguments are totally unfair. I wish we didn't have to get in such big arguments with my dad."

I asked Sam how those arguments made him feel about himself. Sam shot back, "I feel like I'm getting picked on. If I had everything I wanted, we wouldn't need one another." Sam didn't have negative self-assessments when he remembered the upsetting incidents. He was angry. I probed further, "How would you like to relate to your family?" Sam answered obtusely, "If I got what I wanted, they wouldn't be happy." In Sam's belief system, it seemed that the only way the rest of his family could be safe and close was if Sam did not get what he wanted.

I tried another avenue of investigation. "What would your family be like if everyone in the family got what they needed? Can you remember a time when your family was the way you wanted?" Sam thought for a minute. "Right after my brother Joey was born, everything in the family was the way I wanted it to be. Baba was alive.

Everyone got along. We were happy we had a new baby. We were happy we were all together." I decided to reinforce Sam's memories of that tranquil time. "Where can you feel that feeling in your body?" Sam responded, "I feel it in my head and in my mind." I instructed Sam, "Hold that picture and that feeling together." Sam watched my hand move from side to side. When he stopped, he said, "I felt good. I felt loved. We all got along. We all got taken care of." I advised Sam to stay with that feeling, and I guided his eye movement again. Sam said, "That time I got the same thing. We were all taken care of. We're all loved. . . . I always feel we're loved. But sometimes we get in arguments."

I asked Sam whether he would like to be able to control his feelings and his behavior to get along better with his family. Sam agreed that he would like it if his family didn't get him so upset. I asked Sam to describe some of the upsetting arguments that came to mind. He remembered what had happened that very morning. Joey had turned up the volume on his stereo, and the loud music woke Sam, who promptly roared his anger. I decided to do EMDR on several of these incidents, hoping to desensitize some of the triggers that set off Sam's rage. I asked Sam to notice the feelings in his body as he viewed the scene. Sam remembered the noise as he moved his eyes, "I was annoyed. . . . It was noisy. It was annoying music. My brother likes that loud music. The rest of the day went okay."

Next, Sam remembered when his father got angry with him for not mowing the lawn. "I went to my room. Later we argued." When Sam viewed that memory while moving his eyes, it became less upsetting to him. When Sam was finished, he said, "I can do it."

I wondered whether the work on desensitizing triggers would generalize to make other minor conflicts with his family less emotionally charged. "Sam," I asked, "Can you imagine a scene with your family where they push your buttons and you stay in control of your feelings and behavior?" Sam visualized arguing with his brother about which channel to watch on TV. Sam moved his eyes and thought out loud, "He gets there first, and I go downstairs to watch TV instead of pounding on him. . . . I can solve problems and get along better with my family. . . . I felt I could solve any problems I have with my family. . . . Even if I feel mad I can control my behavior."

I asked Sam if there were any other upsetting memories that he wanted to work on. Sam brought up the recent incident when he threw his helmet and bat because he thought that the umpire had made a mistake. I asked Sam what he believed about himself when he remembered that scene. "I felt fine about myself," he replied. Nevertheless, Sam admitted that he felt very upset remembering what had happened. He focused on the memory and his feelings of anger and moved his eyes. Sam's body relaxed, and he commented, "I can keep my cool even when someone makes a mistake."

I asked Sam to imagine being a team with his brothers. "What does it take to be a team?" I inquired. Sam replied, "It takes understanding and cooperation." I asked Sam to imagine being a team leader with his family while I guided his eye movement. He stopped after a minute and said, "It feels kind of good to have someone to play with." I asked him to concentrate again on the feeling of teaming up with his family. Sam concluded, "It feels really good."

A FINAL VISIT

Sam's family was going away for summer vacation, and his parents agreed to come for one follow-up visit at the end of the summer. When they returned, Joy and Cole came alone. "Sam says he doesn't want or need any more therapy, so we decided to come to talk with you." Cole said, "Sam is doing good. He's not having as many emotional blow-ups." Joy added, "He seems more reasonable."

Joy told me a story to illustrate how Sam had changed. "A few years ago, when Sam's older brother, Jerry, started junior high school, we bought Jerry the name-brand backpack he wanted. Sam wanted one too, but we told him he could have one when he started junior high. So this year, Sam is going to start junior high, and he asked for one of those expensive backpacks. We told him that we were sorry, but this year we can't afford to buy an expensive backpack. In the past, Sam would have blown up and shouted on and on about how unfair it was that his brother had gotten that backpack and he didn't. Instead of blowing up, Sam asked his brother if he could have the old one. His brother gave it to him, and Sam washed that old backpack with a toothbrush so he could use it.

He's using that old backpack and hasn't even complained once that it was unfair. Now Sam is no more of a problem than the other four children."

Sam's parents agreed with their son that he didn't need more therapy. I urged them to take Sam back to his therapist for a few sessions to complete the process and to say good-bye.

In the 3 years since our last meeting, I have spoken with Joy twice about Sam's progress. Sam continues to be a bright, competitive, sensitive, and forthright person, and he has not had any further psychotherapy. Since his two EMDR sessions, Sam has felt better about himself, he hasn't been as angry, and he's been a part of the family again. Joy sounded pleased as she told me, "Now Sam can talk about his grandmother's death without being teary. On her birthday, we all went to throw roses into the river as a remembrance. I thought Sam handled that occasion maturely. Sam is the family member who most values family traditions and participates wholeheartedly in birthday and holiday celebrations."

9

NEVER-ENDING LOVE
IS ROUND
COMPLEX, UNRESOLVED GRIEVING

Sam's unresolved grief stemmed from a critical loss at age 6 and was relatively easy to treat with EMDR. Darius, on the other hand, experienced a series of losses at age 3 that continued to stress his family for years. He had ongoing behavioral problems despite months of medication and EMDR-facilitated therapy.

Six-year-old Darius had already been asked to leave four schools, and he was not yet in first grade. When he was 3 years old, he hit and bit so many children that his preschool asked him not to come back. In his next school, the teacher was optimistic. She declared that she would have Darius in shape by the end of 6 months. But before 6 months were up, the teacher had given up. Darius didn't want the children to look at him. He didn't want to sit next to anyone. He tore up every poster on the walls. Finally, he tore up the garden the children had planted, just when they were excited about all the sprouts and buds. His third school experience ended after only 3 days: He threw garbage all over the bathroom then ran out of the school, where it took two adults to restrain him. His fourth school placement lasted 5 weeks. It ended abruptly when he hoisted a chair at his pregnant teacher then curled up in a fetal position and became unresponsive. Now Darius was in his fifth placement, a classroom for severely emotionally disturbed children.

At home, Darius challenged his family as well. Darius's attitude seemed to be "My way is the only way," and he repeatedly became angry and provoked anger. Latisha and Derek, Darius's parents, were also upset about Darius's relationship with his 3-year-old brother, Lewis. It made them sad and angry to see Darius relentlessly taunting, controlling, and provoking his young sibling. It seemed to them that Darius couldn't stand to have those around him happy. He seemed to be stuck in a cycle of stirring up trouble, then feeling remorseful. It was so unpleasant to be with Darius and his brother together that Latisha and Derek even went in separate cars to pick the boys up from school so that neither parent would have to be in the car with both children.

Darius's parents tried everything. They took him to weekly therapy sessions. They arranged for evaluations, including a neurodevelopmental assessment by a developmental pediatrician, psychiatric evaluation, neuropsychological evaluation, pediatric evaluation, speech and language testing, and repeated psychological testing.

Some of the doctors prescribed drug therapy for Darius. He tried Dexedrine and Ritalin, stimulant medications that generally have the paradoxical effect of being calming for children, but Darius's behavior became more irritable and hyperactive. Next he tried imipramine, a tricyclic antidepressant. Darius continued to take 25 milligrams of imipramine from that time on because he showed slightly improved concentration and decreased outbursts. A higher dose of imipramine made him too irritable. Despite the improvement low-dose imipramine offered, a few months later the psychiatrist evaluating Darius recommended day treatment, a special school setting for emotionally disturbed children. Several examiners independently noted that Darius's behavioral difficulties started when he was 3 years old, shortly after his grandfather died.

I was called in to try EMDR with Darius and to manage his medication while his therapist continued to see him weekly. When I read that Darius was fine before his significant losses, I considered unresolved grief and posttraumatic stress disorder as potentially responsible for some of this child's difficulties. I did not know whether EMDR would help Darius with any or all of his problems; but I felt that even if EMDR could only help reduce Darius's anxiety, it might be easier to sort out his other problems.

A CASCADE OF TRAUMAS

At our first meeting, I asked Latisha and Derek about his grandfather's death when Darius was 3. They told me that during that one year Darius had experienced a number of traumatic events: the birth of a sibling, the deaths of his beloved grandfather and two uncles (one was murdered and the other committed suicide), the loss of his special preschool teacher, and the move to the classroom of a teacher who was neither understanding nor kind. To add to his confusion and misery, his loving parents became upset with each other over how to handle matters related to the deaths, and they had turned into angry, fuming, withdrawn adults.

Three-year-old Darius had not just had a "critical incident," he had had a whole cascade of traumas. As one trauma followed another, he was probably convinced that he was being punished for being "bad." In the classroom for emotionally disturbed children, he witnessed children losing control and requiring physical restraint daily. It's not surprising that Darius was also acting "bad."

INTRODUCTION TO EMDR

During Derek and Latisha's first visits with me, we discussed how these traumas may have affected Darius's beliefs and behavior. Derek and Latisha identified the death of Darius's grandfather as their son's most important trauma, and began to speculate about how that event had affected Darius. Latisha guessed that the mental pictures Darius would have of Grandpa might include a memory of being in the park together and a memory of Grandpa in the hospital, unresponsive, with tubes attached to him. I asked Latisha and Derek to imagine what negative cognitions Darius might have about himself in relation to his grandpa's death, beliefs that he still had about himself today.

Latisha and Derek had no trouble generating a list of the self-deprecating beliefs their 6-year-old child demonstrated through his actions and his comments about himself: "I'm a bad boy. I'm stupid. I caused it. I'm in trouble. I lost everything. I'm being punished. I did something wrong. It's my fault." "These statements aren't true about Darius," Derek volunteered, "but he acts like this is what he believes about himself."

It was also easy for Latisha and Derek to come up with a list of beliefs they would like for their son to have about himself: "I'm loved. I am lovable. Grandpa loved me. I loved Grandpa. It's safe for me to love and be loved. I'm a good boy. I'm smart. Things happen and death is part of life. I'm fine as I am. I have Grandpa in my heart. I behave normally." They were curious to see how EMDR might help Darius actually believe that these statements about him are true.

DEVELOPMENTAL CONSIDERATIONS

A 3-year-old is in the midst of developing personality based on a view of himself that is reflected back by the words, actions, and feelings of others. He doesn't have the perspective to see that tragedies are happening to him but are not caused by him. He does not yet have the cognitive processing abilities necessary for understanding what happened to him. He lacks the experience to know what questions to ask. He may not be able to verbalize that he needs information, comfort, soothing, attention, and patience. Even if his parents and his teacher had been emotionally available to nurture him more, the loss of his soul mate would have been overwhelming for Darius.

Young children almost always believe that a traumatic event is their fault. Combining their developmental egocentricity, belief in their own strong magical powers, and limited life experiences, young children initially take the blame for traumatic events. Darius was not yet 3 years old when his grandfather died. Healthy young children think of themselves as very powerful, so powerful that they can make people smile or hurt them. During the preschool years, young children test their theories of omnipotence. Daily experiences of limited power ("No, you may not run in the street.") gradually give the child a more realistic view of his capabilities and boundaries. Developmentally, it makes sense that Darius thought he "caused" his beloved grandfather's death. Even for adults, it may be more self-affirming to believe that a tragedy happened because you neglected to take control, than to accept that the traumatic incident was beyond anyone's control.

DARIUS'S FIRST VISIT: THE FAMILY INTERVIEW

Darius came along with his parents to the next visit. He is a tall, handsome boy with curly brown hair and expressive brown eyes, well groomed and eager to please. When I asked if he'd like to draw a picture of himself with his family, he immediately took out the colored pencils and began working. While Darius drew, his parents and I talked. He listened intently to the "state of the family" message his parents presented. I asked Darius's parents what they liked best about him. Darius looked up curiously. I guessed that it had been a while since he had heard anyone saying what they liked about him.

Darius's parents talked about his strengths, "He has a great face and a nice smile. He rides his bicycle well. He has a good memory. He's loving and affectionate—he's close to his mommy and daddy and grandmother and aunt, and he was very close to his grandpa." They glanced at Darius to see whether he reacted, but Darius kept drawing. They continued, "He's good at math, likes going for rides or going to the park. He's good with his hands—good at building things."

His mother commented that she had never seen a child as neat as Darius. He cleaned his room every night and arranged his toys in a particular way. He lined up his shoes in his closet. He vacuumed his room regularly. Even his mother observed, however, that it seemed unnatural for a child to be that neat and so concerned about order that he straightened his room without ever being asked. Yes, Darius's neatness was beyond the usual range. I wondered whether straightening was Darius's way of bringing order to this world he had reason to believe was unpredictable. The behavior might have gone along with Darius's belief that he had to have things his way in order to be safe. I hinted that a messy room might eventually be a sign that Darius was beginning to relax.

Then I asked what things Darius or his parents would like to have easier. Darius nodded as his parents enumerated: "schoolwork, playing with kids, getting along with people, and acting up." They also mentioned that Darius frequently had unexplained headaches and stomachaches. They hoped that he would feel better. I wondered whether the headaches and stomachaches were posttraumatic, somatic symptoms.

After drawing a picture, Darius wanted to make a sand-tray scene. He spent part of every session playing and doing art work.

I asked Darius if he could imagine a safe place, a place where he could feel good and relaxed and safe. Darius smiled, and arranged some figures in the sand. "A nice place," he said. I asked what the people were doing. "Playing hide-and-seek. They're going home. They see kids." I asked what kind of a day it was, hot or cool. "Hot." I asked whether he could smell anything. "Flowers—red roses." "Anything else you need to feel safe?" I inquired. Darius replied without hesitation, "Grownups—mothers and dads."

I felt encouraged that Darius could imagine a safe place. It meant that he had memorized a calm state in his mind and body, and he was able to retrieve it. I felt hopeful that Darius would be able to come back to his "safe place" if he became upset during EMDR. I also asked his parents to help him practice creating a safe place in his imagination if he needed soothing between sessions. I praised Darius for his good imagination, which helped him think up the safe place and that would help him get over some problems. He beamed at my approval.

Darius came to the next appointment with his mother. He chose the Russian nesting dolls from the shelf and sat on the floor to inspect them. While he played, his mother gave me the story she had written for her son. She had put the typed story in a folder with a picture of 3-year-old Darius on the front.

Here is the story I skimmed as Darius took apart the dolls and realigned them, again and again:

THE HAPPY LITTLE BOY NAMED DARIUS

Once upon a time there was a little boy named Darius who was born to Latisha and Derek Smith. Darius was his parents' first-born child. Darius brought so much joy to his parents' life. Darius was loved by everyone. One person who Darius brought so much joy to was Darius's grandfather. Darius called his grandfather "Grandpa." Darius spent a lot of time with his grandparents. While Darius's mom and dad went to work during the day, Darius's Granny and Grandpa would take good care of him. When Darius got older his grandpa would take him to the park. Darius loved going to the park with his grandpa and he would ask him every day, "Can we go to the park, Grandpa"? His grandpa could never

(cont.)

say no to the small boy who looked at him with so much love in his face. Some days Grandpa and Darius would go to the park twice in one day. The days they went to the park Darius would come back tired and hungry. Oftentimes his grandpa would be so tired he and Darius fell asleep together.

Darius and his grandpa were so close that even on the weekend, Grandpa would stop by. He would say, "Oh I was just in the neighborhood. I thought I'd stop by to see my grandson, Darius."

Darius was getting so big every day. One day his mom and dad decided to have another child. His mom thought Darius needed a playmate. His mom thought to herself, "Do I have enough love for another child?" being that she loved Darius so much. Well, 9 months later another special little boy was born, his name was Lewis. Darius was so excited to see his new little brother. Guess who brought Darius to the hospital? That's right!!! His grandpa.

There were some adjustments that needed to be ironed out when Mom and Lewis arrived home. Darius didn't know his little brother was coming home to stay. He thought they were going to leave him at the hospital. But then his mommy gave him a train that blew smoke out the top that actually came from his new brother. He was okay then.

In the next 2 months to come it would be soon time for little Darius to start school. So, one day his mom took him to his new school. Darius liked his new school. His mom soon had to go back to work. Darius's dad would take him to school. Guess who would pick him up from school? That's right!!! His grandpa.

One day Darius's grandpa became very sick. He was taken to the hospital. Darius's mom didn't want to upset Darius so she said he would be home soon. He was at the doctor's getting better. Well one week went by and Grandpa wasn't getting better. He was becoming sicker and sicker. One day Darius's mom picked him up at school and brought her son to see his grandpa. His grandpa had a big smile on his face when he saw

Darius. Grandpa wasn't able to speak, only smile. Darius was a little afraid at first because his grandpa had tubes hooked up to him. But soon afterwards, Darius was sitting in the bed with his grandpa. When it was time for Darius to go home and take a nap, Darius didn't want to leave his grandpa. His mom promised to bring him back once he woke up from his nap. Sure enough, when little Darius woke up he said, "Okay, Mommy, it's time to go back to the hospital and see Grandpa." When Darius and his mom arrived at the hospital Grandpa was fast asleep. Darius laid next to his grandpa while he slept. When Grandpa awoke, they hugged him and told him how much they loved him. He smiled at them with the same love in his eyes. Darius's grandpa said good-bye to them for the last time. That night Grandpa died.

With Darius being so young, who knew what this smart little boy felt? His mom wanted to keep him from ever feeling the sadness of the loss of his favorite grandpa. But Mom knew that Darius didn't do anything wrong to Grandpa for him to leave them and go to heaven. Grandpa loved Darius VERY MUCH and he wouldn't want Darius to feel sorry for him not being here, but to know that Mommy and Daddy and Granny, his aunt, and even his little brother would take good care of Darius.

Darius is 6 years old and he is the apple in his mommy and daddy's eye. Darius, YOUR MOMMY AND DADDY LOVE YOU SO VERY MUCH!!!! They want you to grow up remembering the love your grandpa had for you, and share that same love with your friends and family.

Darius's parents had written a heart-warming biographical story for their son. The story contained several parts that could be addressed with eye movement, including the "safe place" of parental love and love for his grandfather, the birth of Darius's brother, Darius's first school experience, as well as Darius's grandpa's illness and death. The story was missing some important elements that I suspected related to Darius's current difficulties: the illness of Darius's first teacher, his experience with the unsympathetic teacher with unrealistic expectations of 3-year-old Darius, the deaths of two uncles, the unspoken anger between Darius's parents that lasted for months, Darius's exposure to severely emotionally disturbed children, subsequent school failures, lack of experiences making or maintaining friendships, and anxiety about starting first grade in yet another new school.

FEELING THE LOVE

I asked Darius if he'd like to choose a figure to keep him company while he listened. Darius leaned over to pick up the Russian nesting dolls. His mother began to read. Darius asked, "Who was that boy? Was it me?" to make sure his mother was really telling a story about him.

He smiled and made satisfied noises while his mother described Darius going to the park with his grandfather. I asked Darius whether he could feel himself loving his grandpa. Darius nodded. I asked whether he would watch the dolls move while that feeling of being loved by Grandpa got even stronger. He nodded. I asked where he felt that loving feeling, and Darius pointed to his chest while we used eye movement to enhance and ground the safe feeling of love in Darius's body. Then I encouraged Darius to take a big breath and breathe out slowly, along with me. I asked Darius whether he could feel himself loving his grandpa. He nodded and pointed to his chest, as he began to move his eyes to follow the movement of the dolls.

SIBLING ISSUES

I asked Darius whether he would like to hear more of his story. This time he chose a rattle to help him and settled next to his mother. Latisha read the part about deciding to have another child. She wondered, "Do I have enough love for another child"? I asked Darius, "Do you feel your mom having enough love for you and other people at the same time?" He smiled and nodded. I encouraged him to "stay with that thought" while I used the rattle to do EMDR, giving him both auditory and visual stimulation.

After Latisha read about the birth of Darius's brother, I asked, "Can you feel your brother loving you?" As I moved the rattle, Darius put back his head against the sofa and smiled and cooed while he thought about his baby brother. Then I asked whether Darius could feel himself loving his brother. Darius looked relaxed and peaceful as he experienced his loving feelings for his brother. We had reached another good stopping place.

When Latisha and Darius returned a week later, Latisha reported that Darius had begun to share with his brother! She repeated, "Darius asks his brother to play and then he shares. He's getting along with his brother. I even pick them up together after school." Then she went on, "The problem now is that Lewis can't figure out or believe what's happening. The other day he called Darius "Stupid." Darius cried. I made Lewis apologize. Then they played well again."

ABREACTION: A PAINFUL MEMORY

Darius agreed to hear more of his story. Latisha read the part about Darius visiting his sick grandpa in the hospital. Darius began to clutch his middle and moan, "I have a tummy ache." He doubled up and groaned, "It hurts too much." Latisha looked alarmed. Darius was having an intense physical and emotional experience, what is called an *abreaction*. I thought that this pain was related to the awful pain of losing his grandpa and that resolving the abreaction could help Darius resolve the trauma.

Darius was in too much pain to be able to look at me, so I switched to EMDR tapping techniques and began to soothe him: "Just let go of the pain." Darius became angry and cried, "It's never going to get better." I connected his thought to the trauma by adding an "educational interweave," information that helped clarify his experience. "That was Grandpa who was never going to get better. Darius, you're fine as you are." Darius stopped groaning, his face cleared, and he sat up.

I asked Darius to imagine putting the rest of the story away in the book. I encouraged him to concentrate on the feeling, "I'm fine as I am." I asked Darius how he felt. "Fine," he said calmly. This abrupt drama had left Latisha a little bewildered. She said, "Now I understand why you told me not to do this at home."

IMPROVEMENTS,
BUT MORE WORK NEEDED

Darius's father and mother accompanied him to my office the following week. Darius prompted his parents to tell me how his grandmother had given him his grandfather's necklace. I asked Darius if he'd like for his dad to hear his story. Darius said yes and handed me a rattle. I wondered what his father thought of me treating his son by shaking a rattle.

Latisha read the story again. This time I asked Darius, "Why did Grandpa die?" He replied in a dreamy voice, "Because he loved me." I went to work with the rattle. "Grandpa was happy because he loved you. Darius, ask your mother why Grandpa died." Darius turned to his mother and asked. Latisha answered, "He died because he didn't take his high-blood-pressure medicine."

I wonder whether the whole family had been angry with Latisha's father for not taking his high-blood-pressure medicine. At age 3, Darius may have perceived an undercurrent of unspoken anger and assumed that something bad about him made people angry. He may have felt angry too and wondered whether his angry, upset feelings were so strong that they could cause someone to die. Or maybe he was being punished for the angry feelings by having someone dear to him go away forever.

I asked Latisha whether she has this sickness called high blood pressure. "No." Did Darius's dad have high blood pressure? "No." Did Darius have high blood pressure? "No." I guessed that Darius didn't understand what high blood pressure was, but I thought he'd be happy to know that neither he nor his parents had it.

I checked with Darius several times, "Did Grandpa die because he loved you? Or was he happy because he loved you?" Both of Darius's parents confirmed that Darius's grandpa was happy because he loved Darius. His death didn't have anything to do with Darius. We used EMDR to install or strengthen the positive beliefs Darius now held about himself.

Then Darius began to fidget with his father's ring. "You can't play with that, it's my wedding ring. It means I'm married to your mother, and I have a commitment to her." Latisha added, "It's round because it means never-ending love. It has no beginning and no end." Darius brightened, "Grandpa's necklace that I have is round too. It means I have never-ending love with Grandpa too. Right?" Darius looked at his parents. "Right," they both said, their eyes shining.

LAYERS OF TRAUMA

Despite our good session, Darius had a difficult week. He hit his teacher and called her names. I thought that possibly the EMDR had peeled off a layer of trauma and the next layer was now more visible. Trauma resolution is a process. There are waves of improvement, followed by upheavals of old debris. I hoped that within the next few weeks or months, Darius's behavior would even out. We also stopped Darius's current medicine, imipramine, and tried Tenex® to stabilize his moods.

I steered the conversation to the time when Darius was only 3 years old: He didn't understand what was happening, he was frustrated because he couldn't understand why his grandpa left him to go to heaven, why his teacher got sick and left him, and why he was punished with that teacher who made him feel bad. We talked about how Darius had been upset in the way that any 3-year-old would have been upset.

Then I asked Latisha if she could show us how an understanding teacher could have helped comfort an upset 3-year-old child. Latisha began to talk in a warm, soothing voice and put her arm around her son: "I can see you're upset. I'll give you a hug. You just do whatever helps you feel better. You can draw or play if you want, or just sit here beside me." Darius relaxed into his mother's arm, listening while I tapped his knees. After a few minutes, Darius straightened up and asked if I would show him how to play checkers "by the rules."

Although Darius showed improvement over the next week, he hit a child and called his teacher a name. We weren't through the work yet.

Latisha came to our next session excited to tell how she had arrived at school to find Darius dancing the hokey-pokey with all the children. She smiled, "He looked happy." I asked Darius if he'd like to feel that feeling in his body of having fun in school. Reinforcement of the new experience would help to link positive associations with school. I began the knee tapping. Within a minute, Darius's expression turned from a smile to a frown. I stopped to explore the sullen look, "What are you thinking about?" Darius sulked, "I'm worried about Grandpa." Latisha looked dismayed.

I remembered out loud, "The last day that Darius had fun at school was the day his grandpa got sick. No wonder he's been avoiding good times. Having fun has gotten linked in with danger." I asked Latisha whether she thought it was safe for Darius to have fun at school. Darius looked questioningly at his mother. "Absolutely. Fun times at school can only make people happy. They don't make anybody sick." This time, Darius continued to smile while I tapped his knees.

The following months brought progress, alternating with angry, disruptive behaviors. One day, Latisha said in a satisfied voice, "I feel like we're dealing with the actual person now. Do you remember when you said that we'd know we were going in the right direction when Darius didn't keep his room so neat? You'll be happy to know that his room is a mess!" Darius's family decided to take a break from EMDR sessions over the winter vacation. Darius continued to see his regular therapist weekly for play therapy. He continued to have behavioral problems, but he did not complain of headaches or stomachaches, and he no longer acted as if he alone were responsible for life and death.

"I CAN'T SWALLOW IT"

NOT SIMPLY A CRITICAL INCIDENT

It seemed to be a minor event at the time: Emma choked on a popcorn kernel while she was watching a Disney movie at the theater. She managed to say, "I got popcorn stuck in my throat, and I can't get it down." Emma's mother, Noella, escorted her 7-year-old daughter into the lobby, where the theater manager heard her coughing and offered a soda. He showed concern and repeatedly asked Emma, "Did you get it down yet?" Emma responded, "I'm not sure."

Soon after, Emma began to complain that her throat was sore and that it hurt to swallow. Noella told me about the steps she took to help her daughter. "A week later, Emma was still complaining that her throat was sore, and she said she was unable to eat solid foods. I took her to see the pediatrician, who referred us to an ear, nose, and throat specialist. He examined Emma and said her throat looked fine and prescribed a milkshake diet for 2 weeks." Noella sighed.

"Emma drank her milkshakes," she continued, "but after that she still said she couldn't swallow solid food because 'granules' got caught. She began to complain of headaches and stomachaches. I called Emma's pediatrician again and he said it was okay for me to give Emma a small dose of Tagamet® for her stomachaches, the medication I used to treat my own stomach ulcer. None of that helped, so I took her back to the pediatrician, and he ordered a barium swallow." The barium swallow revealed that Emma was swallowing normally and that there was no apparent obstruction. Noella was relieved her daughter wasn't seriously ill, but the problem wasn't solved.

IT'S HARD FOR A MOTHER TO WATCH

Noella told me, "Even though we were reassured that everything was anatomically normal, Emma began to complain, 'I feel like I can't breathe. I'm going to suffocate.' She began to worry that she would choke or suffocate if she went to school, so I sent her to school with a bottle of water and told the teacher that Emma had to have the bottle on her desk so she would be able to wet her throat. I told Emma to wet her throat if she felt anxious, because that's what helped her feel better in the movie theater. Emma was afraid she might choke if she ate lunch at school, so I brought her home for a milkshake at lunchtime. It was pretty hard for me to leave work at lunchtime, but Emma was so upset—and so grateful that I took her home for lunch—that I felt I had to do it for her, even though it meant I only had time to grab a bite to eat for my lunch."

Noella cleared her throat before she continued, "At dinner time I tried to accommodate Emma's needs for soft food or liquids, so I coaxed Emma to eat special meals of crustless white bread soaked in jelly, or soft Spaghetti-O's with just the right amount of sauce. Emma had already lost 6 pounds in 2 months, and she claimed that she couldn't eat more because it hurt to swallow. It's hard for a mother to watch her child just pick at her food, especially when she's losing so much weight and she was slender to start with."

A MOTHER'S WORRIES AND HOPES

The special care Emma seemed to require and worries about Emma's health were stressful for her mother. Noella felt overwhelmed by her current situation. She and her husband had been separated for a year, and Noella was trying to decide whether to divorce or reconcile. In the meantime, she was essentially functioning as a single mother. She was also dealing with financial difficulties, a demanding job, a needy child, and loneliness. Her older daughter, who had been a best friend to Noella and a second mother to Emma, had left for college in another state a month before Emma choked on the popcorn.

Noella described Emma enthusiastically. "She's a great kid. She's loving and understanding and perceptive. She's strong physically and loves to climb trees and ride horses. She has a strong sense of right and wrong, and she works hard to do well at her parochial school." In response to my inquiries, Noella told me that Emma had been a full-term, healthy baby who nursed well for 9 months. Noella had had high blood pressure with pregnancy, but her hypertension resolved with delivery. Emma had not had any notable illnesses or injuries, and she had not had any specific traumas other than the stress of her parents' separation and her sister's departure for college.

I asked Noella to speculate about Emma's negative beliefs about herself. She generated a list of negative self-assessments that might be related to Emma's choking episode. She responded, "Emma probably has thoughts like, 'I can't get it down. It hurts to swallow. I might suffocate. I can't breathe. I'm choking. It's not safe for me to leave home. It's not safe for me to go to the movies. My throat is sore. Something is wrong with me. I have to have something to drink with me." Noella wanted Emma to believe, "I'm capable of chewing and swallowing normally. My body can deal with food and choking automatically. If I have a problem, I can tell people and get help. It's safe for me to eat in school."

EMMA'S FIRST MEETING

My first meeting with Emma was remarkable in that Emma didn't mention the choking episode. While her mother sat on the sofa facing me, Emma sat beside the sand tray and gently pushed waves of sand from side to side. I told Emma that I like to help make things easier for children, and that we were meeting so that we could begin to get to know one another. Emma volunteered some information about her family. "My mom's father died before I was born. His face turned blue and his cheeks were red, and he died. I was a twin before I was born, and he died before he was ever born." I looked at Noella, and she confirmed that she had been pregnant with twins, but that one of them had been absorbed early in the pregnancy. Emma continued, "Two weeks ago a boy in my school died when he was hit by a car." Noella commented appreciatively, "Emma cares a lot about people."

Emma continued, "I do know how people feel when they're sad. I know all about fighting too. Sometimes the kids at school argue about the rules and whose turn it is to go next in kickball, or they argue about whether the teams are fair, and then people get their feelings hurt because they know their team isn't doing well because they're not good at kickball. My next door neighbor, Tiffany, is my best friend, but sometimes she hurts my feelings. When I have another friend over to play I always invite her too, but when she has someone over to play, she doesn't invite me." Noella added, "Some of the other children haven't been raised with as much respect for other's feelings as Emma has. Her school has religious values, but if the parents don't do their job in raising their children right, the children just naturally can't follow the rules if they haven't been taught properly."

It occurred to me that a kernel of popcorn was not the only thing that Emma hadn't been able to "swallow" lately. At age 7, Emma was acutely aware of the injustice of a child dying in an accident, the incomprehensibility of her own twin's death, the unfortunate death of her grandfather before her birth, and the pain caused by the capricious acts or nasty comments of second-graders. She hadn't mentioned her parents' separation or her sister's leaving, but these events were undoubtedly "hard to swallow" too.

TREATMENT OPTIONS

I considered my options for Emma's course of treatment. Ostensibly, Emma's somatic complaint was the reason for this consultation, and a somatic complaint is the body's way of voicing distress. I was working on the hypothesis that Emma's throat hurt because of some memories and situations that were "hard to swallow."

There were a number of possible treatment approaches. I could meet with Emma's mother alone first, to help her work through her distress and her overly solicitous attitude toward Emma's undesirable eating habits. I could meet with Emma and her mother together to help them negotiate their new relationship as a family of two. I could use narrative methods for reframing the problem and enlisting the parent and child to oust the "choking monster." I could meet with Emma alone and do play therapy or sand tray or art therapy. I could teach Emma relaxation techniques and use cognitive-behavioral techniques to reinforce the safety of eating solid food. I could employ

EMDR to target the choking episode and see how much of the disturbance in Emma's feelings and behavior would clear.

I didn't know whether the choking episode was traumatic in
itself or whether it was representative of some or all of life's difficulties that Emma was finding hard to swallow. An array of treatment options parading before me, I chose to wait and take my cues
from Emma. Children usually reveal their needs, and they give us
opportunities for self-correction if we make a choice that is not
suited to their needs.

FIRST THINGS FIRST

I greeted Emma in the waiting room when she returned for her next
visit. Although I invited Emma to come alone to my office, she
elected to include her mother in our meeting. Emma had taken the
initial decision about treatment options into her own hands.

Emma snuggled next to her mother on the sofa. Noella firmly
urged, "Tell her the problem."

Emma ventured shyly, "I'm having a problem with eating." I
explored the effects of this problem on Emma's life and then asked,
"What would you like to have happen?" Emma assured me, "I'd like
to start eating. I'd like to have lasagna for breakfast." I followed up
with another question, "And if you were free to eat anything you
wanted, how would that change your life?" Emma smiled at her
mother and said, "Mom would let me eat lots of chocolate and veg-
etables I like—like broccoli and potatoes and peas and corn."

"I sure would, honey!" her mother responded.

It seemed clear that Emma and her mother wanted to get down
to business and deal with the eating problem first. I explained
EMDR and said that I didn't know whether it would help, but I
thought it would be worth a try. Emma and her mother agreed.

Emma imagined a safe place, and I guided her eye movement.
Her safe place was a palace with blue and purple walls. Her favorite
room was at the top of the tower with a view of the forest. She imagined her room filled with toys and her own TV. Emma said dream-
ily as she moved her eyes, "My tummy started feeling weird—warm
and strong. I'm safe, and there's nothing to worry about. I feel it in
my tummy."

I asked Emma to remember a success experience—something she learned to do that seemed hard at first, but that she had mastered. Emma recalled learning to write cursive. I guided her eye movement with the wand she chose, and she reexperienced the exciting feeling of accomplishment.

Then I asked Emma to tell me about her experience choking on popcorn. She remembered, "I was eating popcorn when I took in the popcorn shell. I got scared and had to go out and get something to drink and get the manager." Emma's negative cognition was, "It's not safe for me to eat." She wanted to believe, "It's safe for me to eat. I'm fine." She claimed that these beliefs already felt "really true" but she felt maximum disturbance (10 on a scale of 0 to 10) when she remembered the incident, and she felt the anxiety in her throat. Without further discussion, I began to guide Emma's eye movement.

Initially, Emma held her breath for several seconds, then she began to breathe deeply and to speak. "I feel strong, and I could be eating soon." With a few more sets of eye movement, Emma felt increasingly secure. "I feel strong. I feel secure. I feel like I can probably eat more. If I have popcorn, I can have a drink and not be scared." I asked Emma if she'd like to thank her body for knowing what to do to keep her safe automatically—by coughing. I told her she was really safe, even without a drink. I didn't want Emma to think that she needed to have a drink with her at all times in order to be safe. Physiologically, it was her cough reflex, and not the drink, that cleared her airway. Emma concluded her session, "I'm okay. I feel strong and okay. I'm fine. It's safe for me to eat." She imagined herself comfortably eating broccoli.

That night Noella left a message for me saying that Emma had eaten her chicken and potatoes for dinner, but she said that it hurt to eat the broccoli. A few days later, Noella left another message expressing her frustration at trying to get Emma to eat. When an EMDR session ends so positively and the anxiety appears to be gone, it's disappointing for parents to find that the behavioral changes don't always stick initially. I remind them that trauma resolution can be a process with many layers, and that growth, development, and healing seldom proceed in a strictly linear fashion. I expect the vector of change to be in the direction of improvement, even though there may be relapses before consolidation of new, more desirable attitudes and behaviors.

"SPECIAL-DIET GUY"

During the next three visits, we began the process of building stronger skills for coping with stress and restoring the family's equilibrium, as well as using EMDR to desensitize and reprocess the memory of Emma's choking episode. I used some narrative therapy techniques (described in *Narrative Means to Therapeutic Ends* by D. Epston and M. White) to facilitate the process. We chose "Special-Diet Guy" as a name for the eating problem that had taken on a life of its own. Then we mapped the objectionable consequences of letting "Special-Diet Guy" bully the family into changing their diet and eating habits. We agreed to figure out how to empower Emma and Noella so they could take back control of meal times.

Noella resolved to kick Special-Diet Guy out of the house by refusing to prepare special, separate meals. She decided to stop bringing Emma home at lunchtime. Emma was reluctant to stay at school during lunch recess, and I learned that she had trouble with her peers during the loosely supervised lunch period. Emma complained, "Deidre called me a stinking brat, and I don't know whether to play with her anymore. I told the teacher about her calling me names and about Jamal pushing in line in front of me, and then they called me a tattletale." We agreed to work to strengthen Emma's skills for handling problems with peers.

At the beginning of each weekly session for the first month, I asked Emma how upsetting the choking episode seemed. Every week, Emma initially said that her anxiety level was high when she remembered the choking episode, but it diminished to 0 after about 10 minutes of EMDR. During the course of processing that memory, Emma recalled four of her pets who had died or disappeared. Fears about her own death surfaced and receded. The sensation of pain in her throat diminished as she focused on her physical distress and realized that there was "nothing to be scared about," and that she could eat "lots of food." Her headaches and stomachaches diminished. Concurrently, feelings of strength, safety, and self-confidence emerged.

After a few weeks, Noella had done her part to rid the family of

Special-Diet Guy, and Emma was eating a variety of foods comfortably. Finally, she recalled the choking episode by saying that it wasn't scary anymore and that it had happened "a long time ago." Nevertheless, she still felt she couldn't eat certain foods, like lasagna.

Emma began to come in alone for her sessions, and Noella went to her own counselor for support. Although Noella only occasionally came into the office for sessions, she continued to leave phone messages to let me know how she and Emma were doing at home. I found these reports helpful because, like most children, Emma seldom told me directly what was happening in her family life.

TAMING THE ZOO ANIMALS

I made sure that Emma had time to make a picture in the sand tray and tell about it each time we met so that she could express some of her feelings and emotional experiences through play. One day she made a scene with a zoo in which all of the animals were wild because the zookeeper had run away, leaving all of the cages in disrepair. A green, bumpy creature wanted special attention, but the zookeeper didn't like animals anymore and left them out in the rain. I asked Emma what the animals needed. Emma lowered her eyes and quietly told me the animals needed some calm.

I suggested that Emma pay attention to the feeling of calm she wanted. I tapped her shoulders while she gently blew the sand off the various animals in her zoo. Then Emma said, "The animals need new cages, out of the rain, and they need for the zookeeper to notice them." Recognizing Emma's need for structure and positive attention, I later privately encouraged Noella to develop the fun aspects of her relationship with her daughter. Emma could benefit from more attention for being healthy than for having problems. They planned a bike-riding outing together.

MORE CHOKING, MORE PROBLEMS WITH FRIENDS, AND A DREAM FOR THE FUTURE

During the next few months, Emma reported difficulty dealing with children in her class who were mean, lied, copied from her worksheets, or cheated at games. She occasionally reported difficulty eating various foods. One day, Emma choked on chips at school, and after that she was anxious about eating nuts, celery, and various kinds of chips. She wanted to go home for lunches again, but Noella resolved that Emma would stay at school during lunchtime. Despite Emma's ongoing complaints, I was glad to receive Noella's phone reports that Emma was heartily eating a healthy diet at home, and that she had regained her weight.

Every time a food phobia caused difficulty, we used EMDR to process the experience. We also talked about her relationships with friends and role-played ways of dealing with them. Emma made sand-tray scenes depicting her outrage at children's mean behaviors, which she took so seriously. We used EMDR to reinforce skills Emma learned about how to get along with peers, choices she had when someone was mean to her, and choices about who she selected for friends.

With permission from Noella and Emma, I spoke with Emma's teacher, whose policy was to leave children alone to work out their own problems. Emma needed on-the-spot training in how to regard and manage peers' customary teasing and obnoxious playground behavior. Her teacher felt that "kids will be kids" and that Emma needed to learn to shrug it off. Noella, on the other hand, believed that a parochial-school teacher and parochial-school parents should teach the children to behave respectfully at all times.

Emma was stuck in the middle, with righteous beliefs and limited skills for coping with unruly kids. It was not possible to eliminate the tension between Emma's teacher and her family, and Emma experienced ongoing strain. EMDR helped her work through fears about eating; her throat pain, headaches, and stomachaches diminished within a few sessions. But it took months of play therapy, sand-tray work, and role-playing for Emma to work through her indignation about the unfairness in her life and for her to learn to deal with conflicts with friends. EMDR was useful for reinforcing what she learned about standing up for herself in a way that didn't alienate peers, and it helped strengthen her self-confidence.

Finally, some aspects of life were going better for Emma and her mother. Emma had a new teacher in school who had clear rules about children's behavior and taught children to respect each other. Emma's mother decided to change jobs. Emma and Noella spent more time together doing activities that both enjoyed. In one of her last sessions with me, Emma summed up her future in a dreamy voice: "I guess that when I grow up and finish school, I'll marry my boyfriend." She smiled, "Then we'll get married and make babies. I guess everything will be okay."

11

"I CAN'T MOVE"
SOMATIC SYMPTOMS

When I first met 4-year-old Aaron, he had been having peculiar "attacks" for the past few weeks. He would drop on the floor, his body would tense, with legs straight and arms outstretched with hands flexed, and he would writhe as if in pain. Sometimes, just before one of these episodes, he would announce, "My hands feel funny, I can't move." Other times he would grab his penis and moan, "I have to hold my pee. My pee hurts." From time to time he would just say, "My hands feel funny," or "My leg hurts." His parents noticed that these puzzling exclamations were most likely to occur when Aaron didn't want to share with his little brother, when he didn't want to stop playing computer games, or when bedtime approached. Sometimes the attacks just happened out of the blue, without any obvious precipitant. Aaron awoke almost nightly from "screaming nightmares," often crying, "My leg hurts."

Recently, Aaron had been resisting going to preschool. He frequently complained to his teacher that his hands felt funny or that his leg hurt. His teacher was very concerned that Aaron, who was a bright child, no longer seemed to be learning. He was increasingly reluctant to take his turn at any activity and refused to try anything new. He also shied away from playing with children who used to be his best friends. Until the past few months, Aaron had proudly belonged to a group of boys at preschool who called themselves "The Three Bears." These popular, outgoing boys had jauntily monopolized a substantial space on the playground, claimed the climbing structure as their territory whenever possible, and seemed to be first in line for any activity. Recently, however, Aaron preferred to play quietly by himself, and turned down his chance to dominate on the climbing structure. He was no longer one of "The Three Bears" and a replacement had tacitly filled his position.

Aaron's parents were concerned that his "attacks" might be seizures, but their pediatrician ruled out that possibility. They wondered whether a urinary-tract infection might be causing Aaron's penis to hurt. Urine cultures were clear. After a complete physical exam and lab tests, Aaron's doctor was certain that there was no physical explanation for the aches and pains. She thought that Aaron's symptoms were "psychosomatic," that is, Aaron's body was holding an upsetting memory and trying to express it. She referred the family to me.

THE FIRST VISIT

After enumerating their son's puzzling behaviors, David and Naomi told me all they had done to try to help their son. "After the pediatrician reassured us that there was no medical basis for Aaron's pains, we tried diverting his attention when he began to complain about the pains in his leg or hands or penis. We tried ignoring his complaints, but that strategy just made him complain more. When he awoke at night we comforted him and held him until he fell asleep. We resisted his pleas to sleep in our bed, but we agreed to stay with him until he fell asleep every night so he wouldn't be afraid that he would start hurting."

When Aaron cried, "My hands feel funny again," they asked him what his hands wanted to say. He responded, "My hands are whining." They asked why his hands needed to whine, but he frowned his frustration and replied that he didn't know. I've never met a young child who could answer why he suffered from a posttraumatic, somatic symptom. Probably if the child really knew why he had the symptom he wouldn't need the posttraumatic behavior to "speak" for him.

SECONDARY GAINS, SECONDARY LOSSES

Aaron's family had decided to consult me when they had "tried everything." Fortunately, they were consulting me within a few months of the onset of Aaron's problems. The longer posttraumatic symptoms linger, the more deeply entrenched they become. As time passes, they may cause more and more secondary losses. For Aaron, the "attacks" and the pains in his hands, "pee," and legs brought increased attention, and parents who yielded to his requests for company at night. On the other hand, Aaron lost his healthy, age-appropriate, and hard-earned feelings of pride about his independence at night. He lost a sense of confidence in the predictability of his body. He lost the reassurance that comes with having parents who are confident about his ability to cope. He lost his important status as a peer with his friends and younger sibling. This child's symptoms had taken on a life of their own and were interfering with his normal development and sense of well-being.

SYMPTOMS BECOME HABITS AND TAKE ON A LIFE OF THEIR OWN

As fears increasingly dictate the behavior of a child who had been developing confidently, parents become more willing to accommodate their child's pleas for comfort. As the child gains inappropriate power over his parents, his successful bids for special attention actually erode his confidence. He no longer believes he can manage on his own. His parents' actions begin to confirm that there is indeed something to fear and that the child cannot manage without their presence. As the child has his fears confirmed, and gains special parental attention as a bonus, there is no longer a strong incentive for independence. Additionally, if the child loses sleep, and the parent loses sleep as well as intimacy with a spouse, everyone in the household may become tired and irritable. Parents may then begin to disagree about what their child needs and how to handle his demands, and the child may realize that he is responsible for parental discord, which intensifies his anxiety and often compounds the behavioral problem.

I am not suggesting that wise parents should ignore their distressed child. Most concerned parents do their best to ease their child's fears. I am recommending that if a child's fears interfere with family well-being, it would be wise to investigate ways to reduce the stressors. Professional help may be indicated.

BIRTH HISTORY

When I ask parents for the history of their child's experience with trauma, I begin by asking about the period before this child's conception. Although it's impossible to know how prenatal events affect an individual, early history gives me some sense of the emotional ambiance into which the child is born. Aaron's parents had tried to conceive for 3 years prior to his birth, and this was a long-awaited and welcome pregnancy. The pregnancy and delivery went smoothly. Aaron's mother described Aaron as a "good baby" who was breast-fed for 3 months. He developed normally and toilet trained without difficulty at age 2 years, 9 months.

TRAUMA HISTORY

Aaron's parents speculated that his first trauma occurred 3 weeks after the birth of his brother, when his new sibling had to be hospitalized, and Aaron was separated from his Mom for 3 days. When he was 4 years old, Aaron had an upsetting experience when he suddenly had terrible pain whenever he moved his hand or arm. It turned out that Aaron had developed "nursemaid's elbow," a dislocated elbow, which can happen when a child is lifted or pulled by his arm. The condition makes it impossible to pronate or supinate the forearm, and movement is very painful. Aaron's pediatrician manipulated his forearm to return his elbow bones to their normal position, and the problem was solved. I wondered whether that painful experience served as the "template" for Aaron's response to physical pain.

Aaron's parents continued recounting their son's "trauma history." Five months ago, Aaron had broken a leg while playing at preschool, but the doctor said that his leg had healed completely. I explored the details of that experience. I felt sure that Aaron's somatic symptoms were "posttraumatic," and I wondered whether the accident resulting in a broken leg might explain why Aaron felt he couldn't move during his attacks.

RECOGNIZING THE CONNECTIONS BETWEEN SYMPTOMS AND TRAUMA

Frequently, when families come to see me, they don't have a clue that their child's disturbing behaviors relate to a trauma. Often, the behaviors have started months after the traumatic incident, so that parents may not realize that there is a connection. Often the disturbing behaviors are metaphors for some aspect of the traumatic experience. Aaron's behavior of "holding his pee" turned out to be one of those metaphorical symptoms.

THE ACCIDENT

Aaron's mother began telling me about the day Aaron broke his leg. "I was at work when my pager sounded. Aaron's preschool teacher called to say that Aaron had fallen off the climbing structure and was hurt. An ambulance had already been called. When I arrived at the preschool, two ambulances and three police cars had already arrived at the scene. I saw Aaron lying on the ground with his teacher kneeling beside him. The paramedics and police were standing together, waiting. It was really scary. The other preschoolers were sitting in a circle, far away from Aaron." Later she found out that forceful Aaron had persuaded the paramedics to wait for her arrival, "Don't move me until my mom is here!"

Naomi told how the accident happened: "Five boys were playing on the highest platform of the climbing structure. They were all excited about going down the slide in a blue tub, and they were pushing to decide who would get a turn first. Aaron managed to be first in line and climbed into the tub, settling onto his knees for the trip down the slide. Just as Aaron started sliding down, the other boys pushed to be next in line, and one of the boys fell onto Aaron, causing him to hit the ground with enormous force."

Naomi proudly reported that Aaron didn't cry or make a sound when he crashed or while the paramedics put a temporary splint on his broken leg, although the doctor at the hospital later told her that Aaron must have been in enormous pain. For me, Aaron's silence despite evidence of enormous pain meant that Aaron was in shock and that he was literally "scared speechless." This state of shock or numbing is often mistaken for bravery. Furthermore, during this period of shock after a trauma, a person is "hyperaroused," that is, highly vulnerable, alert, and suggestible. The person is scanning the environment for signs of further danger and for clues about the meaning of the experience and lessons to learn about avoiding a similar catastrophe in the future. Any comment heard or any experience can take on a sense of profound significance that can be incorporated into the individual's posttraumatic belief system.

Aaron refused to ride in the ambulance. He insisted that he ride in the front seat of his mother's car, so his teacher improvised a support for Aaron's splinted leg. She gave Aaron a large ball to prop up his leg. He managed to hold the ball in place with his hands, while balancing his leg on the ball. When he arrived at the hospital, a series of X rays confirmed that Aaron had a spiral fracture of his tibia. While the X rays were being taken, Aaron's mother called a toy store and ordered a large toy that Aaron had been wanting. She asked them to have the toy ready so that she could stop for it on the way home from the hospital.

In the hospital, the doctor acknowledged that Aaron was in tremendous pain, and gave him codeine. After several hours in the hospital, Aaron was sent home, with an appointment to return for more X rays in 3 days. Aaron and his mother drove to the toy store, Aaron waited in the car alone while his mother went inside to purchase the toy, and then they went home.

DOUBLE MEANINGS

At home, Aaron didn't want to move or be moved, because the slightest movement caused pain. Aaron's mother described his dilemma, "He was frustrated because he had to pee, but he didn't want to be moved, so he held his pee." It immediately occurred to me that Aaron had been developing a belief system that would prevent further pain if he refrained from any movement of his body, and that his negative cognitions must be something like, "I can't move because I'll hurt" and "I have to hold my pee." Furthermore, the belief "I have to hold my pee" contains two possible meanings: (a) "I have to retain my urine" and (b) "I have to hold my penis." Aaron's exclamations, "I have to hold my pee!" were posttraumatic flashbacks to a painful situation, as well as a belief that "holding his pee" would prevent pain. Posttraumatic behaviors often take on the form of the literal meaning of the experience, such as "I can't move" or "I have to hold my penis."

MORE PAIN, MORE FEAR

When the X rays were repeated in 3 days, the doctor determined that Aaron needed a bent-knee cast. Aaron was terrified. He was afraid that his leg would hurt if the cast were removed—the cast, and immobility, had become his security. Naomi described the sound of the saw used for removing the cast, "It sounded like 10 vacuum cleaners." Aaron needed four cast changes over the course of 6 weeks. The final cast removal was the most upsetting. Aaron had sat in his father's lap and screamed and cried. He didn't want the cast off, because he was convinced that his leg would hurt if he didn't have the cast to keep it from moving.

When the cast was finally off, the doctor said that Aaron was fine, but that he shouldn't jump for 3 weeks. After that, he could resume full activity, without any restrictions. For 2 weeks after the cast was removed, Aaron had refused to walk, and his parents had to carry him. Then he scooted for 2 weeks. Finally he walked.

DEVELOPMENTAL AGE AND TRAUMA

Aaron's accident might not have been as traumatic had it happened at some other age, but at age 4 it challenged many of Aaron's recently attained developmental achievements. Before the accident, Aaron had been able to separate confidently from his parents, he had made friendships with children and adults outside of his family, he had achieved full bladder and bowel control and was totally responsible for his own toileting. He had become physically and socially able to handle playground equipment, including taking turns going down a slide. He had slept independently, in his own bed. He had relished the joy of trying new experiences, sometimes without close supervision. He had been good natured, and not whiny at all.

I reflected on the impact of the accident on Aaron's life, particularly at his developmental stage. For 3 weeks following the accident, Aaron was unable to walk or do anything for himself. He had to be carried everywhere he needed to go. (A younger child would not have felt so insulted. An older child might not have felt such a threat to his autonomy.) He needed assistance removing his pants to go to the bathroom. (Younger children are accustomed to help with toileting. An older child might have managed a system for undressing himself.) He was offered crutches, but was unable to master them. He was given a wheelchair, but his hands were too small to use the wheel controls for maneuvering, so he was dependent on having someone control his movement. (An older child would have been able to use crutches or manipulate the wheelchair, a younger child might have found a wheelchair to be as acceptable as a stroller.)

UNDERSTANDING THE TRAUMATIC EXPERIENCE

I explained to Aaron's parents that I thought that all of his strange behaviors were directly traceable to the accident and its aftermath. "Traumatic memories are stored as visual images," I explained, "as negative self-assessments or, in EMDR terminology, negative cognitions, as body sensations that may resurface as somatic or body-based symptoms, particularly when there has been a physical injury, as affects or feelings, and as behaviors."

I asked Aaron's parents what negative beliefs or cognitions they thought Aaron had about himself as a result of the accident. They generated this list: "I can't move. It's not safe for me to play. I can't pee. I'm a dummy. It's not safe to take my turn. I shouldn't try new things." Then I asked what they would like for Aaron to believe about himself. The positive cognitions or beliefs they wanted for their child were: "It's safe for me to move. I can relax and move comfortably. It's safe for me to play. It's okay to try things even if it feels hard at first. I'm as good as anybody." As an afterthought, his father added, "It's okay to do things when Mom and Dad tell me to do it." I explained how EMDR can help to desensitize and reprocess traumatic events, and they agreed to try it for Aaron.

THE REAL MAGIC

Aaron is a cheerful boy with curly brown hair and appealing blue eyes. But when I met Aaron, he looked serious. "This is Dr. Magic," Naomi announced with an upbeat tone, "and she's going to make you better." I was impressed by her confidence in me and somewhat awed by my advance publicity. Aaron looked impressed too, as he gazed at me with wide eyes and open mouth. I hoped I could live up to their expectations. "Do you know why they call me Dr. Magic?" I returned Aaron's direct gaze, and continued, "They call

me Dr. Magic because I help kids get their own power really strong."
He nodded solemnly. I invited Aaron to explore my office and play
while I talked with his mother.

IDENTIFYING STRENGTHS AND A SAFE PLACE

"What do you like best about Aaron?" I asked, knowing that Aaron
was listening carefully, even as he played with Teenage Mutant
Ninja Turtles. I also wanted Aaron to know that I saw him as someone with strengths, as well as problems. His mother began to enu-
merate, "He plays well with his sister and likes her a lot. He plays
nicely on his own. He's well-mannered. He's special. He has a good
imagination. He can swim under water."

She proceeded to tell me that the teacher had called to tell her
that the boys in the preschool had made Aaron cry because they
wouldn't play with him. I flashed on the image of Aaron's accident,
with the children sitting in a circle watching while ambulances and
police cars, paramedics and police arrived. I wondered whether the
children were traumatized, too, and believed something like "It isn't
safe to play with Aaron." Maybe that's why his preschool friends
were shunning him.

I commented, "Every child in the school deserves to have the
same amount of power." Then I asked Aaron whether he would like
to work on making his power really strong. He nodded approval,
so I asked him to pick out some action figures to help him. He
chose "fighting guys," typical choices for a boy his age. Then I
asked Aaron if he could imagine a safe place. He responded,
"School, with me and my brother there." I asked where he felt the
safe feeling, and he pointed to his neck. Then I asked permission
for one of the action figures to tap his hands while he felt the safe
feeling in his body. He nodded, and we began EMDR with less
than a minute of tapping. Then I asked if he could think of something that made him feel strong. He replied, "playing with Emily."
We did more hand tapping while he concentrated on the strong
feeling.

I advised Aaron that the action figures could help him feel safe
and strong again, even when he remembered the day his leg was
broken. I invited him to pretend he was watching a movie of the

accident while his mom told him the story of what happened and the action figures tapped his hands.

Aaron's mother began the story, "Aaron was on the playground, playing on the climbing structure, getting ready to go down the slide." I used the fighting figure to tap Aaron's hands alternately, as his mother spoke. Then I interrupted, and continued tapping while I asked Aaron, "Is the slide safe?" Aaron replied, "It's boarded up." (I wasn't sure whether Aaron would feel safe around playground slides, or whether he would only feel safe if the slide were boarded up.)

Naomi continued describing how he climbed up on the slide, and how the boys all wanted to take a turn going down the slide. I told Aaron, "It's safe to take turns. It's fair to have a turn." The rhythm of my tapping reinforced the positive cognitions I proposed for Aaron.

Aaron's mother recounted how the boys began to push. I installed another safety cognition: "The 'no-pushing rule' helps keep people safe." I continued tapping while Aaron's mother told her son the story of the accident, and how everyone came to help him when he got hurt, and about the car ride to the hospital, the hospital experience, stopping to buy the toy on the way home from the hospital, and arriving home. We ended our first session with Aaron's mother stating that Aaron had done everything right.

I imagine that our first session would have been a help to Aaron regardless of whether EMDR had been used. Aaron's mother and I acknowledged his magical powers, he had a chance to play, he heard the story of the accident as something that was over, he was taught some reassuring safety rules, and he heard his mother's praise. I counted on EMDR to make the healing process faster and more thorough.

Aaron's father came with him for his second session, a week later. David was optimistic because Aaron was doing better. Over the previous week, Aaron had complained briefly that his hands hurt on four different occasions. One night he had spent the night at his aunt's house, and he had cried, "I want my daddy—my leg hurts." His aunt was able to comfort him easily and he fell asleep quickly. In my office, Aaron chose to play with toys in the sand tray while his father told the story of the accident, just to the point when Aaron arrived home from the hospital. I stood behind Aaron and tapped Aaron's shoulders alternately while he played and listened.

A week later, Aaron returned with his mother. She happily reported, "Aaron's teacher called to say that she had seen 'incredibly good change.' Aaron was more confident, his self-esteem seemed solid, he did not complain at all about pain in his hands or feet, and he was taking turns and learning again. The boys have begun to identify Aaron as a leader, and they are beginning to follow him around the playground again." Quietly, she added that when a child made a mistake, they frequently blamed Aaron for the problem, although it was clearly not his fault. (Perhaps the children who had witnessed the accident, or sat in the circle frightened and waiting when the police and ambulances arrived, had incorporated a belief that accidents, or mistakes happen when Aaron is present.)

NIGHTMARES

Although Aaron's school behavior was normal, Aaron told me that he was still having nightmares. I find that nightmares, night-waking, or difficulties falling asleep are sometimes among the last symptoms to clear when a child is resolving a traumatic experience. It's tempting for families to stop treatment when daytime behavior or public behavior is going well, and the child appears happy, but it's important to continue reprocessing the trauma until symptoms clear completely, so that they don't resurface in another form later. It seems to me that in these final stages of trauma resolution, a new set of beliefs about safety in the world is evolving, a new tenderness and compassion for the child toward his own vulnerable, baby-self is emerging, and this maturational process is nurtured by adult wisdom and protection. Workable beliefs, compassion for and acceptance of one's vulnerability, and new-found confidence in one's self are the ultimate gifts of trauma resolution.

Aaron energetically described his dream of a scary frog. It sounded as if Aaron were describing a real event as he launched into a story of seeing a bumblebee at school that was dead, then came back to life. I invited Aaron to choose figures to make a sandtray picture to help us understand more about his nightmares. He selected several snakes, a frog, Batman's companion, Robin, a "poison hawk," and an astronaut. I asked Aaron to tell me about the creatures he had chosen. He pointed to the large snake and solemnly said, "That's a rattlesnake. It's dangerous." Then he pointed to another snake, "That's a regular snake. It's not dangerous." He appraised the frog, "That is a poison frog and can kill bees." He pointed to the "poison hawk" (a sea gull) and predicted, "That's a poison hawk that can kill every toy, but is not dangerous to me." He smiled confidently, "Robin isn't dangerous." Aaron considered a blue monster-type figure, and he looked perturbed, "I don't know whether that one is dangerous or not."

I was beginning to understand Aaron's nightmare and his dilemma. How could he know when a situation was dangerous? (Is the frog a regular frog or a poisonous variety?) The accident happened when he was participating in an everyday activity, playing on the climbing structure and slide at preschool. Sliding is inherently a little risky, and perhaps scary for a toddler, but for a 4-year-old child, it is usually a safe, comfortable activity. (Fear about playing on a slide came back to 4-year-old Aaron, perhaps surprisingly, the way the dead bumblebee came back to life.) Aaron needed to resolve how it could be safe to resume everyday activities after one such "benign" activity had turned treacherous, seemingly without warning. Were there any clues that his playing would result in such horrible pain?

I decided to focus on Aaron's beliefs about safety. I asked Aaron what helps to keep him safe. "My blankie," he replied without hesitation. "What else?" I prodded, and his mother helped him generate a list, "My teacher, my mom and dad, my grandparents, my aunts and uncles, my baby-sitter, my doctor." We used hand tapping to reinforce the experience of safety provided by his blankie and by the important, protective adults in his life. Aaron looked pensive for a moment and then lifted his head to point to an abrasion under his chin. His mom explained, "The bars at school were slippery, and Aaron fell yesterday. He got a little cut on his chin."

Aaron was reminding me that it's fine to talk about everything that keeps him safe, but he had fresh evidence that he sometimes got hurt, even though he was supposedly safe. "That's right, sometimes we do get hurt even though all those things are helping to keep us safe," I agreed. "Everybody has accidents and gets hurt sometimes. Most of the time it isn't too serious. Can you remember a time when you got hurt, but your body healed?" Aaron showed me a scab on his knee. I confirmed, "That's right, you have a scab. Your body can heal all by itself, so you can play, and you can do what you know to keep you safe, but sometimes you will get hurt. You know what? Your body is so strong and so good at healing—look how your body can help take care of you." He gave me permission to tap his hands while he concentrated on remembering that his body had the power to heal when there is an accident and he gets hurt.

Then I asked Aaron if he could think of safety rules that help to keep him safe. He volunteered, "No bad words. No hitting." He interjected that every day kids hit him, but he reflected proudly, "I'm the toughest." I steered Aaron back to "the rules," and he continued, "No biting. No pinching. Everybody has to take turns." I added that another good way to keep yourself safe is by saying what you need. For example, if kids are pushing while you are trying to take your turn, you need to say, "The rule is 'no pushing'" or "I need time to take my turn." I asked Aaron to imagine that he was about to take his turn on the slide while kids were pushing, and I tapped his hands alternately. I've found that "corrective imagination," reinforced by alternate stimulation, can help a child to learn valuable lessons from his trauma.

TARGETING THE NIGHTMARE

Since Aaron had begun the session by telling about his nightmare, I asked whether he would like to make the nightmare less scary by doing the tapping. Aaron consented. He chose a "wise old man" to tap him while he concentrated on his nightmare. Within a minute, the dreamy gaze left his face, he cleared his throat, and looked calm and alert. I asked whether the nightmare still looked scary. "Nope." I asked him to end the session by thinking about the things that keep him safe. Aaron said, "My parents, and how my body heals itself."

Aaron returned with his father for his fourth session. His father reported, "Aaron is doing great at home and is confident at school. He hasn't had any episodes of pain or writhing on the floor." Aaron asserted himself, "Sometimes I can't go to sleep. My hands and feet feel funny but not funny enough to whine." His father confirmed that Aaron had woken up the night before and had called for his parents, but he hadn't left his bed. Aaron settled himself by the sand tray and began to play with action figures. He asked his father to tell him the story of the accident "from the beginning." I took my position behind Aaron so I could tap his shoulders while he played.

Aaron played casually with the action figures and listened to the story of the accident without showing visible distress. I asked him to pay attention to the pain in his leg when he hit the ground. Aaron said that he didn't feel any pain. I assumed that he was still "dissociated" or numb when he remembered his agony, and I decided to wait and address that pain when Aaron was ready.

Aaron was calm until his father began to talk about the time when Aaron returned home from the hospital and was afraid to be moved because it hurt so much. Extreme physical pain can result in dissociation and subsequent posttraumatic somatic symptoms, stand-ins for the real pain, which is perceived as unbearable. Aaron squirmed uncomfortably as he remembered "holding his pee" because he was afraid of the pain associated with being moved to go to the bathroom. I asked Aaron where in his body he had the feeling of "holding his pee." He pointed to his arms. A moment later, he told me to stop tapping. He picked up a toy airplane, and dramatically crashed it into the sand. He covered the plane with a mound of sand and explained that it was being fixed. When the repair was complete, Aaron lifted the plane into the air and proclaimed, "It's all fixed!" Then he added, "I feel good and strong too."

Aaron's play indicated that he was aware of the mysterious process of healing his "crashed" leg had undergone, that he was accepting more fully that the accident and its attendant pain were over, and that he was in the process of becoming healthy and strong again.

As Aaron flew the plane around the room, I marveled at the play-therapy process, and the magic it works with children. I imagined that if EMDR were not available, Aaron would have responded well to play therapy, but it might have taken months or even years for him to work through the trauma to successful resolution, so that he was confident and free of excessive fear. (Aaron's therapeutic work, augmented by EMDR, took a total of eight sessions.)

POSTTRAUMATIC BEHAVIORS

Aaron's mother accompanied him to his fifth session. Aaron led the way into my playroom, and Naomi stopped me in the hallway to whisper that Aaron had positioned his arms and legs straight out, with hands flexed, about five times during the preceding week, but he seemed to be "faking" or doing it for attention. She had ignored these behaviors, and had given Aaron attention for more desirable behaviors, like doing gymnastics or enjoying playing. I was glad to hear that Naomi was doing her part to tame the posttraumatic behaviors that had "taken on a life of their own." We could give full attention to posttraumatic symptoms and resolve the traumatic aspect of the behaviors in my playroom, but it's important for parents to handle unwelcome posttraumatic behaviors firmly, kindly, and sensibly at home.

Therapy might have taken much longer if Aaron's parents had pampered his fears at that point, indicating that they, too, felt there was some cause for worry. Parents are often "traumatized" by their child's injury. Parents may feel responsible for their child's safety, even when they are not present when an accident occurs. Even very healthy, sensible parents can have irrational reactions to a child's accident at preschool. Some parents feel guilty about working and being away from their young child. Some parents question their judgment and choice of preschool. Others may lose confidence that they can protect their child adequately. If guilt and fear could protect a child, these parents would have a perfect, comprehensive insurance policy. Guilt and fear can be useful in mobilizing parents to change an unsafe situation, but they are absolutely useless in preventing true "accidents." Instead of protecting children, those anxieties and guilty feelings may be transmitted to children, compounding their distress.

When parents participate in the child's therapy process, they can work through their own fears and regain confidence in their power as parents by helping their child get over the upsetting event. When children continually turn down offers to play with me alone in my playroom (I invite them to play with me alone at intervals after the first session), it may be that they sense that it's painful for their parents to separate from them or that they know the parent needs to have the benefit of therapy too.

I think that by alternating weeks for bringing Aaron to therapy and by participating in his healing, Aaron's parents got the help they needed to be confident parents once again. Sometimes parents need to have their own, individual therapy to work on conquering their fears. Sometimes they appreciate separate sessions with me or with a family counselor to plan effective ways of dealing with their own posttraumatic difficulties.

THE RIDE HOME

We entered the playroom, where Aaron had already taken his place by the sand tray, and he instructed his mother, "Start the story where we left the hospital and stopped to pick up my toy at the store."

Naomi began to describe how they drove from the hospital to the toy store with Aaron balancing his splinted leg on the large gym ball his teacher had given him. As Aaron's mother talked, she demonstrated how Aaron had had his legs straight out in front of him, and he had to lean forward awkwardly to hold the ball in place with both hands. I noticed that she was assuming the same posture that Aaron had when he had his episodes of writhing on the floor with his hands and legs extended in front of him.

Posttraumatic behaviors usually represent a behavior that might have magically helped the person avoid further damage at the time of the traumatic incident. I shared my observation, and Naomi nodded in agreement. I said to Aaron, "I guess you had to keep your hands on the ball that way to keep it from moving so your leg wouldn't hurt." Aaron's words burst forth, "I was afraid the balloon would pop!" I reassured him that he had done a good job, that the ball had not popped, and that his leg was all better now.

I continued to tap Aaron's shoulders, and instructed him to stop me when it felt fine to remember how he had felt holding the balloon in place. When Aaron told me to stop, he also said that he had had enough of the story for the day. He played easily in the sand tray while his mother told me that she was proud that Aaron was becoming so confident, that he's a leader, and that he had started taking a gymnastics class. I was glad to hear that Aaron was getting involved in doing a new, fun, physical activity.

THE END OF DISSOCIATION

Aaron's father came to the next session with his son. David reported that Aaron was doing great, with no further episodes of pain or writhing in his "hold the ball still" posture. He said that Aaron had awoken one night, crying for his dad. David asked his son what was the matter, and soothed him back to sleep. Ten minutes later, Aaron awoke again, and moaned, "My leg hurts." His father carried him, and comforted him for half an hour, then Aaron fell back to sleep. The next day he played with two buddies, and went bowling, and was fine. I wondered whether Aaron's night-time experience of pain in his leg, which he denied as we did our work, was the beginning of his acceptance that the pain had been his and that he could now begin to tolerate the memory.

Aaron filled the pause in the conversation, "Tell the story, Dad! Start when I'm home from the hospital." Aaron played with the sand while his father began telling about Aaron's life when he came home from the hospital, and I stood behind Aaron, alternately tapping his shoulders. The story unfolded comfortably until David described how Aaron couldn't walk with his cast, so he had to go to school in a wheelchair, and his teachers had to push the chair because Aaron's hands weren't big enough to control the wheels.

Aaron interrupted anxiously, "Then my friends pushed me around and I was afraid they would push me down." As I tapped Aaron's shoulders, I considered his choice of words. Being "pushed" by kids had caused him great harm when he was playing on the slide. No wonder he was anxious about having kids "push" him in the wheelchair. Although I imagine that Aaron's teachers were deeply sensitized by the accident and would not have allowed young children to push his wheelchair in a place or manner that could have been dangerous, part of Aaron's fear may well have been based in reality. A 4-year-old in charge of a wheelchair could be hazardous, and that realistic fear may have triggered a larger, posttraumatic sense of danger associated with the wheelchair. I tapped until Aaron told me to stop.

He abruptly started telling me about a nightmare he had had that was difficult to explain. I asked if he would draw a picture of the nightmare. He agreed. We put the lid on the sand tray, converting it to a table, and got out the paper and markers. Aaron chose bold red and green markers and began to scribble furiously. He finished drawing and claimed, "I didn't have the nightmare, but both my parents had the same nightmare!" I encouraged him to tell a story to go with his drawing. "Twisters eat you up. Dad is bald and mom is bald. Twister takes you on Dad's head!" He began laughing jubilantly. I guessed that the "twister" was the trauma that twisted his reality in a way that seemed strange and nightmarish. Aaron's laugh seemed like a sign of mastery, as if he were saying, "I get it—it's only a crazy nightmare." I gave the 5-minute notice that our session was almost over, and Aaron quickly said that he was drawing a "good-bye picture." He chose a pink marker and traced his hand. Maybe it was a gentle hand, waving good-bye. Maybe it was Aaron's way of saying he could sense himself owning his body again.

THE GOOD-BYE SESSION

Aaron marched into my room with his mother for what was to be his final session with me. He announced, "I don't need to come here anymore." He boasted, "I got better all by myself, and Dr. Magic did not get me better!"

Aaron's mother was equally enthusiastic. She summed up Aaron's gains: "He sleeps through the night. He's not having nightmares. He does come to our bed about two times a week, but before the accident he was coming in our bedroom every night. He's doing great with friends. He's taking turns. He speaks up for himself. Sometimes he's frustrated, but that seems normal. We can leave him with baby-sitters without a problem. He hasn't had any pain. He is happy, and confident, and he's definitely learning new things."

After that, Aaron surprised me by asking his mother to tell the story, beginning with being home from the hospital. He sat next to his mother and listened quietly. Naomi recounted how Aaron had persevered at scooting around the house in his heavy, hard cast, how he had been frustrated and bored, and didn't want to move. She looked sad when she explained that Aaron's friends had started playing soccer that fall, and Aaron couldn't. They got trophies, and he didn't. Instead he was going around in a wheelchair. Finally it was time for Aaron's last cast to come off. At last the story was over. Aaron said that he was not scared at all anymore. His mother praised him for all he's learned and for how he handled himself and for making new friends.

I congratulated Aaron on facing his fears and told him that he was very brave. I walked to my office door with Aaron and waved good-bye, but he was already racing down the hall, toward the exit.

12

TOO SCARED TO THINK

TEST-TAKING ANXIETY

Nicolas's voice was desperate when he phoned for an appointment. "Please see me as soon as possible," he pleaded, "I really need some help." As I was soon to see firsthand, even a minor trauma in childhood can continue to cause problems years later.

In person, Nicolas appeared upset, despite the composure suggested by his sports jacket, khaki pants, and polished black-leather shoes. Nicolas explained the urgency of his request for help, "In just 3 weeks I have to take—actually, retake—the Bar exam. My career depends on my passing the test, and my family is counting on me. You see, my wife and I are expecting a baby, and she's at bed rest, and if I don't pass the Bar this time, I won't be able to take the job I've been offered. I won't be able to take *any* job practicing law until I pass the Bar, and I won't be allowed to take the Bar again for another whole year. The problem is that I get so nervous taking standardized tests that I can't remember anything. I absolutely panicked last time I took the Bar, and I couldn't think to answer most of the questions, even though I knew the material."

Nicolas continued, "I called you after I saw that *20/20* program about EMDR on television. I know that the man who was a Vietnam vet and the woman who was raped had problems that were different from mine, but they had some of the same symptoms I have. I can't stop thinking about my failure, I can't sleep well, and I have panic attacks. I know enough to pass the Bar exam, but anxiety gets in my way. Can EMDR help me?"

Test-taking anxiety is a common problem for children and adolescents, but it is generally overlooked as a serious, treatable condition. Most individuals do not spontaneously "outgrow" test-taking anxiety. Usually, those who suffer from test-taking anxiety avoid testing situations when they finish school, but this strategy may require them to sacrifice career options. Although many jobs do not involve taking standardized tests, most professions, including law, medicine, psychology, dentistry, and business, do require licensing exams. Nicolas's only apparent obstacle to a successful career was debilitating anxiety when he faced a standardized exam. If Nicolas had been treated for test-taking anxiety while still a teen, he would have been spared considerable time, money, and humiliation.

A PUZZLING HISTORY OF FAILURES

Nicolas had had trouble taking standardized tests for as long as he could remember. Every year in school, with each required standardized test, his panic had worsened. He described what happened when he took the Bar exam: "I was in such a state that my mind went blank. It was terrifying not to be able to think, when normally my mind works so logically. I had practiced and mastered thousands of multiple-choice questions and sample essays from the review course I took, but when I went to the exam, it was hopeless. The 3-day Bar exam was an ordeal for me. I felt my heart pounding, I was sweating profusely, and as I stared at my unanswered exam, I kept thinking 'I don't belong here. I can't do this. I'm not going to pass.'"

Previously, Nicolas had always been able to compensate for his inability to take standardized tests. He was an excellent student who worked hard and produced impressive work. The discrepancy between Nicolas's ability and his performance on standardized tests was dramatic. Although Nicolas had been valedictorian of his high school class with a 4.0 average and many honors to his name, his low College Board scores denied him admission to college. He was such an outstanding student that his teachers petitioned a reputable college and, with considerable effort, were able to persuade the admissions committee to disregard his stunningly low scores.

In college, Nicolas graduated with high honors in history and was commended on his superior thesis. Nevertheless, he scored so low on the LSAT, the standardized test required for admission to law school, that it was a struggle for his college professors to convince any law school to consider him. Finally, he gained entrance to a community law school, where he did very well. He participated in a national trial law competition, and based on his courtroom acumen, he ranked among the top law students in the country. He was then offered a position at a prestigious law firm, contingent on passing the Bar exam.

Nicolas consulted me 3 weeks before the scheduled exam. He had devoted the past several weeks to taking another Bar exam preparation course and practicing sample tests. He had mastered over 3,000 multiple-choice questions that had appeared on previous exams. He was sure that he knew the law "inside and out," but he was terrified that he would panic once again and fail the exam.

Optimally, it is best to begin work on test-taking anxiety at least 3 months before a major exam. This is usually sufficient time to reprocess memories of various experiences that may have contributed to the anxiety. In addition, if upsetting material surfaces, the client will have time to regain equilibrium before taking the test. Finishing the work of reprocessing at least 2 weeks before the exam minimizes the possibility that EMDR may uncover upsetting memories that could interfere with concentration on the exam.

Because there were only 3 weeks left before Nicolas was scheduled to take the Bar exam, I discussed the risks—mentioned above—of using EMDR so close to the time of the exam. I proposed that we could use the EMDR method and protocols without adding eye movement. Nicolas was eager to try EMDR including the eye movement. He felt that he couldn't possibly do worse on the exam than he had the previous year when he had panicked and couldn't think at all. We decided to allocate only one or two sessions for reprocessing upsetting old memories and to use any additional sessions for identifying, packaging, and attempting to put away distressing old memories or distracting thoughts that might interfere with Nicolas's concentration.

TEST-TAKING ANXIETY: A PROCESS PHOBIA

I hoped to treat Nicolas's test-taking anxiety as a process phobia, which would involve desensitizing and reprocessing the first time, the most recent time, and the worst time Nicolas had suffered from anxiety while taking a standardized test. EMDR can further promote a calm approach to test taking by helping the individual visualize himself calmly staying on task. Nicolas was highly motivated to complete this exam successfully and his determination to conquer his fear was a valuable asset.

Nicolas candidly explored some of his conscious fears about taking exams. He admitted, "I sometimes wonder whether my inability to take standardized tests really means that I'm dumb. When I did well in school, I worried that I was a fraud. Maybe I'm just an overachiever who works hard but isn't very bright." Nicolas also worried that his poor performance on tests was an indication that he didn't belong with the top students. It's intriguing that thinking of explanations for fears can lead to the justification and acceptance of negative self-assessments. Insight therapy for this type of anxiety can compound the problem by reinforcing detrimental thought patterns. EMDR, on the other hand, catalyzes the individual's healthy drive toward an affirmation of self-worth.

I chose to proceed with the protocol for process phobias rather than explore Nicolas's understanding of his feelings of low self-esteem. I asked Nicolas whether he could remember the first time he had taken a standardized test. He thought for a moment, searching his memory as he peered at me with his brown eyes. "Yes," he replied, "I was about 8 years old, and I took a test for admission to the gifted program in my elementary school. It was one of those intelligence tests with multiple-choice answers. I remember that I had to stop reading a book I was really enjoying to go to the school library to take the test. I had to work on some logic problems that I did not find very interesting. Shortly after I started working on the test, the school principal came into the room and frowned as he talked to the teacher who was proctoring the test. Then he came over to me and said, 'You don't belong here.' He told me to put down my pencil, and he took me back to my classroom, without explaining anything. To this day, I don't really understand why he pulled me out of the test, but I remember feeling humiliated. I thought I was mentally retarded. It was the first time in my life that I thought of myself as dumb."

"At the time, my parents were having marital problems, and I knew that they were considering divorcing. I was very close to my father, and I was terrified at the thought of him leaving the family. He was a university professor and valued intelligence and excellence in school. I thought that if I were good enough and smart enough and did well enough in school, he would decide to stay with our family. I was afraid that if I didn't get into the program for talented children, my parents' divorce would be my fault." As an adult, Nicolas realized that these childhood fears were irrational. A child's school performance does not influence his parents' decision about whether to leave their marriage. Despite his cognitive understanding of the childhood situation, Nicolas still felt that his performance on standardized tests was linked with his personal worth and his family's survival. His current situation, in which he and his family were relying on his ability to pass the Bar exam, seemed to confirm his childhood worry that his self-worth was linked with success on an exam. For Nicolas, taking another standardized test felt tantamount to risking his life.

Nicolas was eager to get rid of his excessive anxiety as rapidly as possible, and he wanted to try the EMDR method. I guided him to develop his "safe place" and introduced him to eye movement to strengthen his feelings of comfort and relaxation. Next we used eye movement to enhance his feelings of competency and pride, which were associated with winning the national trial competition. I encouraged Nicolas to establish a "light at the end of the tunnel" by imagining the feeling of finishing the exam and knowing that he had done his best. Nicolas experienced relief at the mere possibility that he might pass the exam. When he had walked into my office, he had feared that even the thought of doing his best on the exam was not a possibility.

THE EARLIEST MEMORY OF TEST-TAKING FAILURE

When Nicolas returned for his second appointment with me, he said he wanted to concentrate on the issue of feeling confident enough to be able to perform. We decided to focus on desensitizing and reprocessing the memory of the first time he took a standardized test and felt humiliated. His memory was a visual image of himself in the school library, sitting at a table, and working on a logic problem. He could see the principal enter the room and have a tense discussion with his teacher.

As he remembered the scene, Nicolas's negative self-assessment, which still felt true, was "I am inadequate." It was sad to think that such a gifted student had gone through so many years of school feeling inadequate. Nicolas wanted to believe, "I am adequate and just as capable as the gifted children," but that positive statement only felt partially true (3 on a scale of 1 to 7) for Nicolas. When Nicolas remembered the situation, he felt moderately anxious (7 on a scale of 0 to 10). I asked Nicolas to hold in mind the picture representing the event, the negative belief, "I am inadequate," and the anxious feeling that arose in his abdomen. I guided his eye movement as he thought about what had happened and paid attention to the sensations in his body. Initially he felt increasingly anxious, then angry. His anger subsided, and he felt better, but his sense of well-being faded and was replaced by shame. "I felt hurt that they thought that I wasn't capable. I felt ashamed because I let my parents down."

Nicolas paused, then began to move his eyes again, this time "going with" his feelings of shame. "I felt phony. I felt fake. Like what I was on an everyday basis wasn't true." Nicolas's sense of feeling fake is common among high-performing children who have low self-esteem. They are acutely aware of the discrepancies between their actual performance, their exaggerated feelings of inadequacy, and the judgment of others.

Nicolas continued commenting as he moved his eyes and reprocessed his memory of the old event. "I have this yearning to be considered bright." He pointed to his chest, "I feel it in my heart." I knew that young Nicolas earnestly had wanted to impress his intellectual father with his school success. Furthermore, he believed that his academic success was responsible for keeping his family together. Nicolas continued, "My parents—I'm sad for them. I feel badly for them that I'm not good enough to make everything all right." Nicolas went through several more sets of moving his eyes while he imagined his parents looking at him while they said mournfully, "It's okay to be mediocre."

I decided to intervene because Nicolas seemed stuck with his child's perspective. I asked, "Who gave you the message that you were mediocre?" "The elementary school administrator," Nicolas responded. "What do you want to tell him?" I prodded and guided Nicolas to continue moving his eyes. "I want to tell him he was wrong," Nicolas replied forcefully.

I called on the adult Nicolas to offer his more experienced perspective on the event. "It's unfair. A child takes it so much to heart." Nicolas's facial expression softened as he defended his child-self. He looked startled at his next realization, "I'm fortunate my teachers believed in me. It makes me feel safe. I don't feel I'm putting on an act when I think of them. They judged me on my day-to-day performance, not just on how I performed on one test. When you analyze a logic problem, there can be black and white and gray areas. Really smart people are aware of the gray areas. Objective tests are so hard because you have to choose between black and white areas. You can have a strong analysis and still choose the wrong answer according to the people who wrote the test, but you don't have a chance to defend your point of view."

I asked Nicolas to rate the intensity of his feeling when he looked back at the original incident. He was about half as upset as he had been when he had started EMDR half an hour earlier. He reflected on the memory of the school administrator, "I feel angry with him, and I think he is wrong." He located the source of the feelings in his head. Nicolas focused on these feelings in his body, and resumed eye movement. "A part of me believes it's not an adequate determination. . . . I'll prove them wrong." (He felt that determination in his head and in his heart.)

After a few more sets of eye movement, Nicolas lifted his eyebrows slightly and opened his eyes a little wider. I responded to the change in his facial expression by pausing to ask, "What is coming up for you now?" He thought a moment, then responded, "I get the sense that people do see and are proud and recognize that I'm capable . . . I feel very loved. I feel it didn't matter how I performed on a standardized test; I feel that I still have their love . . . I don't have to earn their love."

Nicolas was intensely involved with the process of realizing that his parents' love for him was not connected to his school performance. Children typically fuse parental approval with parental love. Although some parents do make their love conditional on their child's willingness to meet their approval and achieve high levels of school success, this was not the case with Nicolas's parents. Nicolas, the adult, began to see that his parents loved him regardless of whether he did well on tests and that their decisions about their marriage were independent of his school performance. Although Nicolas the adult felt relieved, realizing that his parents loved him regardless of his test scores, Nicolas the child had imagined that his academic achievements were a source of power that could earn his parents' love for himself and influence his parents' relationship with one another.

Nicolas continued moving his eyes and commenting on his experiences, "I recognize that I love my father. I want him to be proud of me. I wanted my father to be so proud of me that he would want to stay with our family." As an 8-year-old, Nicolas had depended on the only real power he perceived himself to have. At the time, it had been intolerable for him to confront the reality that he had neither the power to improve his parents' relationship, nor the power to keep his father at home, even with stellar school performance. Paradoxically, the importance attached to test taking had turned every test into a "life and death matter," and that desperate need to succeed had fueled enormous anxiety that prevented Nicolas from doing his best.

Nicolas began to look more focused and alert as he moved his eyes, "It doesn't matter what the administrator thought or what he said. It has not really made a difference." He voiced his realizations between sets of eye movement: "I feel much better. . . . It does not seem that important. . . . Even if the tests were true, it does not matter anyway. . . . You're happier when you don't let things like this bother you."

Nicolas had known all this previously. Cognitively, he had understood that tests do not measure your worth as a human being and that being removed from a test for gifted children was not a valid indication of his intelligence or his worth. It was not until that moment, however, that Nicolas appeared to *fully* comprehend that his merit was based on more than whether he had qualified to be in a program for gifted children when he was a second-grader.

Nicolas sat up tall in his chair and exclaimed, "Relief!" He paused for a moment, as if to absorb the magnitude of his acknowledgment that a test has only limited value, that love is not contingent on performance, and that even strong love for a child could not prevent a father from dissolving his marriage.

Nicolas contemplated a range of beliefs that could replace his inflexible "pass–fail" notion about his relationship with standardized tests. He moved his eyes, stimulating the following comments between sets of eye movement. "There's a happy medium. I don't have to force anything to happen. I can just do my best, and opportunities will come. I can do well. I've shown that I can do well. . . . I'm not as bad as I think I am. . . . I couldn't have done what I do if I weren't smart." Nicolas sat silently watching my hand move back and forth. He looked quite serene. He paused and said, "I was feeling good about certain things I've done. I've achieved. I have reason to feel proud of my accomplishments."

I directed Nicolas to look back at the original incident and rate the intensity of his distress. His distress had dropped to 2 on a scale of 0 to 10. He located the remaining tension in his head. I asked him to "go with that feeling," and I guided his eye movement again. Nicolas laughed as he remembered having to leave the test to go back to his classroom. "It was okay. He took me back to the classroom, and I felt happier being in the classroom. . . . I prefer to be in the classroom. . . . One of my best friends was in the program for gifted children, and I felt embarrassed every time I was with him. I remember him telling me that he liked me because I understood his vocabulary." Nicolas laughed heartily. "In the fifth grade they put us in separate classrooms because we were too competitive when we were together."

I asked Nicolas to look back on the original incident and rate his anxiety level. He reported that there was only a little anxiety remaining, and he felt it in his chest. He moved his eyes to complete the desensitization and reprocessing of that old memory. "I don't think I really am upset as I look at it. I was upset that I lost credibility. It didn't really matter. I didn't lose credibility. . . . It doesn't matter what other people think, I know that I'm smart and capable." Nicolas sighed, "Now I don't feel upset at all when I look back at the original incident. I do believe I'm capable. I do believe I can take tests. That incident doesn't matter. I have performed, and I can do it."

He laughed, "I'm actually at an advantage because I don't always feel I'm so right. My attitude makes me more open to considering a range of possibilities. I can see things in many ways." I asked Nicolas to tell me the important learning from our session that day. "I almost believed myself when I thought I could not perform. I took in the negative and ignored the positive. What shifted today is that I feel more confident. It's in me. I always have been able to perform."

The process I had witnessed impressed me. I had intervened minimally as Nicolas had focused on his visual, cognitive, affective, and somatic memories while moving his eyes. He had spontaneously reworked his understanding of a childhood event that had restricted him for years. When he brought his adult knowledge and experience to his child's view of the event, he was able to gain a perspective that had been unavailable to him as an 8-year-old.

If I had had the opportunity to work with Nicolas when he was still a child, I imagine that the process would have required more intervention on my part. I would have interviewed his parents to learn about their perspective on Nicolas's experience. Perhaps I would have recommended a family meeting to clarify that the children in the family were not in any way responsible for their parents' decisions. I could have used EMDR with educational and creative interweaves to provide developmentally appropriate information Nicolas needed to negotiate a self-affirming attitude.

THE WORST AND MOST RECENT MEMORY OF FAILURE

The first EMDR session had helped Nicolas desensitize and reprocess his first painful memory of taking a standardized test. We agreed to focus the second session on his most recent, and worst, experience taking a standardized exam, the failed Bar exam. Nicolas had a vivid mental image of the scene of his failure, "I can see the large, well-lit room with thousands of students and two proctors watching the crowd. The person next to me appeared to be concentrating fully. He was filling in answers as fast as possible. I thought he knew what he was doing. I, on the other hand, felt my heart beating as if it would pop out, and my head was throbbing." I asked Nicolas what negative thoughts he had about himself as he remembered that scene. His negative cognitions were, "I can't do this. I cannot take this test. Everyone will pass except me."

Nicolas wanted to believe what he already knew to be true, but that did not feel true, "I am prepared. I can perform. I will do my best." A feeling of dread overwhelmed Nicolas as he remembered the event. He rated his level of distress as 10, the highest possible rating. He pointed to his chest as the physical site of his dread, and I began to guide his eye movements. Nicolas seemed to be holding his breath. Finally, he swallowed and paused. "I couldn't focus on the exam," he said. I moved my hand again to help him proceed, but Nicolas interrupted. "I had to go to the bathroom because I had had so much coffee that morning. I feel really angry with myself because I had so much coffee, and I hadn't used the rest room before I started the exam. I knew that once the exam started, no one was allowed to leave the room, even to go to the bathroom. I felt miserable." As Nicolas moved his eyes again, I thought about how the "bladder effect" is a well-known obstacle to concentration.

I watched Nicolas's face as he moved his lips silently. When he stopped moving his lips, I stopped moving my hand. "I was having a conversation with myself. I was telling myself, 'Just focus,' but I kept feeling mad at myself for the coffee. I knew I had to go as fast as I could because I only had 1.8 minutes per question, and I needed to concentrate to be able to think that fast."

I observed that Nicolas's pattern was to move his eyes for a minute or two, then to stop and "talk a paragraph." He moved to a different, but related topic in his next paragraph, "I was thinking about a classmate who is a jerk. He said that anyone who doesn't pass the Bar is a moron. I was angry. I rejected his idea, but it hurt. He thought I was going to pass the Bar because I always did so well in school. He told me that I didn't need to worry about passing. Little did he know."

After another set of eye movement, Nicolas moved to another aspect of his anger. (Notice that Nicolas's processing spontaneously proceeds from one memory channel to the next, whereas a school-aged child would probably need prompting to remember another time when he felt angry like that.) "I'm mad at this test. I feel angry with them because they make this test so difficult. It's not fair." . . . "I was talking myself out of it. Everybody goes through it. You don't have to perform perfectly to pass. It is possible. People pass it. Others I studied with passed."

Nicolas moved his eyes again, and then recounted some additional factors that had interfered with his performance, "I do it to myself. When I go into an exam, the physiologic effects take over. . . . In studying, I don't trust my logic. I have to memorize everything, but there is too much to remember."

Then Nicolas began to access his inner resources, his success experiences. "I remember one of the trials when I was under enormous time pressure. I know that the information is in my brain, and I have to trust that it's there for me. . . . I'm remembering other times in law school when I didn't have a lot of time, and I thought I wouldn't do well, but I ended up getting the top grade."

I asked Nicolas to look back at the original incident and rate his level of distress. His subjective units of distress scale (SUDS) score had dropped from 10 to 4. As he moved his eyes this time, he was bolstered by reinforcing images and thoughts, "I'm imagining sitting there. I know what I need to do."

Nicolas reflected, "I care too much about what other people say. I was prepared last time. One associate asked how many multiple-choice questions I had practiced. I had practiced 1,000, and he told me that wasn't nearly enough. Now I've done three times that number. I shouldn't listen to others. I should listen to myself."

Trust and self-trust repeatedly came up as important issues. "Law school is such a big game, and it's so competitive. Even my best friend lied to me about what he had heard would be on a test so that I would be at a disadvantage. My best friend undercut me." Nicolas's frown underscored his disappointment and sense of betrayal. "On the other hand, sometimes others have more confidence in me than I do." I realized that part of Nicolas's anxiety arose from his uncertainty about whom to trust. I asked, "Who should you trust?" Nicolas responded with certainty in his voice, "Myself. I'm the only person I can really trust."

After his realization that he could trust himself, Nicolas's anxiety dropped significantly. "I feel good. I feel everything will be okay. I don't feel bad about this Bar exam. I feel okay about it."

I asked Nicolas to check for any remaining tension in his body. The last remnants of fear unfolded, "I'm so afraid I'll get into the exam and do the same thing." I asked Nicolas to face his worst fear while moving his eyes. "I felt fine," Nicolas sighed. "I imagined myself sitting in the chair, looking at the exam. It looked doable." I suggested that Nicolas imagine doing the previous Bar exam the way he wished he had been able. "I have confidence this time. I felt as though I don't need teachers who have been watching me all semester to know what I'm doing. . . . I don't perform well under pressure. . . . As I imagined it I was able to stay calm and collected. I wouldn't drink so much coffee this time. . . . I can even feel the fun of taking the test and performing under pressure." I added, "Think of what that adrenaline rush can do for you!" Nicolas nodded and smiled. I wanted to encourage Nicolas to interpret the quickening pulse common in a testing situation as excitement, rather than as anxiety.

Nicolas was ready for the installation of his positive cognitions. He held in mind the original picture, the positive thoughts about himself, and the feelings of confidence in his body. Finally, he claimed that these statements felt true, "I am prepared. I can perform. I will do my best." He added, "My best is good enough for me." I was glad to hear Nicolas assert that self-affirmation.

I asked Nicolas to imagine the day of the exam, beginning with his wakening. Nicolas planned his time line, "I will get up at six. I will have coffee and breakfast at seven. The exam begins at nine-thirty, so I'll have plenty of time to use the rest room before I start." He smiled wryly. I encouraged him to mentally practice the day going as he wanted it to go, and to imagine that his body was comfortable as he went through the day. I guided Nicolas's eye movement as he went through that exercise. He concluded, "I imagined a race. I don't dread it. It is fun!"

Nicolas returned for his third and final session with me the day before the Bar exam. Looking back at his last Bar experience, he only felt a little anxious (SUDS = 1), but when he had anticipated taking the Bar the next day, he had had moments of panic. His panic was triggered by thoughts of the consequences of failing the Bar, "I can't take it for another whole year. I won't be able to take the job that is waiting for me. I won't be able to support my family. The stigma of not passing two times would be awful." There had also been moments when Nicolas had thought he would pass the exam. He had been doing extremely well on the practice exams—well above passing.

PACKAGING ANNOYING DISTRACTIONS

I decided to focus my efforts on helping Nicolas to stay calm enough to do his best on the upcoming exam. There was not enough time for any reprocessing of detrimental beliefs or past experiences. I chose to use the peak-performance protocol as described by Sandra Foster and Jennifer Lendl. In this model, the clinician directs the client to identify his "job" during the performance. The "job" must be a task that the client can accomplish. For example, when taking a test, the "job" is to do one's best. It is not the client's "job" to get an A on a test, because he does not have control over what questions will appear on the test or the way his work will be judged by others.

Any thoughts or feelings or memories that get in the way of the individual's ability to do his best are regarded as distractions. The clinician instructs the client to identify distractions, label them as distractions, and "put them away" in an imaginary container while the client is doing his "job" (e.g., taking the test and showing what he knows.) When the "job" is over, and it is safe and appropriate to sort through the contents of the container, the client can then examine the negative self-beliefs and decide whether to reprocess them.

This system, enhanced with EMDR, can help an individual to do his best. It does not ensure that the individual will do well, however, especially if he is not well prepared. I was confident that Nicolas would have an excellent chance of passing the Bar because he had a great store of legal information, an excellent track record for thinking clearly and quickly under time pressure, and he had done extremely well on the practice tests. Treatment with EMDR only removes excess anxiety. If Nicolas had barely passed law-school classes and had not prepared for the exam, his anxiety probably would have been appropriate, his self-assessment regarding his inability to do well would have been justified, and his chances of passing would have been poor even if he had been totally calm.

I frequently use the peak-performance protocol when helping a student prepare to study, to take a test, to give a speech, or to participate in an academic or sports competition, music recital, or theatrical performance. It can be a useful aspect of coaching students with attention-deficit hyperactivity disorder who frequently have to contend with distractions. For a student with ADHD, the "job" might be to focus on the task at hand or to learn new tasks one step at a time. Coping with distraction is an ongoing challenge for the person with ADHD. Although EMDR may not change the underlying dysfunction, it can help to reduce anxiety and self-deprecating beliefs as they arise.

I explained the principles of peak-performance preparation and asked Nicolas to define his task for the next day. His initial response was "To pass the Bar," but he quickly revised and elaborated on his goals, "My job is to do the best I can under the circumstances; to show what I know about the law in the time allotted."

I asked Nicolas to list the obstacles that might interfere with his optimal performance. He enumerated his fears, "I'm afraid I'll be so nervous that the adrenaline rush will hinder me instead of helping. I'm afraid I'll get bogged down in the multiple choice. I'm afraid that I won't pass again, and people will think I'm dumb." None of these anticipatory fears could promote Nicolas in his task to show what he knows about the law in the allotted time. Nicolas acknowledged that these fears could be distractions that could prevent him from staying "on task." He agreed to imagine putting them away in a container so that he could concentrate on the exam. He smiled, "I'll imagine storing the distracting thoughts in the dining-room vase so I can focus on taking the test to the best of my ability."

Nicolas's fear of overwhelming fear or panic is a very common obstacle to optimal performance. Some symptoms of an "adrenaline rush" are almost inevitable when one approaches an important exam like the Bar. I mentally made a note to help Nicolas recognize the physical sensations such as sweaty palms and quickening breath and heart beat that accompany nervousness as well as excitement. It would be important that Nicolas could identify these sensations and interpret them as welcome signs of readiness for a challenging and exciting event, rather than as precursors of immobilizing panic.

A look of concern clouded Nicolas's face, "How can I deal with hard or impossible questions?" He felt unable to put his anxiety about test questions he truly could not answer in the same vase with his unfounded, irrational fears. I asked him what would be an appropriate thing to do with impossible questions on a law exam. Nicolas puzzled over that for a moment and then smiled, "I'll imagine giving them back to the law professor who created them." Nicolas seemed satisfied with his means for dispensing with distractions.

A MOVIE CALLED "SUCCESS"

Now we could use EMDR to strengthen Nicolas's confidence in himself as he imagined practicing and mastering the upcoming test situation. I encouraged Nicolas to imagine a movie of himself calmly taking the test the next day, and I guided his eye movement. He nodded to indicate that he was finished, and I paused. He said, "It was fine. I could imagine myself focused on taking the test." I wanted to strengthen that feeling of full focus that would serve Nicolas well. I asked Nicolas to move his eyes while he stayed with that feeling of concentration and at the same time to press his right thumb and forefinger together as he grasped a pencil. The sensation of pressure on his thumb and finger as he held a pencil to take the exam could serve as a physical anchor for the feeling of confidence and a cue to remind him to stay "on task."

After Nicolas was able to imagine the 3-day testing situation going smoothly, I asked him to anticipate potential problems that could throw him off track. He predicted seeing someone who would say, "Haven't you taken this exam before?" He also felt uncomfortable at the thought of seeing the room full of people, hearing the sound of the person beside him writing and breathing, and hearing people discussing their essays at the end of the first day of testing. I asked Nicolas to concentrate on each of these visual and auditory images while I directed his eye movement to desensitize the images. Then I asked him to imagine encountering an essay question about an unfamiliar topic. Nicolas moved his eyes and imagined scanning related areas of the law that might contribute to a reasonable response. He imagined "winging it" and then moving on to the next question. Finally, Nicolas was able to envision himself concentrating on showing his knowledge of the law, putting aside internal distractions, and refocusing every time an unpleasant or unexpected occurrence caught his attention.

I asked Nicolas to hold together the physical sensation of excitement, the concentration of staying on task during the exam, and the positive body sensation of confidence while I guided his eye movement. Nicolas exclaimed, "It's almost fun! It will be fun in a way. It's not different from anything I've already done. It doesn't matter what I don't know. I feel prepared. I feel confident." Nicolas strode out of my office confidently that afternoon. He felt that he would actually be able to take the Bar exam rather than just look at it and panic.

Several months later, I called Nicolas to follow-up on our work together. When I called Nicolas's home, his wife gave me his number at work. I called Nicolas's work number, and as soon as the receptionist greeted me with the name of the law firm, I knew that Nicolas had passed the Bar. Nicolas enthusiastically confirmed that taking the exam had been "a completely different kind of experience" this time. He had felt competent and prepared as he took the test. Although he had to wait several months for official notification of a passing score, he had walked out of the exam feeling certain that he had passed.

13

"WE DID SOMETHING WRONG"

SECRET COERCION, SEXUAL MISTREATMENT

S exual abuse is devastating to a child's psyche. Research indicates that sexual abuse in childhood is strongly linked with depression and self-injurious behavior in adolescence and adulthood, particularly if the abuse happened repeatedly. This chapter tells the stories of two preschoolers, Ian and Anna, who were sexually mistreated by other children on only one occasion. These children's reactions to traumatic sexual mistreatment are "mild" compared with children who have been raped or sexually abused by a trusted adult. Nevertheless, their stories show how sexual coercion can interfere with a child's self-concept.

IAN'S EXPERIENCE

Five-year-old Ian witnessed the molestation of his little sister Julie by Billy, a six-year-old boy. Billy also tried to force Ian to participate, which left him terrified. Before the incident, Ian had been a bright, active, "cool" kid with a great sense of humor and lots of energy for learning. Ian's beloved pediatrician, who had shepherded the family through illness and various crises, told Ian's parents not to be too concerned about the molestation because no adults were involved. He advised them to just let Ian talk about it, and he would get over it. But Ian didn't get over it. Six months later, his parents declared that Ian had almost turned into a different child.

Now, when confronted with a task, the formerly confident Ian was most likely to say, "I can't do it. I'll never be able to do it!" before he even tried. He had been enthusiastic about preschool until the incident happened, but now his parents described him as "totally stressed out" about the prospect of starting kindergarten in 2 months. He declared, "It's hopeless. I can't do it." Completely toilet trained and dry at night by age 2, Ian surprised his parents by beginning to wet his bed again at age 5, soon after the molestation. He even stopped tying his shoes, a skill he had acquired with pride. He refused to take showers or touch his penis to wash himself. He started lying about little things. Ian seemed ashamed and despairing.

Above all, Ian was ashamed that he had not stopped Billy from harming his sister. Ian was extremely protective of 3-year-old Julie. He shared his room with her, always seemed to know what she wanted, and he made sure that she got what she needed. His unusually strong devotion to his sister began the moment he saw her, when she was a newborn in the intensive care nursery and he was determined to bring her home. Since then he had made it his job to take care of Julie, and this time he thought he had failed.

WHAT HAPPENED?

At our first meeting, Ian's parents, Roger and Shirley, sorrowfully told me what had happened to their children. Roger began, "One Saturday afternoon we left both children to play with Billy, a neighbor who is 6, while we went to help Shirley's mother move into a nursing home. Billy's mom, Jana, told us to leave the children as long as we needed to make the move and urged us to take a little extra time for ourselves."

Shirley continued. "We returned in the late afternoon. We knew as soon as we greeted the children that something was wrong. Usually, when they spent time with Billy, they didn't want to stop playing. This time, the children could hardly wait to leave. As soon as we closed the car door, Julie began to cry. She sobbed, 'We did something wrong.' Billy had told her that if she didn't let him lick her vagina no one would ever like her or play with her again. He threatened that if she ever told, she would get in trouble. He pulled down Julie's pants and licked her genitals." Shirley was visibly upset.

Roger told what happened next. "Julie told us that Billy pushed Ian's head down and tried to force his penis into Ian's mouth. Ian interrupted Julie in tears, sobbing, 'His penis smelled like pee. I feel so bad!' Then Julie told us that she began to scream as loud as she could. Billy's mother came into the room and told Billy to stop."

Shirley dabbed her eyes with a tissue as she explained, "We reassured them that they were good children, and that they had done the right thing by telling. When we were home, and they had settled down, I called Billy's mother. Jana was upset about what had happened and promised that she would talk with Billy so that it would never happen again. She agreed to seek professional help for Billy. She suspected that he had been molested by a baby-sitter and had already made a report to the Child Protective Service." Shirley and Roger were understandably shocked and dismayed that Billy's mother had not supervised the children's play and that she had not told them what had happened. They were concerned about why Billy had behaved in a sexually abusive and threatening way, and they were worried about the effect of the molestation on their children.

After the incident, Shirley and Roger had taken both children out for dinner to reward their bravery. They had reassured Ian that he was a good boy, and that they were proud of his behavior. Although Ian blamed himself for not protecting Julie, his parents responded by telling Ian that a 5-year-old child is not responsible for protecting anybody. They assured him that it was Billy's mother who should have been keeping all of the children safe, and that they would not leave them in her care again. Julie was relieved to hear that she would never go to Billy's house again. She was clear that she never wanted to play with Billy again. Ian, on the other hand, was ambivalent. He certainly didn't want Billy to mistreat him; but Ian had been Billy's friend, and Ian worried about whether he should ever play with Billy again. Ian felt guilty and confused. His parents' wholehearted compassion and reassurance didn't alleviate his doubts about himself.

Julie accepted her parents' reassurance that she was a good girl. She appreciated their praise for her bravery in calling for help and for telling her parents, even though Billy had told her not to tell. According to her parents, Julie came away from the event initially very upset; but within a few days, she was satisfied that she had triumphed over big, mean Billy. She felt angry that Billy had hurt her and her brother. Three-year-old Julie reportedly felt powerful.

Ian didn't feel powerful at all. He didn't believe that he was a good boy. He was ashamed that he had allowed this to happen, that he had not protected his sister, that his little sister had successfully screamed for help, and that he had not. He appeared anxious and repulsed whenever he talked about Billy or the incident. Ian worried that he had gotten Billy into trouble. His parents explained to their son that he had actually helped Billy by telling, because now Billy could get help with his behavior and not hurt other children. Ian was not convinced.

Whereas Julie had learned that she could scream for help and protect herself and her brother, Ian had inferred from his experience that he was a failure. Judging by Ian's attitude, behaviors, and comments about himself, Shirley and Roger speculated that Ian had a list of negative beliefs about himself. They thought Ian believed, "I'm ashamed. I can't do it. My penis is gross. Penises are gross. Everything is hopeless. I'm bad. I let something bad happen to Julie."

Ian's parents told me they were distressed about seeing their son sinking into depression, and they felt sad that their reassurances hadn't been enough to restore Ian's confidence and sense of well-being. I could empathize with their experience of not being able to make things "all better" for their child. I assured them that they had handled the situation well, and that now they could help Ian get over his traumatic experience. I explained EMDR to them, and they agreed to give it a try.

Together, we prepared for Ian's introduction to me, the playroom, and the EMDR process. I explained that some children Ian's age like to come right in and talk about the upsetting incident, some prefer to make a sand-tray picture and tell a story, some like to draw pictures, and others prefer to play in the doll house. I told them that other parents and children had found it helpful to have a story of the incident, both because it could be useful with EMDR and because it helped parents and the child transform the incident into a story that had happened in the past and was now over. They agreed that they would like to write the story of the incident to help themselves, as well as their son, make more sense of the event.

IAN'S FIRST VISIT

My first meeting with Ian was memorable. As soon as I opened the door to my playroom, Ian bounded in and began to play with the figures of animals. He looked right at me and told me that he loves animals. He went on to say that he loves playing with animals, watching TV shows that teach about animals, reading animal stories, and that he likes to visit places like the zoo and the children's farm. His parents added that he has a large fund of knowledge about animals and their habits. Ian's cheerful demeanor reminded me that even children who are depressed, regressed, and generally irritable can look content and normally playful for periods of time.

Children have many different ways of meeting new situations and people. Some children present their brave, cheerful side to me first, presumably because they want me to see how brave they can be, and perhaps they want to take the time to decide if they can trust me before showing their vulnerable feelings. On the other end of the spectrum, some children display their most obnoxious, fearful, or out-of-control behaviors first, possibly to learn whether I can tolerate their "worst" parts.

I always introduce my playroom as a place where children and families come to work on problems that bother them, and that problems have a way of getting worked out. I invited Ian to join us in talking or to play with toys in the sand tray while the adults talked. Ian chose to put figures in the sand tray, while his parents began to tell me more about him. They described their son as "good with his sister, sensitive, smart, imaginative and good-hearted." They said they were looking forward to having Ian get over the incident with Billy. They wanted Ian to feel better about himself.

I joined Ian at the sand tray and asked him to tell me a story about what was happening in his picture. Ian didn't hesitate. "Aladdin walks up onto the dragon (which was hidden under the sand) and then BOOM the dragon comes right out of the sand and then the dragon walks in the sinking sand too. Jasmine comes along on her tiger and then her tiger was in the sinking sand too." The rest of his complex story involved a snake coming out of the sand and biting everyone so that they all sank into the sand where they were buried. I listened with interest. The theme of hidden and unsuspected danger, the sexual symbolism of the snake attack, and the dismal outcome of the story were Ian's first clues to me that he was very distressed.

When it was time to leave, Ian waved and called, "Good-bye, Dr. Love-it-all!" He said "Dr. Love-it-all" as fluently as one would say "Dr. Lovett." Later Ian's parents told me that Ian was convinced that he was saying my name correctly, and every time he saw me, he addressed me as "Dr. Love-it-all."

Ian returned a few days later, eager to make another picture in the sand tray. This time, there was a triceratops facing a mounted knight who was brandishing a sword. I thought that Ian was showing me that he was ready to go on his hero's journey to fight the monster (and I noted that he had selected the extinct variety.)

IMAGINATION EXERCISES

I told Ian that I wanted to show him some imagination exercises so he could make his power strong enough to get over what had happened with Billy. I asked him to think about a safe place. He said, "Home." I instructed Ian to watch the figure of the knight while he felt the feeling of being safe at home, and I began to guide Ian's eye movement, back and forth, with the knight.

Ian complained that his eyes felt "blurry," that he didn't like it, and that he wanted to stop. I praised Ian for telling me what he wanted. Then I asked permission to tap his shoulders while he played. Ian consented. I stood behind him and tapped on his shoulders while he played with the knight and the triceratops. Then I asked him to think about a time when he had learned something quickly. Ian didn't falter. "Eating," he replied. "I'm a born eater!" Ian appeared to enjoy thinking about what a good eater he was as I tapped his shoulders, and he continued to play in the sand.

I told Ian that his parents had written a story, and that we would like for him to listen to the story to see if he could help the kids get over what had happened to them. I decided not to tell Ian directly that the story was about him specifically, because he had not mentioned anything about the molestation experience. I thought it might be easier for him to hear about a generic brother and sister. Of course, if he chose to identify with the children in the story, that would be fine too. Ian was eager to listen to the story. He continued playing with the figures in the sand while his mother read the story.

IAN'S STORY

Once upon a time, not so long ago, in a far-away land, there lived a nice family. There was a mom and dad, a big brother, and his little sister. The children were very nice children and loved by all who met them.

Sometimes they would play "Power Rangers" and save the world. Sometimes they would play animal guessing games. But mostly they liked being silly and telling jokes with their mom and dad. They had lots of friends who would come over and play and sometimes they would go and play at their friends' house. They had their own playroom with lots of toys and neat things for playing imagination. They had one friend whose house they would go to a lot. His name was Billy. The boy and the little girl liked playing with their friend and sometimes they would sleep over and have lots of fun staying up late telling silly stories.

One day, though, it was not so fun. They were all playing in their friend's room. Billy turned to the girl and told her that she had to let him lick her private part. The girl did not want to do this, but Billy told her that she wouldn't have any friends and would get in trouble if she didn't let him do this. The little girl was scared, but she didn't want to get in trouble, so she let him lick her private part. Then Billy turned to the boy and told him to put Billy's penis in his mouth. The boy didn't want to do this either, and he told Billy "NO." But Billy grabbed the boy and tried to force his head down. The boy didn't feel so good. He could smell pee and he felt sick, but the boy was brave, and he wouldn't let Billy do this to him. The girl, seeing how brave her brother was, felt brave too. She made some noise and Billy's mom came into the room to check on them. The kids were safe.

When the parents came to pick up their children, they could see that their children were upset. When they got in the car, the girl was still feeling brave. She told her parents what

(cont.)

had happened at Billy's house. The brother was feeling brave too, and he told his mom as well. Their mom and dad were pretty upset but never at their children. They were upset that someone would try to make their children feel bad. They were very proud of their kids for telling them the truth. They loved their boy and their girl more than anything in the world and wanted them to know that they had been right to make noise and especially right to tell their parents the truth. They were very good children and had not done anything wrong. Dad and Mom took the kids out for a very special family dinner to celebrate their bravery. They explained to their children how happy they were to have such wonderful children and that they could always tell their mom and dad anything.

The kids felt pretty good that they had done the right thing.

"I think I can help the kids!" Ian exclaimed. "I know Billy, and the kids should stay away from him!" I inquired, "How do you know whether it's safe to play with kids?" "Only with an adult there or at my house. Only with the door open." Ian had already figured out a strategy for keeping himself safe when he was playing with friends in the future.

I suggested that Ian's mother read the story again and that whenever there was a scary part Ian's father could tap his shoulders until it looked less scary. I told Ian that I would stop the story to ask him questions, and that he could also stop the story if it felt scary. Ian liked the idea.

After the first paragraph, I asked Ian if he could feel his mom loving him. He said "Yes!" I instructed Roger to tap Ian's shoulder until the feeling was even stronger. I asked Ian whether he felt his dad loving him. "Yes!" Roger tapped again. Then I asked Ian whether he could feel himself loving his parents. "Yes! I feel me loving. My love is strong enough to fight a dragon!" (That's exactly how much powerful love a child needs in order to overcome a trauma.)

DESENSITIZATION AND REPROCESSING

When Billy's name was mentioned in the story for the first time, I stopped the story and asked Ian, "How does Billy look?" "He looks bad and feels bad," came Ian's swift reply. Roger began to tap his son's shoulders. After a minute I stopped Roger's tapping and asked Ian, "How does Billy look now?" Ian answered, "He looks smaller." He held his hands about 4 inches apart, and said, "This big." With my nod, Roger resumed tapping for another minute, and Shirley continued reading.

When she read the part about Billy's penis, I stopped the story to talk with Ian. I wanted to make sure that Ian felt fine about his own penis, that he was clear about when it was appropriate for a boy to expose his penis, and that the smell of urine was not so disgusting nor associated with a feeling of nausea. Roger tapped his son's shoulders while we all talked about "what's appropriate," and Ian's parents developed guidelines for their son. "Of course it's okay to take your penis out to pee in the toilet. The smell of pee is okay in the bathroom. It's okay to touch your own body anywhere, including your penis. You have a fine penis. It's okay to take a shower and wash your penis. It is never okay for a boy to use his penis to make someone feel bad." Roger tapped, and Ian nodded when each statement felt true.

EMPOWERMENT

Ian said, "I'd like to tell Billy it's not okay to show your penis to anybody." I encouraged Ian to imagine telling Billy. Ian said forcefully, "Put your penis away." Then he added, "I'd like some ants to itch him." I knew that once Ian was able to feel angry with Billy, instead of terrified by him, his sense of power and well-being were beginning to return. I was satisfied that our first session had gone well, but our work was not over.

Two weeks later Ian returned with his mother for his third visit. They had just come from his "getting acquainted" visit at kindergarten. Shirley was happy that Ian seemed fine and "ready to go." Not only had his reluctance about starting school vanished, but, during the past 2 weeks, he had become more active and bolder than he had been since the molestation. He had started swimming lessons and had learned to put his face in the water. He didn't seem anxious any more. He had not wet his bed even once since our last session. He was sleeping well.

Ian had taken his place at the sand tray. "What do you think about Billy?" I asked directly. Ian replied, "I feel okay because I know I'll never go to Billy's house again. He's not a close friend any more. Right, Mom?" Ian looked to his mother. "Right!" his mother affirmed. Ian played with the triceratops. He volunteered, "Kids are supposed to protect their mom and dad by not letting the bad guy get them." "Where did you get that idea?" I wondered aloud. "I just knew it," Ian mused. Shirley added, "Lately he's been intent on helping me get over my fear of reptiles. I've been afraid of snakes ever since I was terrified by one as a child."

I looked at Ian's sand-tray scene. Aladdin and triceratops were covered with sand. Taz, a small figure, rescued Aladdin, and the dinosaur got himself out of the sand. The dinosaur hit Aladdin, and he fell. Then Aladdin was buried again. I surmised that we were out of one trap, but the story indicated that we were about to encounter the next episode in the hero's journey.

THE SECOND LAYER OF THE TRAUMA

Ian returned with his father a week later. Roger was pleased with his son's progress. "Ian's confidence is right back up. His lassitude has evaporated. He has a different tone when he talks about Billy." "How's Billy?" I asked Ian. Ian responded, "He's in trouble. He's grounded for being bad. I acted better than him."

Roger read the story of the molestation. I asked Ian how scary the story was now. I placed my hands about 10 inches apart and said, "If this is the scariest you can imagine and," placing my hands together, "this is not scary at all." Ian positioned my hands about 4 inches apart. He said, "This is how small Billy looks now." He held his fingers a few inches apart. I urged Ian to think about Billy while I tapped his shoulders. "Now he looks this big." Ian moved his fingers closer together. I tapped some more. "Soon he'll be invisible." A minute later, he sighed, "He's invisible."

For our next session, Shirley and Roger came alone, without Ian, to discuss Ian's progress. Shirley declared that Ian was back to himself and was pushing the limits again. She was unsure about whether his limit-testing was age appropriate or more than normal. "He's confident and happy and is doing great in kindergarten. He sleeps through the night—no more bedwetting. He's stopped lying. He's really honest now. He's started tying his shoes again. He takes showers and washes himself without a problem."

Roger agreed that Ian was definitely doing much better, but he felt that something was still bothering Ian because he seemed to be trying to get into trouble. His misbehavior was a subtle change from normal but still significant. Ian was acting as if he believed, "I'm ashamed. I deserve to be punished because I let something happen to Julie."

We agreed to schedule another session with Ian to check whether he was still experiencing problems from the molestation. Ian came into my playroom and settled himself in front of the doll house. "I've been thinking about Billy," Ian commented, before I had a chance to say anything. He went on to say, "I want to hear the story." While his mother read, Ian began to pull up the skirt of the little girl doll and put her on the toilet. I stopped the story and asked, "How scary does Billy look now?" Ian replied, "Not very spooky." "How spooky?" I prodded. "Not spooky at all now," Ian said with certainty.

As Ian listened to the story, he undressed the little girl doll. As soon as Ian's father had read, "Billy told the little girl that she had to let him lick her private part," I stopped the story and asked Ian, "How scary is that part of the story if 0 means not scary at all and 10 means the scariest you can imagine?" I held my hands together to indicate not scary at all and moved them 10 inches apart to indicate the most scary imaginable. Ian flung his arms wide apart and said, "It's 100 scary." I tapped his shoulders while he stared at the naked doll and became agitated.

FOR A CHILD "RESPONSIBILITY" OFTEN EQUALS "FAULT"

Ian began to talk, even while I tapped his shoulders, "I'm responsible for Julie. I should have made a noise and gotten the parents to come. I opened my mouth but no words came out." Ian looked very distressed. I stopped tapping and asked Ian if he had heard the expression, "scared speechless." Ian shook his head, "No." Ian's mother reminded him that he had read a book called *Goosebumps* in which someone was so scared of a monster that he couldn't scream. I added that when something as scary as this happens, it's normal not to be able to scream. In fact, I've seen many adults who were "scared speechless" when something like this happens. Maybe Julie was able to scream because she was too young to realize how scary it was.

Ian was still agitated and ashamed that Julie had been able to make noise, and that he couldn't. He lamented, "I was responsible for Julie, but I couldn't scream. Julie made her own noise and took care of herself." Ian's mother reassured him that it was okay for Julie to take care of him, too, but Ian would not be consoled.

Remembering how Ian loved animals, I talked about how animals react when something scares them. I talked about how animals, like people, have certain responses to danger. Animals' hair stands up. People get goosebumps. Both can feel their hearts beat fast, so they're ready to run if they need to escape. Both can be so frightened that they can't run and can't make a noise. I wanted to convince Ian that his response to the trauma was normal, and certainly not a character flaw. My animal analogies did not help Ian.

Ian remained upset that he had not been able to protect Julie, and I realized that we would have to address his unrealistic expectations about his responsibility toward his sister. Ian had been only 2 years old when Julie was born, but his traumatic experience at the time of her birth had dictated his belief that he was bad if he didn't take care of Julie. He wouldn't heal from this molestation experience until we went back to his earlier experience to alleviate his guilt about not keeping Julie safe. Unlike an adult, who might have spontaneously reprocessed earlier, linked memories contributing to current anxiety, young children appear to store these memories in discrete memory channels.

Shirley finished reading the story, and Ian contemplated his experience. "In my book I can scream 'cause I can do anything in my imagination, but in Billy's room, I couldn't. It's over. We'll just work on it in my book." Indeed, his story was turning into a book, and we would have to investigate another chapter. Ian wanted to make a sand-tray scene before he went home. He made up a story about a boat being overcome by a tidal wave of bees. The people on the boat called the giant Viking for help. I asked Ian what he had learned today. "That's how I felt with Billy—he was like a big tidal wave of bees." Then Ian showed me how the boat survived the tidal wave and learned to keep going.

THE 2-YEAR-OLD BLAMED HIMSELF

Ian's father brought Ian back the following week, and said that school was going well for Ian, but he could tell that Ian was very angry sometimes. At Julie's birthday party, Ian had taken his turn swinging at the piñata with a bat, and when he found his target he had beaten it to shreds, with uncharacteristic vengeance. He had also wet his bed one time during the week.

We began to talk about Ian's relationship with his sister, and Roger proceeded to tell me about the first time Ian had seen his baby sister, Julie. On the day Julie and Shirley were scheduled to go home from the hospital, Roger had told 22-month-old Ian that he was the big brother, and that it was his job to bring his baby sister home. Ian had been proud of his title and his job. When they arrived in the newborn nursery, Roger told me, baby Julie had just had an apneic episode while nursing and had turned the color of "pocket lint." As Ian caught a glimpse of his sister, the nurse was hastily taking her to the intensive care nursery for blood tests and a lumbar puncture, and Shirley burst into tears. At the time, Ian didn't say a word. He just clung to his sobbing mother.

Now, at age 5, Ian had plenty to say about the event. He became excited and upset as he told his version of the story, "I went to the doctor's office to see if Julie was going to die. I got there too late to protect Julie. Was she an orphan when the nurse took her away?" Roger patiently explained that Julie was not an orphan, and that she had come home 3 days later, when the doctors were certain she had not had an infection. Ian interjected, "I was going to bring my baby home. I should have."

I reminded Ian that he had been less than 2 years old when Julie was born. A 2-year-old can't be responsible for taking a baby home from the hospital. Ian disagreed, "I should have knocked the nurse over and brought Julie home." Five-year-old Ian believed that he should have been all powerful when he was 2! He had been primed for the role of big brother at age 2, but this is not unusual. He just happened to arrive at the hospital a moment after Julie stopped breathing and turned dusky while feeding, saw his sister being taken away, and felt his parents' intense fear about the life of their newborn. Twenty-two-month-old Ian had concluded independently that this drama happened because of him, and he had vowed that he would protect his baby, his parents, and himself from future trauma by always taking care of Julie.

We used EMDR to desensitize and reprocess Ian's early memory of his first meeting with his sister. I call this early experience a *template memory* because it set up the blueprint for Ian's core beliefs about his safety in the world. From this early experience, Ian concluded that his well-being was integrally linked with Julie's safety. "How does the story of Julie as a baby look now?" I asked as we finished. "It looks like a little worm story now, Dr. Love-it-all," Ian chuckled. "It was scary before, but not any more."

After that, our final session addressing the molestation went smoothly. Ian's memory of Billy molesting his sister faded to "a little worm story," too. The story was over, and Ian's energetic, confident, delightful nature was restored.

Ian had demonstrated that even young, preverbal children conceptualize themselves as enormously powerful and therefore ultimately responsible for everything that happens in their world. Before the age of 2, Ian had learned well the lesson that his young psyche embraced in an attempt to prevent trauma in the future. After that, his behavior and his attitude demonstrated his belief that it was his responsibility to protect his sister. Normally, belief in his power as the responsible big brother might not have caused a problem for Ian, although the children's parents indicated that Julie had been slow to talk because Ian did most of her talking for her. His remarkable closeness to his sister was not viewed as problematic until the trauma of the molestation challenged Ian's exaggerated sense of responsibility.

The molestation incident itself, although handled extremely well by Ian's parents, had distorted Ian's regard for his own body, had made him leery of friendships, and distrustful of adults. It had shaken his view of his own competence and reliability. It had eroded his self-esteem to such a degree that he had lost well-established developmental milestones. His depression and anxiety had also threatened his ability to progress in school. Undoubtedly, his sexuality would have been threatened by the molestation.

Was Julie really spared the damaging effects of the molestation? I don't know. I never met her. Perhaps the posttraumatic effects of molestation would lie dormant until Julie was old enough to have an intimate, sexual relationship. Shirley and Roger told me that their 3-year-old daughter had expressed an interest in coming to see me because "she had feelings too." They felt that Ian needed attention first, because his symptoms were so dramatic and disturbing. The family moved to another state shortly after my final session with Ian. I encouraged them to take Julie to a therapist who specialized in working with children when they settled into their new home.

Even though the "perpetrator" in this case was only 6 years old, he had managed to paralyze his victims and render them powerless. The traumatic experience had scarred Ian with repulsive intrusive thoughts, loathsome visual memories, nauseating physical sensations, and feelings of terror and paralysis. Molestation by a trusted adult, repeated molestation, or molestation that is denied or punished by parents can be even more devastating for a child. Without swift and effective treatment, children who have suffered molestation may be doomed to a lifetime of debilitating symptoms, yet they may identify themselves, rather than an incident in childhood, as the problem.

ANNA'S EXPERIENCE: SECRETS ARE LIES

Anna's parents knew she needed help within a month of the incident. Beginning the night two boys pulled her pants off to play "doctors," 4-year-old Anna had awoken nightly, screaming "No!" and grabbing her crotch. She was not simply having nightmares, she was having night terrors during which she screamed for 45 minutes and could not be consoled. She begged her parents to check on her "a million times" during the night. She said she was afraid that her toys would come to get her while she was asleep.

Ellen and Mark, Anna's parents, identified four recent events as contributing to Anna's anxiety. Anna had been confident and outgoing until the past few months in preschool, when one of the boys started bothering her. He would run up to Anna while she was playing and hit her as he ran by. Anna's teacher advised her to just ignore Jason, or just walk away from him. Finally, when Anna complained that Jason had chased her and stomped on her ankle, Anna's mother called a meeting with the boy's parents and the teacher. The boy's father came alone to the meeting and his nonchalant message was "Boys will be boys." The teacher said she would try to get Jason to stop bothering Anna or to keep the children apart. After the meeting, Anna continued to complain about Jason, and her parents were concerned about how to handle the situation.

A CLUSTER OF TRAUMATIC EXPERIENCES

One evening, Ellen and Mark were in their living room discussing the situation with friends while Anna played with their two sons in her bedroom. She had played with these boys, ages 6 and 8, many times before, but usually her 9-year-old brother was there too. That night, he was spending the night at a friend's house. When the guests had gone and it was time for bed, Anna wanted her mother to sleep with her, which was unusual. She said she was afraid of the dark, which was also unusual for her.

For several days, Anna guarded the secret the boys had warned her to keep. They had been playing "doctors." The boys had showed her their penises, then they had pulled off Anna's underpants and scratched her vulva, despite her protests. She had screamed, "No!" and finally the boys left her alone, but first they threatened that they would not be her friends if she told.

The day after the incident, Anna and Ellen took a hike and Anna climbed a fence beside the trail. All of a sudden, the fence collapsed and Anna fell backward. If she had fallen forward, she would have tumbled 70 feet into a ravine. Anna and her mother were both upset and crying at the realization of what might have happened.

A week later, Anna and her mother went to see *Toy Story*, a movie about toys that come alive. Anna was terrified. She began to have nightmares that a toy dinosaur came alive at school and chased her. She had nightmares that she fell off a cliff and struggled to climb back up. Movies frequently disturb young children who are susceptible, especially if they are in the process of recovering from a trauma. Young children are not mature enough to protect themselves from the impact of menacing characters, themes of violence and abuse, or scary emotional overtones that movies, videos, and television shoot at them. I recommend that parents carefully monitor any media their children watch, especially if they already have symptoms of anxiety. Anna continued to have night terrors during which she screamed inconsolably, held her crotch, and whimpered or shouted "No."

When Anna told her mother what had happened when she had "played doctor" with the boys, Ellen immediately called the boys' mother. Confirmation about what had happened came from one of the brothers, and later that day they delivered a package with beautiful stuffed animals and a note saying the boys were sorry. The gifts and apology only seemed to confuse and agitate Anna further. She became mopey, reticent, fearful, and unsure of herself in almost every situation. She also began to complain about stomachaches.

PARENTAL ISSUES

Anna's parents came to me to discuss how they could help Anna and how they could deal with their own distress. Ellen had begun to feel that she couldn't protect her daughter. Even the "fun" outings—the hike and the movie—she had planned for Anna had literally turned into nightmares. Mark was concerned that his previously sturdy daughter was afraid of boys, lacked self-confidence, and was having nightmares.

We focused on their concerns about Anna. Ellen and Mark postulated the negative beliefs they thought Anna had about herself: "I can't protect myself. I can't rely on grown-ups to protect me. I'm not safe with boys. I'm not safe in the world. I'm not brave. I'm powerless. I'm not strong. I'm not beautiful." They wanted her to believe, "I'm strong. I'm capable. My words have power. I'm powerful. I'm beautiful. I'm smart. I can trust my own judgment. I can share anything with my parents regardless of what anybody says. I can rely on trusted adults to help me. I'm lucky. I can solve problems." Anna's father smiled as he added, "I want her to believe about herself, 'I'm a delight to all who know me.'"

Both parents brought Anna to our next meeting. While Anna

played or snuggled, they warmly told me that Anna is a wonderful child who likes stories, music, art projects, and gymnastics. They described her as generous, sweet, and funny. They said that Anna was good at sharing, making friends, and using her words. They expressed their hope that it would soon become easier for Anna to sleep well at night, and to relax during the day. Anna's mother agreed to take on the task of writing a story about the events that had upset Anna.

ANNA'S STORY

Once upon a time there was a little girl who was very happy and very loved and very confident. She liked her life very much. She had lots of good friends, lots of fun at school, and a very happy family life with her parents and cat.

One day at school a little boy hit her, and this scared her. This little boy hit her a few other times at school and she started to become very frightened. Her mom talked to her teachers and asked the adults to protect the little girl.

One night at home, two boys came to play with the little girl. The children played "doctor" in the bedroom while the parents talked together in the living room. The boys showed her their penises. The boys pulled her pants down and started to touch her vagina. They scratched her on her private part. She asked them to stop and they wouldn't. They didn't hear her. The little girl had to scream "No!" in a very big voice to get them to stop.

But guess what? They stopped when she used her powerful words in a powerful way. The little girl is very strong and powerful to have gotten the older boys to stop. Then the boys told her not to tell anyone or they wouldn't be her friends anymore. That night the little girl was very scared and she needed her mom to lie down next to her to go to sleep.

The next day the little girl and her mommy went for a hike. The little girl ran down into a clearing and climbed a fence. The fence collapsed. This was very scary because the collapsed fence was very close to a steep cliff. The little girl was very lucky that she fell backwards.

The little girl and her mommy came home. The little girl started school again. She was very brave to tell her mommy what happened with the boys. The little girl became very scared to go to sleep at night and had some scary nightmares. Back at school the little boy who hit the little girl started to bother her again. She became very frightened of him. She became frightened of her room at night and frightened of the dark.

THE NEED FOR A STABLE ENVIRONMENT

The story was a clue about which issues were unresolved for Anna's mother, issues that would have to be addressed so that the family could "sleep easy" again. The story revealed that neither Anna nor her mother viewed Anna's school environment as safe. When Anna could be safe and secure in school, it would be easier to resolve her fears.

I agreed with Anna's mother that the teachers were supposed to protect the little girl, but what was Anna to do when the teachers were not doing a good enough job of protecting her? Before Anna could feel safe at school, several things had to happen: The teachers had to take on the job of taming Jason and insisting on the "no hitting" rule and coach Anna to stand up for herself, and Anna's parents had to be confident that the school was doing this job well. In addition, Ellen and Mark needed to feel empowered and trust that their daughter could learn the skills she needed to be able to defend herself from a bully.

Anna came to her next session with her mother. We talked about making things less scary for Anna. I asked Anna to choose a wand she liked and then used the pink feather wand to tap her hands alternately while she felt the good, safe feeling of "being on Mom's lap." Next she chose the Blue Fairy figure to tap her hands while her mother read her the story.

Anna and her mother returned a week later. Ellen told me that Anna had gone to bed easily and slept well for several nights following our first EMDR session. For the past few nights she had climbed into bed with her parents in the middle of the night, however, saying that her bedroom and her toys were scary. Anna chose to draw a picture while her mother read her story again. I tapped Anna's shoulders with Strawberry Shortcake, whom Anna had selected for a helper.

I stopped the story to ask Anna how scary the boys' penises looked, and she indicated that they were very scary. I continued tapping until they didn't look scary any more. Then I asked Anna to remember when the boys had warned her not to tell what they had done and threatened not to be her friend any more if she did tell. Anna stayed upset even though I continued tapping, and I realized that Anna needed more information before she would be able to successfully reprocess the troubling memory of her experience.

EDUCATIONAL INTERWEAVES

Anna needed to be able to distinguish a secret from a surprise. Simply put, a surprise feels good, and a secret feels bad. She needed to know that a surprise, like not telling what birthday present is in the package, is fine because everyone will be happy about it. A young child should be taught never to guard a secret, because it is a lie. Anna needed to learn to stand up for herself by never keeping a secret from her parents even if someone warned her not to tell.

Anna's mother added that the boys were sorry about what they had done, and that they had brought Anna presents as a way of saying they were sorry. I asked Anna how she felt about the boys hurting her and then bringing presents for her. She said, "What they did was okay because then they gave me presents." It became evident that Anna needed to be taught that even if someone apologizes and gives you a gift, that doesn't mean that the mistreatment is acceptable. No wonder Anna seemed confused.

A 4-year-old can understand and use simple, direct explanations or rules. Anna needed to know exactly what was all right and what was not. No, it was not okay that the boys had forced themselves on her. No, it was not okay that they had threatened to stop being her friend if she told. No, it's not okay to keep a secret that feels bad. Yes, it was right that the boys apologized, but that still did not mean that what they did was all right. Those are a lot of rules for an inexperienced 4-year-old to digest.

Anna, who had been silently drawing, began to roar. She started quietly saying, "Roar." Then she took a deep breath and exploded "Rooooar!" I acted frightened. Anna smiled and growled again and again. I pretended to cower. Anna's roars swelled to an intimidating volume. Anna looked quite pleased with her newfound courage, and I cringed appreciatively as she roared. I was satisfied that Anna was practicing displaying her power, but I noticed that tears were sliding down Ellen's cheeks. Ellen said she was crying because she could see how frightened Anna had been. I complimented Anna on her impressive roars, and invited Ellen to come for a session alone.

ADDRESSING PARENTAL ISSUES

Ellen came to the session saying that Anna was sleeping better, but that she, Ellen, was very upset over the preschool's inadequate response to the problem with Jason. When Ellen thought about what was happening at preschool, she believed, "I can't protect my child." She wanted to believe, "I can effectively protect my daughter. I can teach her how to take care of herself." Ellen outlined a plan of action. She would go to the school board to insist that there be better supervision of the children.

Ellen returned alone for her next session. In response to Ellen's complaints, the preschool had decided to designate a teacher to "shadow" Anna and protect her. Anna had told Ellen that Jason didn't hit girls any more, and she thanked her mother for her help in stopping Jason's attacks. Ellen was still upset by the series of events that left her feeling powerless to protect her daughter. We agreed to use EMDR to help her develop a "safe place" for herself and to help her trust that she could teach her daughter to take care of herself. When we finished her brief EMDR session, Ellen felt calmer and more confident that she could handle the situation.

When Anna came for her next session, she brought me a card she had made to thank me for helping her be less afraid. Although she was less afraid, she was still being harassed, now by one of the girls at preschool. "Words just don't work with these kids," Ellen lamented. We began to talk about how Anna had to "stand up for herself." I started to say, "Standing up for herself is—" but Anna interrupted and completed the sentence, "hard."

PRACTICING

I decided that Anna could benefit from practicing "standing up for herself" by role-playing. Fearful children are easy targets for bullies and repeatedly become victims. Preschool bullies are usually reluctant to bother children who are assertive and self-assured. I took one of my marionettes from the wall and invited Anna to choose a marionette for herself. She chose an elegant doll wearing a full-length gold dress. Anna's figure had plaster legs, one of which had broken off and been repaired. I knew that lifting her gown would reveal a prominent scar.

"Hi!" our dolls started a conversation. "Let's play kick," my doll proposed. I swung her feet toward Anna's doll and tapped her doll's leg. "Oh," I said in my own voice, "let's see if your doll got hurt." I lifted her doll's skirt to disclose the scar. Anna and I examined the "injury." "Don't tell," I spoke for my kicking doll. I asked Anna, "Was it okay that my doll hurt your doll?" Anna shook her head, "No." "That's right. Should your doll keep the kicking a secret?" Anna wasn't sure. If her doll told, maybe no one would play with her again. We reviewed the rules about secrets.

Then I took a tiny toy package from the shelf and gave it to Anna's doll. I said to Anna, "My doll gave your doll a present. Is it okay that she hurt your doll?" Anna said, "Yes, because she gave her a present to say she was sorry." I explained, "No, it was not okay for my doll to hurt your doll. It was good she said she was sorry, but that does not mean that hurting her was all right."

"Let's play again," my doll invited Anna. We both picked up our dolls. "Let's play kick," my doll challenged again. Anna just waited and watched, so my doll kicked hers again. We examined her doll's injury again. "Was it okay that my doll kicked yours?" I asked. Anna replied, "No."

"Anna," I instructed, "let's teach your doll how to stand up for herself. Get her to say, 'I don't want to play kick,' in a firm voice." Anna spoke up for her doll. My doll kicked hers anyway. I advised Anna, "Tell her the rule is, 'no kicking allowed' in a voice that says you mean business, and if she doesn't listen to that, you can give her one of your mighty roars." Anna said, "No kicking allowed," in an uncertain voice.

My doll kicked again. "Tell her that in a voice that lets her know that no one is allowed to bother you," I urged. "No kicking," Anna bellowed, and then she began to roar, and between roars she smiled. She was getting the idea. My doll backed away and said she was sorry, and that she wouldn't kick again. We practiced for a while until Anna's rehearsal was totally convincing. Finally, I asked Anna to watch my marionette swinging back and forth, to think, "I can stand up for myself," and to feel the brave feeling in her body. I guided her eye movements again while she thought, "I can say what I want. I can say what I don't want."

Anna left with confidence that she could command respect by expressing herself, and her mother had learned how to coach her daughter through role-playing. That was my last visit with Anna and her family. I would have liked to have played with her more, but it was time for her mother to take over the job of teaching Anna to be bully proof. EMDR had taken the upsetting charge off of the incidents, and her mother could now teach her the skills required for taking care of herself.

I talked with Anna's mother a few weeks after our last visit and again, a year later. She told me proudly that Anna had started kindergarten in a different school and was taking care of herself quite well. She was confident and happy, and she slept well at night. I was delighted to hear that Anna was having fun again.

14

MONSTERS COME OUT AT NIGHT

SLEEP DISORDERS

Everyone has trouble sleeping from time to time, but for some children getting to sleep can be a nightly struggle that takes over their lives. This was the case for Hanna, Henry, and Emily.

HANNA

"I lie in bed watching the clock. I think, if I don't fall asleep soon, I'll be too tired tomorrow. Something is wrong with me. Everyone else in the world can sleep except me. I feel really babyish. I'm all alone. I'm not in control, but I want to be. I feel so pressured to sleep. Being the only one awake makes me nervous." Twelve-year-old Hanna sighed with discouragement and pushed her black hair away from her face as she described her experience trying to fall asleep at night.

Falling asleep was not Hanna's only problem with sleeping. Several times a week, she awoke in a panic, drenched in sweat, with her heart pounding. She felt agitated, frustrated, and frightened. Jolted awake, she had trouble falling asleep again. Hanna dreaded bedtime for good reason.

Hanna's parents had different responses to their daughter's distress. Her mother, Mieko, empathized with Hanna, "I know how much Hanna wants to be able to sleep easily. When Hanna can't sleep or wakes up terrified, I rest on the floor beside her bed and help her to focus on happy memories, remind her to "calm down," and keep her company until she finally dozes off."

Hanna's father, Ken, was impatient with the whole problem. "I think that Hanna should just decide to go to sleep on her own and then do it." He thought that his wife was babying Hanna. Hanna's mother assured me that she preferred to sleep with her husband rather than on the floor, but that by the time Hanna came to her bedroom for help, she was seriously distressed and needed her mother. Hanna knew that her parents were upset about her problem, and she felt "babyish" for needing them and guilty about causing conflict. It's very common for parents to disagree about how to handle a child's sleep problems (or any other behavior problem), and it's typical for the child to feel guilty that she caused friction between her parents. Sometimes parents consult me for a verdict about which parent has the "right" approach.

Hanna's bedtime ordeal also stood in the way of her being able to spend the night with friends or go to sleep-away camp. She was motivated to consult me because she wanted to go to sleep-away camp with friends and had signed up for a 2-week session, beginning in 1 month. As July approached, she feared that she wouldn't be able to tolerate being away from home while having so much difficulty falling asleep. Recently, she had started having stomachaches in anticipation of going to camp. Hanna's mother had loved summer camp as a child, and she wanted her daughter to have a happy camp experience. Everything indicated that Hanna and her parents sincerely wanted to resolve this problem. They were all experiencing secondary losses as a result of this problem. No one was profiting.

WHEN DID IT START?

Mieko recalled that Hanna had always been a lighter sleeper than any of her other three children, but she had not had any significant difficulty sleeping until she was 9 years old. She had had trouble falling asleep for about a year, between the ages of 9 and 10, and had managed by sleeping with the light on. Then she seemed fine for about a year. The current problem had begun when Hanna was 11 and had gotten increasingly worse over the past year.

Hanna's fearfulness at night seemed out of character. She presented as a friendly, outgoing, articulate adolescent. She was an excellent student, a strong athlete, and a popular friend. Nevertheless, as Hanna began to describe her first and only experience at sleep-away camp, she looked like a frightened child. At age 10, she had tried camp for only 5 nights. Those had been 5 very long and difficult nights. She remembered crying and telling the counselor that she felt homesick. The counselor had brushed off her fears by saying, "You're too old to cry." Hanna stifled her tears and went into the bathroom, where she had diarrhea, and cried some more. Hanna felt that she shouldn't be crying and had concluded, "I'm really babyish." When she returned to her bunk, one of the other campers came over and whispered, "It's all right." Hanna lay awake, muffling her sobs with her pillow, long after everyone else had fallen asleep. She kept thinking, "I'm the only one awake."

Mild sleep difficulties had begun before Hanna's first camp experience, so I directed my questioning to Hanna's early history. I asked about birth, illnesses, injuries, and traumas, exploring the possibilities for a "template experience." Between the ages of 3 months and 2 years, Hanna had had multiple ear infections and had needed pressure-equalizing (PE) tubes inserted in her ears to help them drain. That had solved the problem. Although Hanna had no conscious memory of the series of infections or the medical procedures, I kept in mind that her body had recorded the events, and that those somatic memories could be contributing to her anxiety about sleep.

Mieko paused to think over her daughter's childhood. She said she wasn't sure whether this was relevant information, but she went on to add that she had had a tumor when her daughter was a baby. It had been treated successfully by surgical removal, and there had never been a recurrence. The experience was so upsetting, however, that she had given up her career as a TV broadcaster and decided to stay home full time with her children. Traumatic events can be pivotal in informing life decisions. I wondered whether this talented and successful woman had adopted the belief, "It isn't safe for me to work away from home" as a magical talisman, intended to protect her from harm.

Then she told me that when Hanna was 3 years old, Hanna had had a lump on her shoulder. The doctors were uncertain about what the lump was, so they decided to "wait and watch" for a few weeks. During those 3 weeks, Hanna's parents' anxiety swelled as they worried that the mass might be malignant. Hanna's mother described herself as "terrified" for her daughter's life. Finally, with no change in the mass, the doctors decided to do a biopsy to make a diagnosis. Hanna went to the hospital for the surgical procedure under general anesthesia. Hanna's memories of the event were sketchy. She remembered seeing her parents "in white robes" and remembered struggling as she was "pushed down" by the nurses. The mass turned out to be a hemangioma, a harmless collection of dilated blood vessels, and no treatment was required.

Hanna's childhood injuries included broken fingers and a broken wrist, but discussing memories of those events didn't provoke any upset feelings. All in all, Hanna had had a safe and healthy childhood. Her family was supportive and child centered. Her mother expressed her confidence in Hanna, "She's resilient. She has come through disappointments, and I know she's strong. I also know she's determined to go to camp and to be happy at camp."

STARTING THE PROCESS

Hanna and I looked more closely at her unpleasant first camp experience. She had a mental image of herself lying on the top bunk and seeing her counselors. Her negative thoughts about herself were, "I am all alone here, and I have no control. There's nobody who can help me. This is terrible. I can't fall asleep. There's something wrong with me." Hanna wanted to believe, "I believe in myself, and I'm okay. I'm normal. I'm safe. I can comfort myself. I can do this." Although Hanna cognitively knew these statements to be true, they didn't *feel* true. I explained EMDR to Hanna and her mother and asked their permission to combine EMDR with some other methods for helping resolve the sleep difficulty and Hanna's low self-appraisal with regard to sleep. They were open to trying any methods that I thought might help, especially when I emphasized that Hanna would be in charge of saying exactly what she wanted.

When Hanna returned for her first session alone with me, we decided to practice applying eye movement to situations that felt good for Hanna to help strengthen her feelings of confidence. She chose the image of being at the beach, and enjoyed imagining the ocean breeze in her face, and sensing the feeling of relaxation in her body. Hanna liked the way eye movement enhanced her feelings of calm and relaxation, so we used eye movement to enhance several other memories. She thought about her pet and how happy she felt with him. She imagined stroking his silky fur and feeling his warm tongue on her cheek. She remembered kicking the winning goal in a soccer tournament, and felt the feelings of strength, power, and success in her legs. She recalled receiving a "spirit award" for soccer and feeling proud, excited, and honored. Eye movements strengthened her positive feelings.

I asked Hanna whether she would like to imagine how the future would be, when she would be able to sleep easily. She remembered a time when she had slept over at a friend's house and had successfully fallen asleep and stayed asleep all night. She imagined how nice it would be to be able to count on herself to sleep easily every night. She reported feeling dreamy and normal and tired and relaxed. The absence of obstacles to Hanna's view of a healthy future encouraged me to believe that EMDR would help her.

DESENSITIZING TRIGGERS

There was no critical incident directly responsible for Hanna's anxiety, so I decided to begin by desensitizing the environmental triggers for anxiety. I asked Hanna to visualize her bedroom clock, her visual cue for nightly anxiety, and I encouraged her to move her eyes. She immediately became aware of her heart beating fast and her growing anxiety at the idea of trying to sleep. She continued moving her eyes until the image of the clock no longer evoked anxiety. I asked her to visualize her pet and notice the feelings in her body evoked by his presence. Hanna smiled as she thought about him. Then I suggested that she pair the image of her clock with the body sensation of relaxation that came with thinking about her puppy. Bedtime began to look much less scary.

Hanna returned the next week feeling pleased that she had not had any trouble falling asleep except on the night preceding this session. She had dealt with her mild anxiety by thinking about her pet, and she soon relaxed to sleep. She asked what else she could do at night to help herself if she felt worried. I suspected that there was anxiety from some old memories still interfering with Hanna's ability to "let go" at night, and that reprocessing those old memories would clear the anxiety, but I also wanted to respond to Hanna's request for something she could do at night. Even though I believed that EMDR would catalyze the process of erasing Hanna's nighttime anxiety, there would still be times when stresses in her life could interfere with sleep, and she was wise in wanting to learn ways to soothe herself.

I asked Hanna whether she would like to learn some self-hypnosis or visualization to help herself relax. She enthusiastically agreed. She readily followed my instructions to look at the ceiling until her eyes felt tired and then to pay attention to her body relaxing. I reminded her that she was fully in control, even when she was very relaxed. I instructed her to lift her finger when imagery began to come to her that would help her at night. In about a minute, Hanna lifted her right index finger. She remembered being a young child on a float being pulled easily through the water by her father. She had felt happy and free. The image of a blue star came to her, and she said she would keep the image in mind to remind herself that she could be happy and free, and that she could feel relaxed and safe in the world. We ended Hanna's hypnosis session. Hanna was pleased that she could access her image of the blue star and its symbolism. I asked whether she would like to use eye movement to reinforce the feeling that she could learn ways to help herself relax, and she said that she would. First, I guided her eye movement to reinforce the belief, "I can learn ways to calm and relax myself." Then I asked Hanna what she had learned. She responded, "I can use my imagination to help me. I can imagine holding the blue star and I can feel free." We used eye movement to strengthen the feeling of freedom and relaxation in her body.

DESENSITIZING AND REPROCESSING OLD MEMORIES

I recommended that we begin to desensitize and reprocess scary old memories that might be contributing to her current anxiety. Hanna chose the memory of her camp experience at age 10. She pictured herself lying in her bunk in the dark. Her negative cognition was, "I'm alone." She wanted to believe, "I'm safe. I can do this. I can relax and get tired." When I asked her to check her body to determine how true each of these statements felt already, she said that she already felt safe, but it only felt about half true that she could relax and get tired. She felt anxiety when she looked back at the picture of herself in her bunk. Her anxiety rated a 7 on a scale of 0 to 10. Over the next 15 minutes, she desensitized and reprocessed the old memory. She spontaneously realized that it is normal for a 10-year-old child to feel homesick her first time at sleep-away camp, and that it was the counselor's job to help her feel better. It had been inappropriate for the counselor to shame her for her normal reaction to being away from home for the first time. I asked her to imagine being a counselor and calming an upset first-time camper. Soon Hanna felt calm looking back at the old memory, and all of her positive cognitions felt true.

Hanna returned for her third EMDR session in a few days. She had fallen asleep easily and slept well for a few nights, but the night before coming to see me, she had had trouble falling asleep. Hanna had practiced her self-hypnosis technique and had relaxed to sleep. I discussed treating Hanna's sleep problem as a process phobia. We agreed to desensitize some sleep-related memories systematically— the first time she had trouble with sleep (surgery at age 3), the worst time (when she had a panic attack looking at the clock), the most recent time (which had occurred in the previous week), and the next time (that very night, after our session).

That day, we focused on her memory of surgery at age 3. Hanna closed her eyes and thought for a moment. A picture came to her. The nurses were putting the gas mask on her and lying her down, and she was screaming. Negative beliefs that still felt true 9 years later were, "Something's wrong with me. I'm uncomfortable. I'm a baby." Hanna wanted to believe, "I can cooperate. I can do this by myself. I'm regular. It's over now." When she checked her body to determine how true these beliefs felt, she found that the only belief that did not already feel true was, "I'm regular. I'm fine."

Hanna noticed anxiety mounting as she looked at the memory of her surgery at age 3. She felt, "Something is wrong with me." Her anxiety rated 9 on a scale of 0 to 10. As she moved her eyes, Hanna imagined herself lying down and "going to sleep." She kept repeating in a dubious voice, "There is nothing to worry about. I was fine. Nothing was wrong." I wondered whether the doctors and nurses had forgotten to tell 3-year-old Hanna that she was normal, and that she didn't need to worry any more. I asked Hanna to imagine the doctors, nurses, and parents all relieved and happy that she's healthy. Hanna moved her eyes as she remembered the scene, then she exclaimed, "Everybody was happy I was okay, and we didn't have anything to worry about. I was healthy!" Hanna's anxiety dropped to 3.

Hanna continued to reprocess her experience, "I did what I was supposed to do. I shouldn't be upset. Why were they pushing me down when I could do it myself?" Three-year-old children often feel quite insulted when someone does something for them that they are capable of doing for themselves. I suggested that she imagine the scene the way she would have liked it to have happened. Hanna continued, "I could do it myself. I could just lie down and get relaxed and go to sleep. I could just be happy the whole time. I didn't have to worry at all. I could do it and then, later, I could go out for dinner." I realized that Hanna's psyche had confused "being put to sleep" against her will with going to sleep. No wonder nights had become a struggle for her.

Hanna's anxiety dropped to 1 on a scale of 0 to 10. She said, "I'm still worried something is going to be wrong with me. I'm worried something bad is going to happen to me." A picture of Hanna's mother and her worries about recurrence of her tumor came to me. Unlike Hanna's mother's medical problem, Hanna's hemangioma was benign and had resolved over time. It had never been a threat to her health and never would be. As a young child, Hanna had naturally taken on her parents' worries as her own. I asked Hanna to imagine giving her parents' worries back to them. Their worries had nothing to do with her. After a set of EMDR, Hanna's anxiety cleared completely. She explained, "I think I'm regular. I'm fine. I can picture myself walking into the room feeling happy. I picture myself lying down. I'm regular. I'm healthy. I'm fine. Everything was okay. The operation went fine so there was nothing to worry about in the first place."

Next, we looked at Hanna's memory of the worst time she had had going to sleep. She remembered looking at the clock, with her teeth chattering, and thinking, "I won't be able to do this." She wanted to believe, "I can relax and get tired and go to sleep on my own." Although that belief felt almost true, Hanna still felt extremely anxious remembering her most difficult night trying to fall asleep. With EMDR as catalyst, she quickly desensitized and reprocessed that memory, and concluded with an image of herself falling asleep. She described her mastery of the situation: "I told myself I could do it, and I did. I told my body to calm down and to get calm, and it did."

Finally, we focused on her most recent difficulty falling asleep. She remembered glancing at the clock thinking, "Come on. Come on. Why isn't this working? I've done it before. I work myself up when there is no need. I expect too much of my body and when it doesn't meet the expectation, I get worried." Hanna wanted to believe, "I can fall asleep when I'm ready." She began to move her eyes and to talk, "I can take care of myself even if I'm awake at night when others are asleep. I can be calm while I'm still awake. I can accept myself as I am. I can stay relaxed and fall asleep when I'm ready. My mind and body can work together. I can keep myself company while I wait to fall asleep. I am all alone. I can imagine happy thoughts. I can relax myself when I'm the only one awake. I have control over myself. I'm not worked up any more. It's okay with me." Hanna no longer felt anxious at all looking back on her recent difficulty sleeping.

Hanna was ready to look ahead to her upcoming camp experience. She imagined her 2 weeks at camp, as if she were watching a video. "I had fun and didn't worry about whether I could sleep or not. I just enjoyed the new experience." Hanna gleefully shared an image that came to her representing her anticipated camp experience, "It's like cookie dough. You make it yourself and you mold it and whatever it turns out to be, it is. At least you know you made it yourself."

FACING FEAR

Hanna returned for her final session a few days before she left for camp. She reported that she was sleeping fine, but she was feeling nervous about the possibility of getting nervous at camp. Fear of fear is often the last symptom to dissipate, even after fear associated with old memories has diminished, and new skills have been taught. Sometimes it just takes time and experience, rather than imagining, to convince a person that she can handle a situation calmly and competently. For children, playing can be a wonderful way of trying out new ways of being in the world. Sometimes, a child faces her fears by playing out the worst outcome she can imagine.

Hanna elected to spend our time together playing. She chose to use small toys for making a scene in the sand tray. She selected Snow White to represent herself and three dwarfs to represent three other campers. The first dwarf, the "mean" one, said to Snow White, "You are a baby. I don't feel homesick." The second dwarf said, "It's okay. I get homesick too." The third dwarf added, "It's my first time at camp, and I miss my home." The mean dwarf looked at the homesick campers and said, "You're weird."

Hanna created another scenario in the sand tray. Snow White and six other campers (represented by dwarfs) were sleeping in their bunks, tended by two counselors, Barbie and Power Woman. One of the campers sniffled, "I'm feeling homesick, and I can't fall asleep." Power Woman comforted her, "That's okay. Nothing to worry about. You're safe. You have friends. We're here. It's okay if you worry. Good night." One of the dwarfs showed concern for the homesick camper, "Are you okay? Just relax, and you'll be okay."

I remarked to Hanna that if she felt homesick and wanted to go home, that might just be a sign that camp, at least this camp, isn't the right place for her at this particular time. Lots of people don't like camp, and that's normal, too. Her 2 weeks at camp could be a learning experience, to decide whether she's someone who likes camp or someone who doesn't.

A few weeks later, Hanna called and left a message to thank me for my help and to say that she was doing great and had loved camp. She hadn't had any problems with sleeping, either. That evening I called to thank Hanna for her call, but I missed her. She was spending the night at a friend's house.

A year later, when I called to ask permission to include her story in my book, Hanna told me she was looking forward to going back to camp—for a month this time.

HENRY

Henry's parents consulted me because Henry was anxious and his anxiety was interfering with his life. Ten-year-old Henry especially had trouble sleeping at night. He would toss and turn for a while, and then he would go to his parents' bed where he would quickly fall asleep. Lydia would sleep with Henry, while Greg slept in his son's room. Henry's parents were not particularly distressed by this arrangement, but they did think it was time for Henry to become more independent. When Henry did fall asleep in his own bed, it took him a long time to fall asleep, and he felt tired the next day. Henry's parents asked me to teach their son some relaxation exercises so he would be less anxious about sleeping.

Henry wanted to spend the night at friends' houses, but he was afraid that he wouldn't be able to sleep, and he admitted that he just felt better staying home. Henry was especially anxious whenever he had to stay home alone, however. If he arrived home from school and knew that his mother would meet him there 15 minutes later he was fine as he waited for her, but if she was even 2 minutes late, he became "hysterical." He frequently complained about stomachaches.

Sleep problems often bring families to see me, because fears can cause an obvious problem at bedtime. Children can usually avoid spending the night away from home, but they can not avoid bedtime indefinitely. Usually, when children have sleep problems, they also have other behavioral indicators of stress. Henry had difficulty separating from his mother, as well as trouble sleeping.

CLINICIAN'S VIEW: MAKING A DIAGNOSIS

When a child has a sleep problem, I have to sort out whether there is an organic cause, like sleep apnea; a functional cause, like a diurnal clock that is "off"; or a physiologic cause, like drinking too many caffeine-filled sodas. When I think about trauma related to sleep problems, I wonder whether a traumatic incident actually happened at bedtime, or whether difficulty falling asleep without a parent makes separation anxiety more obvious at bedtime. Traumas that are not directly related to bedtime can affect sleep too. Worry delays sleep for some people. Nightmares about a traumatic incident can interrupt sleep regardless of whether the trauma occurred during bedtime or during the day. So nighttime problems become an indicator for all kinds of traumas.

All families have experienced traumas. When Henry's mother started telling me about her health problems, it quickly became apparent that Henry's worries about his mother's well-being had been justified at some point in the past. Possibly, Henry's current difficulties stemmed from his concerns about her. One morning, when 3-year-old Henry was home with his father, his mother was in a serious automobile accident. The next time Henry saw her, she was lying in a hospital bed, confused from a head injury, and she had slurred speech and double vision. She didn't seem to recognize Henry. She had multiple injuries, including a fractured pelvis, and she could barely move. To a young child, this experience might be as shocking as having one mother one day and a different mother the next day. The year and a half that followed were marked by frequent medical tests, strenuous rehabilitation, doctors visits, and anxiety about her future. Just as life was beginning to settle down, about a year later, seizures sent Henry's mother back to the hospital. Finally, she recovered quite well, her seizures were controlled by medication, and she had not had major medical problems in over 5 years.

HENRY'S FIRST VISIT

When I met Henry for the first time, I was impressed by this tall, athletic 10-year-old who told me his troubles and outlined his goals. "I can't go to sleep without my mom, but I know I'm too old to go to sleep with her. Too much stuff goes through my head, and I get stomachaches on and off. I like going to friends' houses, but I can't sleep there either. I want to be able to sleep easily, to be calm and not worry at friends' houses. I'd like to not worry about my parents getting hurt or about someone kidnapping me. I want to be able to go to sleep-over basketball camp." Henry told me that his troubles with sleep began when he was 6 or 7.

I asked Henry whether he remembered when his mother had been sick. He said he vaguely remembered seeing her in the hospital. He described his recollection, "I don't think she was conscious. I think she was asleep." I asked Lydia whether she would write a story for her son so that he would have a better understanding about what had happened. She readily agreed.

A HYENA STEALS A BABY

When I saw Henry alone, he chose to make a sand-tray picture. He had a hyena steal a baby and then laugh at a group of figures, calling them sissies for not wanting to steal a baby too. I had the sense that Henry was showing me the experience of having someone precious taken away and then feeling shamed for having strong feelings about his loss. Henry was allowing me to witness this visual representation of his emotional experience.

"THE SLEEPERS" VS. "THE WORRIES"

I absorbed the scene in the sand tray, then asked Henry if he could imagine a safe place, where he could feel exactly as calm and safe as he wanted to feel. He visualized a small neighborhood with nice people who all looked out for one another. I asked if he would name the helpers he would need in order for him to feel safe like that. He named his allies "The Sleepers" and the guys who prevented them from doing their job "The Worries." We agreed that our job was to give "The Sleepers" more power and make sure that "The Worries" had less power.

During the next five sessions, Henry and I worked together to empower "The Sleepers" and to acknowledge, but shrink "The Worries." I taught Henry some visualization techniques for relaxation. I offered EMDR to enhance the feelings associated with the safe place to strengthen Henry's vision of the future when he would be free from the grip of "The Worries"; and to desensitize the nighttime triggers for anxiety, including the clock, the bed, and the thoughts, "It's getting late, and I have to go to sleep." Sometimes Henry chose to use EMDR and sometimes he preferred to make scenes in the sand tray.

Henry made sand-tray pictures entitled "The Rainforest," depicting the yet undetermined fate of the wonderful plants and animals of the rainforest and "Undersea," in which oceanographers were trying to decide whether the sharks were truly dangerous or whether they were just scary looking. In "Rainforest," I thought Henry wanted to show me his love and appreciation for his mothers' life, without whom life was unthinkable, yet whose future was uncertain. In "Undersea," I inferred that the risks were mysterious, even for the experts.

I imagined that Henry was struggling with questions of whether his mother's health was secure, whether it was safe to relax, or whether his anxiety actually played a role in keeping her safe. Sometimes, when anxiety follows a traumatic event, the child believes that the anxiety itself is keeping the trauma from recurring. It seems reasonable that Henry was grappling with the question of whether it was safe to give up his anxiety.

HENRY'S STORY

When Henry was ready to use EMDR to address his anxiety about his mother's injuries and illness, I asked Lydia to read Henry the story she had written. She told me that writing the account had helped her to gain perspective on what had happened, and she hoped that it would also help her son to realize that she was fine. She chose to end her narrative in a way that gave Henry permission to move forward with his life, "Everyone was getting older, and their lives were evolving. They were all changing and Mom's health problems stopped being a major part of their lives." Lydia read the story to her son, answered his questions about her health, which was currently stable, and then left the room so that Henry could have privacy while he did EMDR on feelings that the story had stirred up.

Henry started with a visual image of his mother in the hospital. He wanted to work toward the positive cognitions, "I'm fine, I can take care of myself, and I'm confident I can handle whatever happens." In the course of working toward acceptance of these positive cognitions, we reviewed the steps Henry could take if his mother were injured or ill. Later, with his mother present, we outlined an action plan to deal with his mother's habit of arriving home later than she had planned. She agreed to try to be on time, but concurred that Henry should call his father and designated adults if she were more than half an hour late.

When Henry returned for a follow-up visit, his sleep was no longer a problem, he had not had any more stomachaches, and he was able to sleep away from home. Nevertheless, he said that EMDR had not helped because "I know I'll never get the worries out of my mind." He did concede that "The Worries" now felt small and manageable, and he was ready to handle them on his own.

EMILY

Ten-year-old Emily, her hair in two long braids, presented me with a candid inventory of her troubles. "My dad favors me because I'm his first child and all four of my grandparents favor me too. This makes my brother and sister mad, and they tease me." Emily was clearly upset by her favored position in the family. "My parents are divorced, and my dad won't listen to my mom. I have enough problems without them teasing me. I worry about falling off a bridge. I worry about being eaten by a shark. It doesn't even help that I know it's highly unlikely. I can't sleep at night because I worry about being murdered or kidnapped. I'm afraid of the dark. I can't sleep, or when I do, I have nightmares about being murdered. I'm tired and have headaches every day, and then I have to deal with my siblings on top of that."

I asked Emily to tell me about the time when she first started having trouble sleeping. She had slept fine until one memorable night, 3 years previously. "One night when I was 7, I had this really scary dream. I got hot and thought someone was there, breathing on me. He was wearing black, and he had a knife. He was swearing at me and telling me he'd murder me some day. I woke up so scared, and since then, I've been worried that something terrible would happen to me." This nightmare occurred during the process of Emily's parents' divorce.

Emily was aware that her fears were just fears. She was quite sure that no one would murder or kidnap her, that she would not fall off a bridge or be eaten by sharks. I asked her how "The Fears" convinced her to believe them even though she *knew* they were irrational. She replied, "All I have to do is to watch a movie or the news. People are always being murdered or kidnapped. Polly Klaas's kidnapping was on every TV channel. It was sad and tragic. Even though I think terrible things won't happen to me, I know that they can happen."

When I asked Emily to imagine a "safe place," she described heaven. "I feel safe when I imagine heaven, where angels are guarding me. I'm wrapped in a golden cocoon, and the angels are watching me. I can imagine a golden cocoon wrapped around the world. There would never be any wars. In heaven, no one eats meat, but if you like meat, you can eat imitation meat so no one is killed. No harm could be there. Everyone in heaven gets a halo and wings. In heaven, people stay with their perfect mates. I have a warm cozy feeling in my heart and a gold feeling coming from my heart."

Emily chose to draw a picture to let me know more about herself. She drew a picture of a girl with braids standing beside a Christmas tree. She volunteered, "I like Christmas."

TRYING EMDR

I explained EMDR and asked Emily whether she would like to try some eye movement to strengthen some of her happy, safe feelings. Emily agreed. I guided her eye movement as she focused on various pleasant images including the "Christmas feeling" in her heart, the "fourth-of-July feeling" she felt all over, the image of the golden cocoon keeping the world safe, and her experience of learning something new—diving from a diving board.

Next, I encouraged Emily to move her eyes while she thought about how it would be when she could sleep comfortably and easily. She moved her eyes in slow circles (her preferred eye movement) and said, "I'd be rested, alert, and able to concentrate during the day, and I'd spend the night with friends." I was impressed by Emily's rich imagination, her ability to enhance positive feelings, and her clear vision of a future free from sleep problems and excess fears. She appeared to be ready to shed "The Fears."

When Emily returned for her next session, she was ready to begin working immediately. She plunked herself on the sofa and said, "I want to work on sleep." I asked Emily to list the nighttime thoughts or objects that were signals for "The Fears" to start. She reeled them off, "The dark, the closet, my window that doesn't have a curtain, noises, the thought that someone is in my room, the thought that someone will hurt me, nightmares, and the scary feeling itself." I asked her to rate each of these items as to how scary they looked. Most items rated a 10.

A GUARDIAN ANGEL HELPS

The items looked so scary that Emily thought that she would be unable to even look at them or think about them. I wondered aloud whether a protective angel could help her. Emily brightened.

I asked Emily to imagine that a guardian angel was keeping her safe while she imagined looking at the darkness, feeling the scary feelings, and moved her eyes. Soon, Emily felt no distress as she viewed the darkness from a position of safety. When I asked her to view the darkness by herself, she was frightened again, but less than before. She was able to focus on her image of the darkness and move her eyes until the darkness no longer looked frightening at all. We went through the list desensitizing each item, while imagining the guardian angel present, until Emily's anxiety level was manageable. Then Emily faced each fear alone and desensitized each memory until she felt calm and relaxed as she imagined looking around her room at night.

The last item on her list was the memory of the nightmare that had precipitated "The Fears," 3 years earlier. The memory lost its upsetting charge within seconds. I suggested that Emily move her eyes while she remembered the nightmare and thought, "I'm safe even if I have nightmares." Next, I asked Emily to let her body know that she could sleep and feel safe and know that even while she was sleeping comfortably her body could pay attention to any *real* danger. Emily considered that idea, moved her eyes, and nodded.

At the end of our session, I instructed Emily to "run a movie" of leaving my office, going home and enjoying the evening, and then sleeping comfortably and easily all night long. Emily watched my moving hand until her "movie" was over, and then she said, "I think I can do it."

MOM HELPS

When she returned in 10 days, Emily announced that it was much easier to sleep now. She felt safe, the scary thoughts were gone, she was able to sleep alone, and she was having nice dreams. The only trouble was that she was tired in the morning. Emily diagnosed the problem herself, "I go to bed too late. I need for Mom to say, 'Go to bed now' so that I go to bed at 9 o'clock instead of staying up until 10 or 11 to play." Emily ended the session that day by enlisting her mother's help in enforcing her bedtime.

FIGURING IT OUT: IT'S NOT MY FAULT

Emily came for three more appointments with me. She drew pictures, assembled collages, made sand-tray pictures, and told stories about her art work. Out poured her ideas about getting along with many kinds of people and her theories on marriage and why some work and others do not. Children almost always believe that their parents' divorce is their fault. Emily concluded that if a person marries the wrong person, it isn't anyone's fault, and they get another chance to find the perfect mate. I know that she was trying to understand and make peace with her parents' divorce. I wonder whether Emily's recurrent nightmare had represented her terror that her parents' divorce was her fault, a crime punishable by death.

Emily's appointments spanned Christmas vacation, and Emily had an important realization just before Christmas. "I'm not worried about my brother and sister teasing me about being the favorite any more. It's not my fault that I'm the favorite. If I get presents they like for Christmas, it's not my fault." After that realization, not only did Emily sleep easier, she also got along better with her siblings.

AFTERWORD

The mysteries described in *Small Wonders* have been solved. Once again, Sam is free to love, Aaron is a confident leader in school, and Hanna can enjoy a good night's sleep—at home as well as at camp. It is deeply gratifying to know that I have helped these children reclaim the healthy childhoods they deserve. In turn, they have given me deep respect for the healing potential within each of us.

Families continue to offer me new mysteries, each story beginning with a familiar theme of distress and confusion. Parents often feel that their child's problems imply their own inadequacy or failure. They ask, "What is causing my child's behavioral problems? What did I do to cause the problems? We've tried everything we know to help our child—what can be done to help us now?" The pain of their perceived failure echoes through their history-telling.

Most parents do their best to take care of their children. They do not want to be quick to label their children with problems; neither do they want to ignore obstacles to full growth and development. It is often difficult to know when behavioral problems call for a "wait and see" attitude and when to consult a professional. Reaching for professional help when a child's development has gotten off track, however, signals great courage and trust, not failure.

We cannot always predict or control what life brings us, but my own experience and the experiences of others have taught me some important lessons. We all deserve love and care and safety; we all have tremendous reserves for healing. Being able to give help to others and being able to receive help when we need it are among the greatest gifts in the world.

QUESTIONS FREQUENTLY ASKED ABOUT EMDR

Children may ask you or their parents about EMDR: what it means and how it works. The following appendixes are examples of the handouts I share with my clients and their families.

WHAT IS EMDR?

Eye movement desensitization and reprocessing (EMDR) is a method that helps relieve posttraumatic stress. It is used for reducing fears and anxiety as well as for strengthening feelings of calm and confidence.

WHAT DOES "DESENSITIZATION" MEAN?

Desensitization is the process of becoming comfortable with a memory of an event that was scary, but is currently over or harmless. For example, you might be scared to ride a bike again after falling while riding. Remembering the accident might be so scary that it prevents you from riding a bike again—at least for a while. If you practice riding slowly, first on grass, then on the sidewalk, and also talk about the frightening experience, the memory of the accident could become "desensitized" so that the thought of riding is no longer as scary. Remembering the event becomes comfortable, like looking at an old photo or movie. In fact, when desensitization is complete, riding a bike could be something fun and exciting, not scary at all.

If it's reasonable to expect that an incident will never happen again, desensitization can allow you to look at the memory calmly. If the event is something like a medical procedure that you will face again, desensitization of old memories will make it easier to prepare for the future. EMDR can help desensitization of upsetting memories happen quickly.

WHAT DOES "REPROCESSING" MEAN?

"Reprocessing" is a psychological term that means to work on understanding a memory so that the memory becomes useful instead of just scary. Going back to the example of the bike accident, you might have thought, "I'm not good enough to ride a bike. I can't handle new experiences. I'll get hurt if I try anything new." If you continued to believe that, you might be miserable and miss out on a lot. If you "reprocess" the memory of that experience, you might think, "It's over now. I am good enough to ride a bike. It's safe for me to try new activities. I can handle normal risks." EMDR lets people "reprocess" memories in a way that helps them be more comfortable and confident when it's appropriate to be calm.

HOW WAS EMDR DISCOVERED?

In 1987, Dr. Francine Shapiro discovered that eye movement can help to make memories less upsetting. One day when she was walking in the park, she was bothered by some disturbing memories. As she walked, the memories became less disturbing. She wondered what she had been doing that made the memories less upsetting, and she realized that she had been moving her eyes quickly back and forth.

At the time, Dr. Shapiro was a psychologist helping war veterans. She wondered whether her clients would feel less upset by memories of war if she guided them to move their eyes back and forth. It worked! Since that time, EMDR has evolved into a sophisticated method for treating trauma, anxiety, and stress.

IS EMDR HYPNOSIS?

No, EMDR is not hypnosis. During hypnosis, EEG readings indicate that there is an increase in alpha, beta, or theta waves, which has been associated with an increase in suggestibility. EEG patterns of people during EMDR therapy show brain waves that are within normal waking parameters. In EMDR, the person is actually less susceptible than usual to information that is not correct.

HOW AND WHY DOES THE EYE-MOVEMENT COMPONENT OF EMDR WORK?

We don't know exactly why the eye-movement component of the treatment is effective, but we have some theories. EMDR may work in a way that is similar to rapid-eye-movement (REM) sleep, the period of sleep during which we dream while moving our eyes. Dreams often help to clear up small traumas so that they aren't upsetting anymore. EMDR, like dreams, may stimulate our natural brain process that makes difficult experiences more acceptable, or at least less upsetting.

When something traumatic or very upsetting happens to us, information about the event seems to go around and around in our brains, probably so that we will avoid any situation that reminds us of the traumatic event. Getting upset every time we remember isn't very helpful. EMDR helps to get the old memory "unstuck," or "desensitized and reprocessed," so that it will become useful information, rather than upsetting information.

WHAT DO YOU DO WHEN YOU "DO" EMDR?

EMDR may involve moving your eyes while you focus on your memory of an upsetting event. You may choose a wand or a sand-tray figure to watch while I move it back and forth. It may feel upsetting or scary to remember the traumatic incident when you begin. The memory will become less and less upsetting while you move your eyes.

Remember, while you do EMDR, you are in charge. You may close your eyes, turn your head, or put up your hand to indicate that you want to stop to rest or to talk. Please say which direction and speed of eye movement feels best to you. Some people like to move their eyes back and forth for a minute or two, rest, then continue eye movement; others like to keep moving their eyes for a while, until they feel very relaxed.

If you don't like moving your eyes, we can try alternately tapping your hands to stimulate your brain to start processing the upsetting memories. We'll practice using different techniques. You can choose the one you like best.

HOW WILL WE BEGIN?

We will probably begin your introduction to EMDR by doing some imagination exercises. For example, I may ask you to imagine a "safe place." (You may prefer to remember a time you had fun or a time you learned something. That would be fine too.) The safe place can be somewhere that you can feel safe, relaxed, and comfortable. You can choose a place that is real or imaginary. When you have the picture of the safe place in mind, I'll ask you to concentrate on noticing the feelings of safety, relaxation, and comfort in your body.

You might practice using your imagination to "dial up" those feelings so that they are stronger or so that the relaxation spreads through your body. Next, we may use EMDR while you focus on the safe place so that you may experience how EMDR can help to strengthen the soothing work your imagination has already begun.

Later, when you are ready (usually not in our first meeting), you can begin to "desensitize and reprocess" upsetting memories. When you begin to concentrate on the traumatic memory you may feel anxious. You may notice tension in your body. Gradually, you will notice that EMDR prompts your natural healing system to erase excess fear so that you can feel calmer and more confident.

WHAT DOES EMDR FEEL LIKE?

Some people say that EMDR feels relaxing. Some say dreamy. Others say "weird." When you move your eyes while thinking about a painful memory, your anxiety may decrease right away or it may increase before it subsides. Sometimes it helps to imagine that you are just watching the event on a video or that you are viewing it through a train window. Any way you feel is okay. All you have to do is notice. EMDR can work to help you feel more confident, calmer, and happier, regardless of whether you experience it as relaxing, dreamy, weird, or even annoying. While you move your eyes, you may notice that mental pictures, thoughts, feelings, or body sensations come to your attention. This is normal. You may not have any particular visual images, thoughts, feelings or body sensations. This is normal too.

AM I CRAZY? CAN EMDR HELP?

People who suffer from posttraumatic symptoms sometimes wonder if they are crazy. It feels crazy to worry all the time and to think the same bothersome thoughts over and over. It feels crazy to let fears get in the way of doing things you want to do. You are not crazy, and you will feel much better when EMDR helps you make the best of what has happened to you.

WHAT CAN EMDR DO FOR ME?

EMDR can help you get in touch with your own inner power so that you can look back on old memories calmly, get over fears, and prepare for stressful events. It can help you feel braver and more confident. It can help you believe what is useful and self-enhancing, so that you develop more self-esteem. EMDR can only prompt you to erase useless information or excess anxiety and can only reinforce what is true.

WHAT CAN'T EMDR DO FOR ME?

EMDR cannot make you feel safe if you are not safe. That is, EMDR cannot take away appropriate protective fear responses. For example, EMDR cannot make someone feel safe riding on a steep, rough road if he doesn't have the skills or equipment to do it. EMDR can only help you be calmer (which could help you to think faster in an emergency).

EMDR can't get you to do something you don't want to do or to like something that you don't want to like. For example, if you were pressured into riding a bike and you don't want to do it, EMDR can't change your true opinions.

CAN I TRY EMDR ON MY FAMILY AND FRIENDS?

Please do not use EMDR on anyone. Although EMDR may appear simple, it is actually a sophisticated method that requires special expertise. Only licensed professionals who have trained in a program approved by the EMDR International Association should use EMDR. Sometimes upsetting memories unexpectedly come up during EMDR, and professionals know how to keep the "desensitization and reprocessing" safe and successful.

FOR PARENTS: WHAT TO EXPECT WHEN YOUR CHILD DOES EMDR

HOW LONG WILL IT TAKE MY CHILD TO GET OVER A TRAUMATIC EVENT OR FEAR?

It is not possible to predict how long it will take for your child's symptoms to resolve. EMDR helps therapy to go faster, but not necessarily fast. The length of time it takes a child to get over a traumatic event may depend on many factors, including the type and severity of the trauma, the age at which the trauma occurred, the extent to which other family members have gotten over the trauma, the stability of the child's current environment, your child's personality and level of functioning before the traumatic event, and whether your child is able and willing to participate in doing EMDR.

WHERE CAN I LEARN MORE ABOUT EMDR?

Two books on EMDR were published in 1997.

EMDR: The Breakthrough Therapy for Overcoming Anxiety, Stress, and Trauma, by Francine Shapiro, Ph.D. and Margot Silk Forest, published by Basic Books, explains how EMDR works and gives case examples (including a case of mine).

Transforming Trauma: EMDR. The Revolutionary New Therapy for Freeing the Mind, Clearing the Body, and Opening the Heart, by Laurel Parnell, published by Norton, explains how adult clients have benefited from EMDR.

The EMDR Institute will provide a list of references supporting the efficacy of EMDR as well as referrals to qualified clinicians who are skilled in the EMDR method:

PO Box 51010
Pacific Grove, CA 93950-6010
Phone: (408) 372-3900
Fax: (408) 647-9881
e-mail: www.inst@emdr.com

HOW SHOULD A PARENT PREPARE A CHILD FOR DOING EMDR?

I will introduce your child to EMDR, so you don't need to do anything special to prepare your child for the experience. Parents who are informed about EMDR and have had their own questions answered about the method usually feel confident that EMDR can help, and that confidence is transmitted to the child. Parents can reassure their child that it is the child who is in charge of the process, that the child's own brain is doing the healing, and that the clinician is there to make it easier for the child. You can let your child know that EMDR is a way to help her get over an upsetting event, fear, or nervousness.

THE PARENTS' ROLE DURING EMDR

If you are present during your child's EMDR session, we will talk about how you and I can work together to help your child get over the traumatic incident. Sometimes, just having a parent present is comforting for a child. Sometimes the child will look to his parent for additional information or confirmation about what happened. Sometimes, a parent recounts what happened at the time of the trauma, while I guide eye movement or tapping, to facilitate the child's processing of the event.

Some children like to play while doing EMDR. Some prefer not to have a parent present. That is fine, too. Because you are the most important person in your child's life, your attitudes, confidence, and support will help your child heal from the trauma.

ARE THERE ANY CONTRAINDICATIONS TO DOING EMDR?

A person who has had a history of a detached retina should not be encouraged to move his eyes rapidly. However, alternate tapping or auditory tones are safe for anyone. A qualified professional with training in the EMDR method can evaluate whether EMDR is the best way to help an individual.

ARE THERE ANY SIDE EFFECTS MY CHILD MIGHT EXPERIENCE WHILE DOING EMDR?

Some people complain that moving their eyes back and forth makes them feel dizzy. Changing the direction of eye movement or using tapping instead of eye movement alleviates this temporary discomfort.

Some people initially feel anxious when they begin to process an upsetting memory. Occasionally, a child will want to stop EMDR because he doesn't want to feel anxious. Usually, continuing EMDR for a few more minutes will help the child to get over the scary part of the memory, and he will begin to feel relaxed. I encourage, but never force, children to use EMDR to help them get over painful memories. To date, we are not aware of any long-term problems that have arisen from doing EMDR when it is used correctly.

WHAT SHOULD PARENTS EXPECT AFTER AN EMDR EXPERIENCE?

After an EMDR session that involves desensitizing and reprocessing traumatic memories, a person may feel relieved, and he may feel exhausted. Plan for your child to have some quiet time or some choice about his preferred activity after the session.

Some sessions are "complete," that is, the entire traumatic memory seems to have been cleared during the session. Some sessions have to be stopped, before the traumatic memory has been cleared, either because there hasn't been enough time to finish, or because there are many parts to the traumatic experience. In the case of an "incomplete" session, I will help your child to put away the upsetting memories. If you notice that your child continues to be upset between sessions, however, you can remind her to imagine putting the worries in a container and opening it again when back in my office. You can also encourage your child to practice visualizing her "safe place" and noticing the safe, relaxed feelings that go with the image. Most children feel fine after a session.

Some children say that they don't notice any differences in how they feel between sessions, but parents often notice marked changes in their child's behavior and moods. Your observations can help me know which symptoms have cleared and which symptoms to target at our next session. Please feel free to call me with any questions about your child's experience with EMDR.

GUIDELINES FOR WRITING A STORY FOR YOUR CHILD

The purpose of writing a story for your child is to help your child begin to make sense of what has happened to him and to put the events in their place in the past. Together, we can develop a story to teach your child healthy ways of viewing himself in relation to the trauma that disturbed his life. The story will make it easier for me to apply EMDR to desensitize the painful memories and to reprocess them so that your child can feel safer and more confident.

A "successful" story is one that your child will like, one that provides a resolution for the overwhelming, difficult-to-understand issues presented by the traumas, and one that gives your child developmentally appropriate beliefs about himself that will help him go on with life. Several pointers will make it more likely that this story will be a success with your child.

1. The language in the story should be simple and easy to understand.
2. The length of the story should be similar to the length of a familiar bedtime story.
3. The story should be written about "a boy" or "a girl" without using the names of individuals. Some children claim the story as their own, other children find it easier to hear a story about "a child." Let's leave it up to your child to decide whether he prefers to hear a story about himself or someone "like him." Regardless of your child's preference, the story establishes the traumatic event as something that can happen to children, and proposes ways that a child can deal with such an upsetting event.
4. The story, or chapter, should have a beginning, a middle, and an end.

The *beginning* of the story may identify your child and present something positive about him that will catch his interest. For example, "Once upon a time, there was a boy who lived with his mother, his father, his brother, and his fluffy yellow cat. They all loved him, and he loved them." Right away, the child may guess that the story is about him, even though his name isn't mentioned. He may be willing to experience the feeling of being loved and of loving while doing eye movement or while being tapped on his hands or knees. This positive introduction to EMDR will prepare him for desensitizing and reprocessing distressing memories later.

The *middle* of the story should include pertinent events leading up to the trauma, as well as the trauma itself. The traumatic event should be described in detail, including sights, sounds, smells, tastes, textures, and feelings that may have been experienced at the time. If your child experienced a series of traumatic events, it may be a good idea to devote a separate "chapter" to each part of the trauma.

Mention current symptoms that seem to be related to the trauma. For example, "After that, he was afraid to sleep by himself in his own bed at night, and he began to have stomachaches. Sometimes he woke up with nightmares about the accident." We will use EMDR to desensitize and reprocess each incident and each symptom related to the trauma.

The *end* of the story presents the resolution of the trauma and includes the positive beliefs you want your child to have about himself. For example, "When the accident was all over, some things were different about the family, but the little boy was safe. He started to feel comfortable with his new baby-sitter, he liked playing with his friends, he slept happily in his own bed at night, and his body felt fine. He knew that he was brave, and strong, and loved."

Include any rules for safety that will help your child feel competent and powerful. For example, "The boy learned that he could use his voice to call for help. He could soothe himself by remembering his mom's love for him."

Remember that your child will probably add his own ideas about why the trauma happened or what he felt and thought as he remembers the trauma. We will modify the story to accommodate his memories and to meet his needs. It is important for us to be flexible. We will let him listen to the story and take it in at his own pace.

Your child may become comfortable with the story of the trauma and get over the symptoms quickly, or it may take a number of sessions. Some children prefer to hear the whole story many times, each time doing EMDR on one of the upsetting parts. Others choose to work on only a part of the story in each session. Your child may need encouragement to listen to the story and do EMDR, or he may need time to play. EMDR can be used to help him master his fears as he plays. Your story can serve as a model for helping him to imagine ways to overcome his fears or worries and to feel safe and confident again.

Between sessions, please notice which problems have cleared and which posttraumatic behaviors persist. If possible, observe what seems to trigger these behaviors. For example, "He's no longer afraid to go in the kitchen when the stove is hot, but he still worries about a fire when he hears the sizzling sounds of food frying."

Some parents like to keep a log of their child's posttraumatic behaviors so that we can have an inventory of symptoms that require treatment. The log might look like this:

Date	Situation	Behavior	Trigger
7/10	in kitchen while dinner is being prepared	crying; worried about fire	grease sizzling

Being aware that the sounds of sizzling trigger the child's anxiety will let me know to use EMDR to target the auditory cues that provoke undue anxiety. The story and your feedback about your child's progress enable us to work together to help your child.

GUIDELINES FOR CLINICIANS

USING STORYTELLING AND EMDR TO TREAT YOUNG CHILDREN FOR CRITICAL-INCIDENT TRAUMA

The following guidelines may be adapted to meet the needs of individual families and clinicians. The storytelling approach should always be guided by a qualified EMDR practitioner with expertise working with children. This approach is useful for treating critical-incident trauma in young children.

THE FIRST VISIT

On the first visit, meet the parents without the child present so that they can give information or express concerns that they may not want to share with their child. During the meeting, cover the following areas:

1. THE TRAUMATIC EXPERIENCE

a. Ask parents to tell you the story of their child's traumatic experience in as much detail as possible.

b. Ask for current posttraumatic symptoms. (For example, bed-wetting, fears, and so on.)

c. Ask parents for negative cognitions they imagine their child has. (For example, "I can't do anything right" or "It's not safe for me to take a turn.")

d. Connect posttraumatic symptoms to the trauma and to negative cognitions. (For example, "Maybe she is afraid of clouds because they remind her of smoke" or "Maybe he is afraid to take his turn at school because the accident happened when it was his turn to go down the slide.")

2. HISTORY

Ask about the pregnancy, labor, delivery, neonatal history, illnesses, injuries, hospitalizations, and other traumatic experiences. The history may reveal previous traumatic events or template experiences that must be addressed before the child's anxiety will subside. Young children may not spontaneously reprocess earlier memories, and the clinician may have to guide the desensitization and reprocessing of each individual critical incident.

3. POSITIVE COGNITIONS

a. Ask parents for positive cognitions they want their child to have. (For example, "I am strong. I can do what I want to do.")
b. Ask for the child's strengths and examples of his or her imaginative powers. (For example, "He sometimes helps his little brother." "She tells wonderful stories with funny characters in them.")
c. The clinician can use EMDR to reinforce true and self-enhancing beliefs.

4. SAFETY CONCERNS

Ask parents for their beliefs about safety—"How is your child kept safe? How can she protect herself?" (For example, she is kept safe by family, trusted adults, friends, siblings, love, religious beliefs. She can protect herself by using her voice to express herself, by saying what she needs, by calling for help, by turning away or running, by using her imaginative powers.)

Young children may be confused about why they were hurt in an accident even though they wore a safety helmet or seat belt to "keep them safe." The clinician and parents can work together to determine developmentally appropriate explanations for a young child.

5. THE STORY

Ask the parents to write the story of their child's traumatic experience, in language their child will understand, using the third-person narrative style. The story should begin with everyone safe, lead up to the trauma, describe details, and end with positive cognitions and everyone safe. If they do not want to *write* a story, they can just prepare to *tell* the story. For more guidelines on storytelling, see Appendix 3.

The story offers a structured way to desensitize a critical-incident trauma for a child who may not be able to describe or make sense of the event. The story may also serve to restore the parents' belief that they can help the child resolve the trauma.

6. EXPLAIN EMDR

Explain EMDR and let them know that together, you and they can help their child get over the trauma. They will tell their child the story and provide a safe base while you use EMDR to make it easier to get over the painful memories of the trauma.

THE SECOND VISIT: MEET WITH PARENTS AND CHILD

Meet with parents and child together to establish your office as a safe place where the child and family can resolve problems.

1. ASK PARENTS

a. Ask parents for their child's strengths and qualities they like best about this child.
b. Ask about the child's imaginative power.
c. Ask about developmental challenges you already know the child met easily—learning to walk, talk, toilet training, or to sleep through the night. This helps to remind the child and parents that they can resolve difficult problems.

2. ASK THE CHILD

a. Ask the child if she would like to choose a sand-tray figure or wand to help her get her own power (or magic) really strong.

b. The child can sit with parent or on parent's lap if she likes.

c. Give choices—which side of hands should the figure tap, front or back? Would she prefer knee tapping?

d. Ask the child to imagine a safe place.

e. Ask the child to remember a time when she felt really strong or learned something new. Ask the parents if the child can't think of anything (remember meeting a developmental challenge, as mentioned previously).

f. Practice a "stop" signal and speed of tapping, with child in control.

THE THIRD MEETING: EMDR

Review the story the parents have written and decide whether to use the story or whether to meet with parents alone again to discuss the story. The story may reveal further unresolved issues that the parents have that should be addressed before you attempt to work with the child.

1. EXPLAIN EMDR TO THE CHILD

Meet with the child and parents to begin to desensitize and reprocess memories of the critical incident. Tell the child, "Today we're going to work together to get your power (magic) really strong so you will feel safe even when you remember the fire"; or "So you'll feel fine even when you think about the accident or ride in a car," and so on. Use the positive cognitions the parents presented.

Continue as follows: "You can choose where to sit and whether you want a figure or a wand to help you. Your mom/dad will read a story to you while I tap your hands/knees, and your power/magic will help it feel less scary."

2. PARENTS READ STORY DURING EMDR

As parents read the story, stop them to ask the child questions. For example, "Can you see the fire? Let me (or sand-tray figure) know when the fire doesn't look scary anymore."

"Can you smell the smoke? Let me know when it smells okay."

"Can you hear the sounds the fire makes? What do they sound like? Let me know when they sound okay."

"Can you feel the heat? Let me know when you feel just right."

"How do you feel now? Is it scary to look? Where do you feel the feeling in your body? Let me know when you feel calm and safe."

Keep reading. Only read as much of the story as the child can tolerate easily in one session.

3. ENDING THE SESSION

a. Ask the child to imagine putting the story away until the next visit.

b. Ask the parents to observe and bring in a list of behaviors and triggers to target during the next visit. See Appendix 3 for parents' guidelines for the log format.

THE FOURTH MEETING

Again, meet with parents and child.

READ THE STORY

Read the story again. Concentrate on the parts that are still scary. Incorporate posttraumatic symptoms and behaviors into the story. For example, "Tell Magic Lady about the scary sound the toilet makes. Did the big fire hoses make a noise like that when they came to help put out the fire? Can you see the hoses? Can you hear the sound of water rushing to help put out the fire? Make the noise and let Magic Lady know when it isn't scary anymore."

Install parent's positive cognition: "It's safe for me to flush the toilet."

FURTHER VISITS

Meet parents and child for as many sessions as necessary to desensitize and reprocess all components of the traumatic memories. Consider asking the child to listen to the story with her eyes closed and tell her to open her eyes if anything in the story is scary—then tap or use eye movement while reviewing the upsetting part of the story. Respect the child's pace. Use sand tray, play, or art work as necessary, according to your clinical judgment and experience.

FINAL VISIT

In the final session, read the story again and ask what the child (or the child in the story) learned, or what the child would tell another child who had to go through a similar experience. Repeat positive cognitions that have been selected by the parents while tapping or guiding eye movements. Praise the child for her bravery.

EMDR RESOURCES

EMDR Institute
PO Box 51010
Pacific Grove, CA 93950-6010
Phone: (408) 372-3900
Fax: (408) 647-9881
e-mail: www.inst@emdr.com

The institute offers EMDR training internationally for licensed professionals and has trained more than 25,000 clinicians since 1990. It also provides an international referral service to EMDR Institute–trained clinicians.

EMDR International Association (EMDRIA)
PO Box 141925
Austin, TX 78714
Phone: (512) 451-5200
Fax: (512) 451-5256
e-mail: www.emdria@aol.com

EMDRIA is a nonprofit organization that sets standards for EMDR training programs, sponsors an annual international conference and specialty training, maintains a membership directory of EMDR-trained professionals, publishes a newsletter, and supports research on EMDR.

EMDR Humanitarian Assistance Program (EMDR-HAP)
PO Box 1542
El Grenada, CA 94018
Phone: (415) 728-5609
Fax: (415) 728-2246

EMDR-HAP is a network of EMDR-trained professionals who volunteer their expertise to help victims of natural disasters or violence. This nonprofit organization also provides pro bono training in

EMDR for mental health professionals. EMDR-HAP volunteers have provided services in Bosnia, Colombia, Croatia, El Salvador, Hungary, Israel, Kiev, Northern Ireland, Oklahoma City, and Rwanda.

REFERENCES

Chemtob, C. M. (1996, November). *Eye movement desensitization and reprocessing (EMDR) treatment for children with treatment resistant disaster related distress.* Paper presented at the International Society for Traumatic Stress Studies, San Francisco.

Copeland, L. (1995). *The lice buster book.* New York: Warner Books.

Epston, D., & White, M. (1990). *Narrative means to therapeutic ends.* New York: Norton.

Foster, S., & Lendl, J. (1996, August). *Eye movement desensitization and reprocessing: Applications to competition preparing for athletes.* Paper presented at the 104th Annual Conference of the American Psychological Association, Toronto.

Levine, P. A., with Frederick, A. (1997). *Waking the tiger: Healing trauma.* Berkeley, CA: North Atlantic Books.

Parnell, L. (1997). *Transforming trauma: EMDR. The revolutionary new therapy for freeing the mind, clearing the body, and opening the heart.* New York: Norton.

Shapiro, F. (1995). *Eye movement desensitization and reprocessing: Basic principles, protocols, and procedures.* New York: Guilford.

Shapiro, F., & Forest, M. S. (1997). *EMDR: The breakthrough therapy for treating trauma, stress, and anxiety.* New York: Basic Books.

van der Kolk, B. (1996). *Traumatic stress: The effects of overwhelming experience on mind, body, and society.* New York: Guilford.

van der Kolk, B. (1997). The psychobiology of posttraumatic stress disorder. *Journal of Clinical Psychiatry, 58* (Suppl. 9), 16–24.

van der Kolk, B. (1997). *Current understanding of the psychology of trauma.* Paper presented at the July 1997 EMDRIA Conference, San Francisco.

Wildwind, L. (1992, April). *Working with depression.* Paper presented at the Advanced Clinical Applications of EMDR Conference, Sunnyvale, CA.

Wolpe, J. (1991). *The practice of behavior therapy* (4th ed.). New York: Pergamon.

BIBLIOGRAPHY

Brazelton, B. (1992). *Touchpoints—Your child's emotional and behavioral development.* Reading, MA: Addison-Wesley.

Fraiberg, S. (1959). *The magic years: Understanding and handling problems of early childhood.* New York: Scribners.

Gallagher, W. (1994, September). How we become what we are. *Atlantic Monthly,* pp. 38–40.

Greenwald, R. (1994). Applying eye movement desensitization and reprocessing to the treatment of traumatized children: Five case studies. *Anxiety Disorders Practice Journal,*83–97.

Greenwald, R. (1998). Eye movement desensitization and reprocessing (EMDR): New hope for children suffering from trauma and loss. *Clinical Child Psychology and Psychiatry, 3,* 279-287.

Herman, J. L. (1992). *Trauma and recovery.* New York: Basic Books.

Manfield, P. (Ed.). (1998). *Extending EMDR.* New York: Norton.

Marcus, S. V., Marquis, P., & Sakai, C. (1997). Controlled study of treatment of PTSD using EMDR in an HMO setting. *Psychotherapy, 34,* 307–315.

Miller, A. (1997). *The drama of the gifted child.* New York: Basic Books.

Pellicer, X. (1993). Eye movement desensitization treatment of a child's nightmares: A case report. *Journal of Behavior Therapy and Experimental Psychiatry, 24,* 73–75.

Pipher, M. (1994). *Reviving Ophelia: Saving the selves of adolescent girls.* New York: Ballantine.

Puffer, M. K., Greenwald, R., & Elrod, D. (1998). A single session EMDR study with twenty traumatized children and adolescents. *Traumatology,3*(2).

Rothbaum, B. O. (1997). A controlled study of eye movement desensitization and reprocessing (EMDR) treatment for posttraumatic stress disordered sexual assault victims. *Bulletin of the Menninger Clinic, 61,* 317–334.

Scheck, M. M., Schaeffer, J. A., & Gillette, C. S. (1998). Brief psychological intervention with traumatized young women: The efficacy of eye movement desensitization and reprocessing. *Journal of Traumatic Stress, 11*, 25–44.

Shapiro, F. (1989a). Efficacy of the eye movement desensitization procedure in the treatment of traumatic memories. *Journal of Traumatic Stress, 2*, 199–223.

Shapiro, F. (1989b). Eye movement desensitization: A new treatment for posttraumatic stress disorder. *Journal of Behavioral Therapy and Experimental Psychiatry, 20*, 211–217.

Shapiro, F. (1996). Eye movement desensitization and reprocessing (EMDR): Evaluation of controlled PTSD research. *Journal of Behavior Therapy and Experimental Psychiatry, 27*, 209–218.

Teicher, M., Ito, Y., Glod, C., Anderson, S., Dumont, N., & Ackerman, E. (1997). Preliminary evidence for abnormal cortical development in physically and sexually abused children, using EEG coherence and MRI. *New York Academy of Sciences, 821*, 160–175.

Terr, L. (1992). *Too scared to cry: Psychic trauma in childhood.* New York: Basic Books.

Wilson, D. L., & Silver, S. M., Covi, W. G., & Foster, S. (1996). Eye movement desensitization and reprocessing: Effectiveness and autonomic correlates. *Journal of Behavior Therapy and Experimental Psychiatry, 27*, 219–229.

Wilson, S. A., Becker, L. A., & Tinker, R. H. (1995). Eye movement desensitization and reprocessing (EMDR) treatment for psychologically traumatized individuals. *Journal of Consulting and Clinical Psychology, 63*, 928–937.

Wilson, S. A., Becker, L. A., & Tinker, R. H. (1997). 15 month follow-up of eye movement desensitization and reprocessing (EMDR) treatment for posttraumatic stress disorder and psychological trauma. *Journal of Consulting and Clinical Psychology, 65*, 1047–1056.

Wright, K. (1997, October). Babies, bonds, and brains. *Discover*, pp. 75–78.

Zeenah, C., & Scheering, M. (1996). Evaluation of posttraumatic symptomatology in infants and young children exposed to violence. *Zero to Three, 16* (5), 9–14.

INDEX